Schleiermacher and Palmer

Schleiermacher and Palmer

The Father and Mother of the Modern Protestant Mindset

JUSTIN A. DAVIS

PICKWICK *Publications* · Eugene, Oregon

SCHLEIERMACHER AND PALMER
The Father and Mother of the Modern Protestant Mindset

Copyright © 2019 Justin A. Davis. All rights reserved. Except for brief quotations in critical publications or reviews, no part of this book may be reproduced in any manner without prior written permission from the publisher. Write: Permissions, Wipf and Stock Publishers, 199 W. 8th Ave., Suite 3, Eugene, OR 97401.

Pickwick Publications
An Imprint of Wipf and Stock Publishers
199 W. 8th Ave., Suite 3
Eugene, OR 97401

www.wipfandstock.com

PAPERBACK ISBN: 978-1-5326-6733-6
HARDCOVER ISBN: 978-1-5326-6734-3
EBOOK ISBN: 978-1-5326-6735-0

Cataloging-in-Publication data:

Names: Davis, Justin A., author.

Title: Schleiermacher and Palmer : the father and mother of the modern Protestant mindset / by Justin A. Davis.

Description: Eugene, OR : Pickwick Publications, 2019 | Includes bibliographical references.

Identifiers: ISBN : 978-1-5326-6733-6 (paperback) | ISBN 978-1-5326-6734-3 (hardcover) | ISBN 978-1-5326-6735-0 (ebook)

Subjects: LCSH: Schleiermacher, Friedrich, 1768–1834. | Palmer, Phoebe, 1807–1874. | Protestantism—History.

Classification: LCC BT98 D19 2019 (print) | LCC BT98 (ebook)

Manufactured in the U.S.A.   08/13/19

To Hugh, Kathy, Randy, and Bev
Thank you for your continual love and support

Contents

Preface | ix

*Introduction: Schleiermacher, Palmer, and Pietism
in the Nineteenth Century* | xiii

   I Friedrich Schleiermacher (1768–1834) | 1

  II Theology of Schleiermacher | 37

 III Phoebe Palmer (1807–1874) | 76

 IV Theology of Palmer | 113

  V Holiness, Pentecostals, and Liberalism:
The Direct Heirs of Schleiermacher and Palmer | 146

 VI Fundamentalism and Neo-Orthodoxy:
The Qualified Heirs of Schleiermacher and Palmer | 174

VII Conclusion | 192

Bibliography | 199

Preface

STUDIES OF NINETEENTH-CENTURY PROTESTANT Christianity often begin with Friedrich Schleiermacher, but very few include Phoebe Palmer. Often her legacy is left to a footnote when addressing American revivalism, but her impact went well beyond that. Palmer is the mother of the Holiness movement, which took Wesley's notion of Christian perfection and transformed it into a central doctrine reshaping the Christian life. At its conception the Holiness movement advocated for a second conversion, a conversion to a higher level of Christian life where their outward lives would resemble the transmitted holiness of Christ. How this transformation looked and what shape it had varied depending on how any community chose to interpret the call to be holy. In many ways Holiness became the default position of all forms of evangelical Protestantism in America as well as Europe. The other major theological trend which dominated Europe and Mainline Protestantism in America was Liberalism. Liberalism is a theological movement that reaffirmed an individual's relationship with the divine, as well as asserting that scripture is valid as it relates to the individual; it is a movement which readdressed Christianity to the modern world by speaking the language of modernity. Schleiermacher was the first to successfully attempt this dialogue and as a result he justly earned the moniker the father of modern liberal Protestantism. Liberalism and Holiness grew to dominate nearly every aspect of Protestant theology and ecclesial practice by the dawn of the twentieth century, yet this Father and Mother are never comprehensively treated together.

To my knowledge there is no other work which seeks to address both Friedrich Schleiermacher and Phoebe Palmer together. Even books focused on nineteenth century Protestant theology do not address these two or the natural connection they possess. This is due in part to the bias of mid-twentieth century theology against non-German Protestant theologians, or a singular focus on English or American religious life. This bias can even be found in Karl Barth's *Protestant Theology*, as he failed to mention Kierkegaard, with whom he was intimately familiar, and Palmer, who was influential on both sides of the Atlantic. In the 1970s, the late Claude Welch, an early modern theological historian, notes this discrepancy in the treatment of nineteenth-century theological thought.[1] Still any work that fails to mention both Schleiermacher and Palmer while attempting to describe Protestant Christianity at this time is guilty of an egregious oversight that leaves the readers with an incomplete picture of the religious landscape that gripped the century.

These two do possess a real connection. Both inherited similar theological training, and many aspects of their lives were surprisingly analogous. They were both Pietists, the trend within Protestantism towards experiential rather than scholastic or rational approaches to the divine. As Helmut Walser Smith describes it, "a Protestant religiosity that emphasizes subjective experience of Christ—'Christ within us.'"[2] Both Schleiermacher and Palmer inherited a form of Moravian piety, Schleiermacher a Reformed version of Moravianism from his father. Palmer learned about Methodism, John Wesley's version of Moravianism, from her father.

Linking Schleiermacher and Palmer demonstrates how wildly different Pietism can be and yet remain a single cohesive structure. By any account the theologies developed by these nineteenth-century luminaries are antagonistic, if not antithetical to one another. Schleiermacher identifies experience as the feeling of absolute dependence upon God, while Palmer was opposed to conceiving of feeling as an essential aspect of the religious life, believing that faith should present itself outside of emotions. They each present their reconstruction of Pietism and remain within the experiential tradition handed down from their fathers and earlier Pietists, using their conception of the experience of the divine to construct their larger theological systems.

While the name Schleiermacher is commonplace in discussions of nineteenth-century theology, the treatment of Palmer's impact is largely overlooked. Not only does Palmer expand our understanding of Pietism beyond continental Europe and acknowledge the impact women played in the construction of modern theology, she is deserving of her place as the mother of the Holiness movement. Her works achieved unprecedented success; The Way of Holiness went through fifty-two editions, and her preaching career brought her all over the United States and England.

1. See Welch, "Problem of a History."
2. Smith, *Continuities of German History*, 56.

Understanding Palmer is essential to understanding Anglican Methodism[3] in the nineteenth century, and thus Pietism in the nineteenth century as well.

This study will contextualize the works of Schleiermacher and Palmer, as an expression of dogmatizing Pietism. While Palmer and Schleiermacher were prominent members of their society, they created a theology that reaffirmed their outsider status.

Continuing in the revival of scholarship addressing Schleiermacher, Palmer, and to a degree Pietism, this book seeks to weave these histories together, emphasizing the dominant strands of this theological tapestry, in a way that has not been done before now. Schleiermacherian and Palmerian studies have gained in popularity within the last decade or so. Karl Barth's influence on Schleiermacher has loomed large throughout the twentieth century, yet Barth's word is no longer the final one on Schleiermacher. New generation of scholars are once again attempting to come to terms with Schleiermacher's ideology and how it relates to modernity outside the Neo-Orthodox lens.[4] Palmer was widely popular during her life time and immediately afterwards, but within a generation this strong feminine voice was widely forgotten. Only recently have scholars rediscovered her foundational importance and impact upon American Methodism, Pentecostalism, and the early role of women preachers in America and Britain.

Pietism is a growing field for historians of religion. Recent scholarship from Strom, Lehmann, Shantz and others on Pietism focuses primarily upon the fields of ethics and politics. Pietism's role in politics largely relates to its role in nationalism, as well as a possible reason for the rise of the Hohenzollern state. The ethic of Pietism may be a connection to the militarism of Brandenburg-Prussia. Using the current studies on Pietism and nationalism, I will show how Schleiermacher and Palmer had key roles in building their respective states. While my work will primarily treat Pietism as a system of beliefs and not a political movement, existing scholarship may aid in understanding how these beliefs were received in their states, as well as illustrate why Palmer's views were so popular in America and less so in England. With this new outpouring of Pietistic scholarship, very few have looked at Pietism, codifying its belief system into distinctive theologies.

---

3. More often identified in America as "Methodist Episcopalian."

4. The recent monograph series put out by Princeton and edited by Wilcox, Tice, and Kelsey—as well as several other new publications—demonstrate a resurgence of interest in Schleiermacher.

Introduction

Schleiermacher, Palmer, and Pietism in the Nineteenth Century

> Every utterance presupposes a given language . . . Communica-
> tion necessarily presupposes the shared nature of the language,
> thus also a certain acquaintance with the language.[5]

THE LANGUAGE OF FRIEDRICH Schleiermacher (1768–1834) and Phoebe
Palmer (1807–1874) was not only German and English respectively, but also
a distinct dialect of Protestant Christianity. This dialect is known as Pietism,
or experiential Christianity. The simplest definition of Pietism that I can
offer is to identify it as the experiential strand of Protestantism, or more
precisely, as those Protestants who prioritize experience over scholasticism
and rationalism. This emphasis on experience also leads to an antipathy
towards the larger society and a view of themselves as outsiders. Pietists
whose engagement with the divine through prayer and reading of scripture
provides an individual and personally meaningful relationship with God.
It is this tradition which birthed the modern Protestant worldview as
interpreted by the distinct theologies of Schleiermacher and Palmer.

Only recently has Pietism emerged as a source of study, and scholar's
treatment of Pietisms impact in the nineteenth century is still in its infancy.
When nineteenth-century Pietism is addressed, the discussion surrounding
Pietism generally fails to illustrate how Pietism differs within itself. There
is no single Pietistic theology. In equating the discussions throughout
the Protestant world to a single voice, we lose out on understanding an
important religious movement that helped to shape the modern world.
While no universally agreed upon definition of Pietism exists, I define this
strand of Protestant Christianity as a quasi-mystical experiential revivalist

---

5. Schleiermacher, *Hermeneutics and Criticism*, 8.

movement, found within Lutheran, Reform, and Anglican Protestantism of every age, which seeks to understand and rework their world, both inside and outside of themselves along lines of personally meaningful relationships between themselves as individuals and God, while maintaining a general antipathy or outright hostility to the greater Christian culture and religious formalism which dictates that culture's norms and practices.

The Pietists found homes throughout all Protestant areas of Europe and America, where they would gather in small communities and dedicate themselves to Bible reading and self-reform. Pietists were inter-confessional, found within Lutheran, Reform, and Anglican denominations. As per their ideology, they never existed as a single unified block; rather there have been many "Pietisms" that took the shape and flavor of the larger communities in which they lived. Some found refuge and even gained control in Brandenburg-Prussia, or the isolation of the New World. In areas where Pietists were the minority, they often faced forms of economic and political persecution by the dominant culture. This maltreatment served as confirmation of their theological presuppositions.

As Doug Shantz and Richard Vierhaus point out, much of the political persecution faced by Pietists abated at the beginning of the nineteenth century, with the greatest political freedom found in Germany and America. Pietists found the most freedom in areas where they had a large degree of influence in the educational systems and where there was little control over the religious lives of congregants. In areas where their influence in education was minor, such as Scandinavia, they would continue to face forms of persecution.

The nineteenth century experienced dramatic social change in Europe and the Americas, yet the relationship of Pietism within the long century has not been adequately addressed. Given dramatic social change, revivalist movements are forced to adapt their message or fade away. Oddly enough the key challenge of Pietists in this century was not open persecution or a refusal of ideas, rather the challenge of Pietists, like all revivalist movements, was to maintain an outsider status within the larger society. Elements of Pietism became normative in society, specifically the subjective and individualistic focus for which Pietists were criticized in the previous centuries. Largely this was due to the success of secular movements like Romanticism, the Enlightenment, and nationalism. Hartmut Lehmann, a historian of Pietism and nationalism, argues that one of the greatest effects of Pietism was felt in fostering early nationalist sentiments. These sentiments evoked Romantic ideals of patriotism. Lehmann suggests that much like the Roman Empire, the religion that was once persecuted by the state would be used to shape it. Secular success was the largest hurdle to spiritual success. The outward form of a Pietistic culture was completed in the seventeenth and eighteenth centuries, but the spirit was animated by theologians in the nineteenth. The nineteenth century evidences dramatic and dynamic Pietistic theologians and a resurgence of religion in the public sphere.

In this work, I discuss the development of Pietist theologies in the long nineteenth century, as advanced by Schleiermacher and Palmer. Schleiermacher wrote in Berlin, the capital of Brandenburg-Prussia, and Palmer began in New York and continued her writings in England before returning to America. Both of these theologians had different cultures and attitudes which their Pietism was reacting to, yet they each produced a unique theology that was Pietistic. Their theologies maintained an oppositionary force against the secular cultures they lived and worked in, each with their own personal, historical, political, and sociological events. They both added to the theological edifice of Pietism, but not always in ways that were complementary to one another. Furthermore, these nineteenth-century Pietists dismantled part of the edifice, removing what they perceived to be unfitting in order to remake Pietism in such a way that it addressed the specific intellectual and spiritual challenges of their day.

Looking at key theologians as opposed to religious congregations will give us a better perspective on the history of ideas in the nineteenth century and how Pietism influenced and was influenced by them. Protestant historian Fred Van Leiburg has called Pietists a Church within a Church, as they did not establish new congregations, but found homes in existing churches. Thus to look at existing churches, we would miss out on both the scope of Pietism throughout the world and the depth of theological discussions had by those who formed key schools of thought within Pietism specifically and Protestantism as a whole.

Context is key to understanding the life, theology, and impact of Schleiermacher and Palmer. This work seeks to provide that much needed context. Palmer and Schleiermacher are both treated first as historical realities, wherein their biographies are addressed before their theology. This context will draw parallels with earlier Christian theologians, including Pietist leaders such as William Perkins, Johann Arndt, Philip Jakob Spener, August Herman Francke, Count Nicholas Ludwig von Zinzendorf, and John Wesley.[6] Earlier Christian mystics such as Angelina da Foligno, Johann Tauler, and Thomas á Kempis will also be mentioned, as their mystical writings impacted Pietism as a whole and the theological framework that both Schleiermacher and Palmer lived in.

---

6. To better understand the first few centuries of Pietism, I recommend reading my earlier work, *Pietism and the Foundations of the Modern World.*

The Pietistic theologies produced by Schleiermacher and Palmer emerged to define Protestant piety over and against the culture at large. For these theologians, their immediate cultures were undergoing a period of great change during their life time. Schleiermacher's Brandenburg-Prussia had emerged stronger after the dissolution of the Holy Roman Empire in 1806 and French occupation (1806–1815). Brandenburg-Prussia also had a long history where the Hohenzollerns, the ruling family of Brandenburg-Prussia, supported Pietism. Palmer's ministry existed before and after the American Civil War. The dramatic social change in America encouraged different religious attitudes, fluctuating between Holiness, unity, inter-denominational discourse, teetotalism, women's rights, and of course slavery.

While both theologians lived in a time of dramatic change, their lives followed similar patterns, sharing a remarkably similar biographical outline. Their parents were rather devout, though each had a family guilt or shame which shaped the upbringing of the children. There were great social changes in their formative years, they lacked faith in their adolescent years, they had a conversion experience and by modern and contemporary standards had atypical gender roles or relations. Each produced a theological message consistent within the Pietist framework outlined by F. Ernest Stoeffler and myself, yet each theology is distinct.

Palmer and Schleiermacher further demonstrate the influence that Pietism had within the nineteenth century outside of the ossifying institutionalized forms that grew to dominate eighteenth-century Pietism. The radical transformation and impact of the long nineteenth century serves primarily as a backdrop to the intellectual history and as a context to understanding not only the wider cultures that Pietism found itself in, but also the challenges revivalist movements face when many of their formative ideas are adapted in a wider profane culture. By studying Schleiermacher and Palmer's lives and theology we can better understand not only the tension of the modern world but also further illuminate discussion on nineteenth-century history and theology in general.

The theologies that they produced quickly dominated not only Pietist circles in Germany and America, but all of Protestantism. Schleiermacher and Palmer become the father and mother of the modern Protestant mindset. I conclude this work by demonstrating how their theologies transformed Protestantism. Nearly all Protestant theology following Schleiermacher and Palmer is a consequence of them, either for or against their Pietist thought. Reactions come from not only Liberalism and the Holiness movement, but also fundamentalism, Pentecostalism, and Neo-Orthodoxy. Furthermore, Palmer's Holiness movement is often credited with fostering interdenominational discourse in America and laying the foundation for female ordination in American and English churches. Neither Palmer nor Schleiermacher sought to create a new system, rather they both reworked their Protestant and "Pietist" worlds along the lines of personally meaningful relationships between themselves and God. While the culture around them came closer to their ideal than in previous centuries, these leaders, as well as many more, still held a general antipathy to the greater Christian culture and formulated Pietism with their new norms and practices. The mystical experiential revival must be revived once again. Protestant Christianity must once again be reworked along the idealistic and pietistic lines, which now face an advanced modernity and entrenched Pietism, where despite centuries of success, the experience of piety is seemingly elusive.

Before taking a look at the theologies of Schleiermacher and Palmer we will consider their nineteenth century context. Biography informs theology, and once the lives of these nineteenth-century Pietists are examined, their theology will come into view. Their experiences directed their theological concerns and provided the opportunities for them to express themselves as outsiders, both theological and culturally. Pietism's antipathy towards Christian cultural and the culture at large is also best expressed in the biographical narratives of Schleiermacher and Palmer. The specific theological issues concerning God, justification, sanctification, and ecclesiology, as well as their primarily theological contributions will be addressed in the chapter following their individual biographies. From the vantage point of their lives, their theologies are contextualized as a reconstruction of Pietism. The work concludes by addressing how Schleiermacher and Palmer give birth to nineteenth and twentieth-century Protestantism. This includes their theological children, namely Liberalism, Holiness, and the Protestant Ecumenical Movement, as well as their ideological grandchildren Neo-Liberalism, Neo-Orthodoxy, Pentecostalism, and fundamentalism. Many of these ideological descendants take aim at Schleiermacher, Palmer, or both, but their existence is at least due in part to them. With such a swath of theological and ecclesial movements indebted to Palmer and Schleiermacher, it is only right that we treat these two luminaries of the faith in one work and examine how they produced the Protestant world that surrounds so many of us.

I

Friedrich Schleiermacher (1768–1834)

TRAINING IN PIETISM, ENLIGHTENMENT, AND ROMANTICISM

"A Christian child is welcomed with love and joy, and ever remains embraced by them, furnishes a guarantee that the Spirit of God will dwell in that child."[1]

SCHLEIERMACHER WAS THE UNLIKELY hero for many reasons. The first and most obvious reason is his lineage. While in Prussia, the Schleiermacher's were not Lutheran, but Reform. This confessional identity suited the Hohenzollerns, although the vast majority of Prussia, including the only major university, remained Lutheran. In many ways Friedrich was destined to become a pastor. He was the eldest son of an eldest son, and third in a line of Reformed preachers. His paternal grandfather, Daniel Schleiermacher, born 1695, was at odds with both the Lutheran majority of Prussia and the Reform minority. Daniel was charged with sorcery and witchcraft in 1749. The charge came about due to some unfortunate associations he made with some Rhenish sectarians, a quasi-Pietistic group. Daniel's wife and son Gottlieb were forced to testify against him. To avoid incarceration, Daniel fled to Holland, where he stayed with his sister Arnheim. Following the trial he never preached again. Daniel Schleiermacher died in exile.

Friedrich Schleiermacher's father Gottlieb fared better than his father. By all accounts he was an exceptionally bright child, completing his

---

1. Schleiermacher, *Christmas Eve*, 52. Unless otherwise noted, all section header quotes in chs. 1–4 are quotes from the works of the subject of that chapter (i.e., chs. 1 and 2 are from Schleiermacher and chs. 3 and 4 are from Palmer).

1

theological training by nineteen. Following the Rhenish sectarians demise, Gottlieb chose to become a teacher in Magdeburg in 1758. It was at this time that he distanced himself from his father's Pietism and grew increasingly attracted to the Enlightenment. It was good timing to shift ideological allegiances. The Hohenzollern dynasty was moving away from the piety of Frederick Wilhelm I, to the Enlightenment supporting Frederick II. A dozen years later in 1760, Gottlieb began serving as a chaplain in the Prussian army, during the middle of the Seven Years War. Shortly after the war Gottlieb married Katharina-Maria Stubenrauch.

Katharina-Maria Stubenrauch was the daughter of a Reformed pastor, Samuel Ernst Timotheus Stubenrauch, a professor of theology at Halle. Little is known about the life of Katharina-Maria. The brief mentions of her focus on two areas. The first concern her death. The remaining accounts concern her deep piety and her love for her three children. The first of Gottlieb and Katharina's children was a daughter named Charlotte (1765–1831). Friedrich (1768–1834) was the second child, born November 21, and often referred to his older sister as Lotte. The youngest of the three was Carl, born in 1772.

Friedrich Daniel Ernst Schleiermacher was so named in honor of his grandfathers and the monarch. Daniel was given to honor his paternal grandfather. While Daniel Schleiermacher was discarded and in exile, Gottlieb still wanted to honor his father. Daniel was also the absentee godfather to Friedrich when he was baptized on the sixth day on November 27. Ernst was taken from Katharina-Maria's father, surprisingly it was not his first name, Samuel. A possible connection exists with Daniel Ernest Jablonsky, the Moravian Bishop in Berlin in 1737 who met with Count Nikolas Ludwig von Zinzendorf. While it is unlikely that Friedrich was named in honor of the Moravian bishop still a decade out from his father's conversion, there may be an intentional connection heretofore unnoticed. The name Friedrich was derived from Gottlieb's affinity for the Prussian monarch who he served under in the Seven Years War.

Gottlieb's fondness for Frederick II likely waned in 1778. Gottlieb distanced himself from his father's version of Pietism in his youth and embraced the *Aufklärung*. From April to June of 1778 the Prussian troops to which Gottlieb was the chaplain were quartered in Gnadenfrei. While in Gnadenfrei, Gottlieb encountered a Moravian community that transformed the pastor's spiritual understanding. This experience was a change to a full belief in Christ as the Son of God and reconciler of human beings to God. Gottlieb's spiritual journey moved from schismatic Pietist to Enlightenment theologian to Moravian, one of the established Pietist groups whose spiritual legacy traces back to Zinzendorf. Gottlieb never formally joined the group. This was likely due to his fear of ending up like his father and being incriminated through formal associations. His forced testimony incriminating his father was not a lesson he would soon forget.

Friedrich was now ten years old, but his future was bound with his father's new conversion. For the next five years Friedrich, his sister, and his brother internalized their father's conversion. Each did so in a different manner. Friedrich, like his father, was inquisitive and bright from a very early age. His mother recalled that "that he began to read at the age of four; and while other children played games, he busied himself with translating French and Latin." His brother Carl was not as bookish as his older brother. According to their mother "Fritz is all spirit, and Carl all body."[2] The young Friedrich likely focused on the spirit rather than the body because his own body was not very strong. Friedrich had poor health. He was nearsighted and had a number of stomach disorders that bothered him most of his life. He was also noticeably short and overall a diminutive adult.

Katharina-Maria became ill in 1783. Unsure how to best care for the children, the decision was made to send them to a Moravian boarding school at Niesky, furthering their Pietist education. The three children packed up and arrived in Niesky on June 14. They never saw their mother again as she died on November 17 1783. Niesky was the logical place to send the children. The Moravian school sought to keep the students away from the evil world. The best way to do so was a strict program filled with pious activities. This Moravian school resembled the schools instituted by another Pietist leader, August Hermann Francke, in many respects. Francke was well known for reforming religious education in Glaucha, the slums outside of Halle. The one noticeable exception was the church services resembled the long and numerous liturgies of the Moravians rather than the strict promethean Lutheran Pietism which Francke advocated. Every day there were four services and students were expected to go to confession once a month as well as take communion at least that often.

Though Friedrich's time here was short, only two years, it was rather influential in shaping the life of the adolescent. It was at this school where he became a Moravian both outwardly and inwardly. It was here that the experience of experiential Christianity was finally grasped by Friedrich. He marks this time as the "birthdate of his higher life." The letters that survive from this time are filled with the talk about the Savior's love, his unworthiness, and how he longs for a deeper spiritual experience. Schleiermacher's conversion took place along similar lines to Francke. Both had a period of adolescent rebellion only to have a born again experience.

2. Schleiermacher, *Servant of the Word*, 1.

While Francke records a specific prayer that launched his conversion we do not have a clear statement of a conversion experience from Schleiermacher. If Schleiermacher did not undergo a Francke style conversion experience, he likely deepened his faith at this time following the example of John Wesley or Zinzendorf. The central change focused on his understanding of his connection to Jesus as his personal savior.

In 1785 he transferred to the Moravian theological seminary at Barby. Accompanied by ten other graduates, they began the rather long walk in September. After taking only five days to traverse the hundred and fifty miles, they arrived on September 22. Schleiermacher was now in the center of Moravian theology. The school had 225 students, and was filled with Moravian theologians and pastors. The purpose of Schleiermacher's attendance at Barby was ordination. Barby was farther away from Niesky than the hundred and fifty miles, at least for Friedrich. While he was still enthused by his religious awakenings at Niesky and still held an affinity for the Moravians, outside influences crept in.

The two prevailing and destructive influences were Immanuel Kant and Johann Wolfgang von Goethe. The school viewed these thinkers as damaging to the spiritual wellbeing of the students and attempted to silence these competing ideologies. The lure of the *Aufklärung*, which gripped his father, now gripped him. Friedrich found a group of fellow students who smuggled in these works and developed their own educational program. This new underground program did not focus on Zinzendorf, rather their attention was solely Kant and Goethe. Kant's lure was his radical distinction between the knowledge of the world on the one hand and religion on the other. Kant's positive conception of religion reordered theology for Schleiermacher. Goethe's writing was so deep and nuanced that Friedrich found a new literary hero. Both Kant and Goethe appeared so full of life and hope that even the Moravian theology appeared as an arid metaphysic to Friedrich.

Eventually the schools requested Friedrich and the others to leave in 1787. In many ways it was already too late. Schleiermacher penned his father several times throughout the two years he was in Barby. On one occasion he hinted to his father that "his teachers fail to deal with those widespread doubts that trouble so many young people of the present day."[3] His father did not understand that the doubts belonged to Friedrich. The letter Friedrich composed in January of 1786 left little room concerning whose doubts the teachers overlooked. Friedrich wrote his father informing him of his radical turn of faith. Friedrich believed that reason must accompany faith and

3. Gerrish, *Prince of the Church*, 25.

began to deny many Moravian doctrines. The most troublesome doctrine to Friedrich was the doctrine of substitutionary atonement. Gottlieb reacted in a passionate repudiation of his son, calling Friedrich a denier of God. Eventually this paternal condemnation was rescinded. Father and son reunited as pastors and preachers, but likely not in person before Gottlieb's death on September 2, 1794.

Even with his father's denunciation, Friedrich did not believe that he was a denier of God, only a denier of bad theology. He maintained that he was "a Herrnhuter,[4] only of a higher order."[5] This half denial is often overblown in biographical accounts of Schleiermacher. Unfortunately for Friedrich, the seminary at Barby and his father could not see the distinction either. Schleiermacher expressed honest concerns, but the school failed to comprehend how to address doctrinal division. With the success of the movement, Moravianism found it difficult to understand criticism and questions which it had easily shaken off with Zinzendorf.

Friedrich considered himself a Moravian even though the Moravians did not consider him one any longer. Schleiermacher still echoed the words he wrote his sister years earlier, "Verily, dear Charlotte, there is not throughout Christendom, in our day, a form of public worship which expresses more worthily, and awakens more thoroughly the spirit of true Christian piety, than does that of the Herrnhut brotherhood!"[6] As a young man Schleiermacher left the seminary at Barby, but remained a Pietist. Schleiermacher was in the process of remaking Pietism, rejecting only the newly formed theology in favor of a Kantian method in interpretation, and not the insistence upon experiencing Christianity.

If anything, Schleiermacher internalized the habitus of Pietism to a greater extent with his break from Barby. Pietism's centuries long history emphasized experience over doctrine. Schleiermacher rejected the new orthodoxy of the Pietist schools in favor of a deeper experience of the divine. Zinzendorf argued that "Religion can be grasped without the conclusions of reason."[7] If reason was requisite for faith, then only scholars or intelligent people would be capable of religious knowledge. Schleiermacher echoes this same sentiment, but this time with an experience that the established followers of Zinzendorf disapproved of. This new experience included both Kant and Goethe, the cultured yet marginalized figures for the eighteen year

---

4. Herrnhut was the name of the first Moravian settlement under Zinzendorf and is often used as shorthand to designate a member of the community even outside the settlement.

5. Tice, *Schleiermacher*, 4.

6. Schleiermacher, *Friedrich Schleiermacher*, 15.

7. McGrath, *Christian Theology Reader*, 120.

old Friedrich Schleiermacher. Only recently are scholars understanding how his later development was dependent upon his Moravian heritage.

This early period of Schleiermacher's life does more than lay the groundwork for his education and theological development. It also is the beginning of his life as a social critic. Schleiermacher spent most of his life critiquing the world around him. Even from these early accounts in the Moravian schools, he was actively engaged in any controversy that presented itself. During this time, Schleiermacher criticized the strict regime and inflexibility of the school. These early critiques prepared Schleiermacher to train his critical eye on institutions and people that he loved and admired. From here it was an easy step to become a critic of the world around him. Later in life he criticized his friends in Berlin and the Prussian monarch whom he served. The letters he wrote his father and expulsion from the school produced a period of isolation. It is this isolation that made Schleiermacher into a Moravian of a higher order.

Following his expulsion from Barby, Gottlieb concluded that Friedrich would be served best at the University of Halle. The universities theology department was founded by Pietist leaders Phillip Jakob Spener and Francke under the Reform Hohenzollern monarchy to combat the influence of Lutheran Orthodoxy coming out of Saxony. In 1787 Friedrich moved to Halle and stayed with his uncle Samuel Stubenrauch, a theology professor at the university. Friedrich was a theology student, but one could hardly tell by his course load. Friedrich spent far more time in the philosophy department than he did in the theology department. While engaged with the philosophy department, he continued to concentrate on Kant and Baruch Spinoza (d. 1677), despite his father's protestations. His father was not the only one to disapprove of Friedrich at the university. Many of the Lutheran students were opposed to a Reform student in their midst. During his two year stay, he was called an atheist, a crypto-catholic, and a Spinozist. Other labels, such as a Herrnhuter and Reformed heretic were a little more fitting. For the Lutherans, all Reformed were heritics to one degree or another.

Oddly enough the comfort he found was not with his uncle; it is unlikely that Friedrich attended any of his theology courses. Rather Schleiermacher's respite was in the philosophy department surrounding Johann August Eberhard (1739–1809). Writing on Aristotle in 1788, Schleiermacher infused his piety, Kantian philosophy, and excitement into philosophy, giving us the dictum that "we live deeper than we think."[8] Still, the time at Halle was just as short as his stays in Barby and Niesky. By late

---

8. Crouter, *Friedrich Schleiermacher*, 31.

1789 Schleiermacher's uncle took a job in Drossen, and reluctantly Friedrich accompanied his uncle.

Even away from Eberhard and Halle philosophy, Schleiermacher continued to read Kant. It is probably best that Schleiermacher left Halle during this period, as his political leanings were thoroughly Kantian and the Enlightenment ideas were increasingly coming under suspicion at Halle. The Enlightenment became the enemy of the Prussians now that the French Revolution was underway. Censorship grew to the point that the minister of Silesia ordered the arrest of anyone who mentioned the French Revolution, and all Kantians at Halle were denounced as spiritual and temporal Jacobins.

While Schleiermacher avoided imprisonment, the year away from Halle was not much better. As the year progressed, Schleiermacher fell into a depression. To combat this depression, he decided to pursue ordination. Initially the shift to reading theology only served to further depress him. He abandoned his recent love for a pragmatic future. This uninspiring reasonable decision to pursue ordination bore unexpected fruit. By the time he took his ordination exams, a new love for theology had grown. In August of 1791 he wrote to his father the exciting news "My heart is properly cultivated . . . and is not left to wither under the burden of cold erudition, and my religious feelings are not deadened by theological inquiries."[9] Ordination and theology gave Schleiermacher a new life, much like his earlier experiences in Niesky.

Ordination also provided a degree of freedom from his father and his uncle, as he could now find his own employment. The family of Count Dohna in Schlobitten, East Prussia were looking for a tutor and Schleiermacher took the job. The job as a tutor also afforded Schleiermacher some time to preach occasionally. The preaching opportunities helped to cement Friedrich's relationship with his father. He sent samples of his sermons to his father and uncle for criticism and sought to develop his own distinctive Pietist preaching style. Like William Perkins, whose work *The Art of Prophesying,* served as a template for Pietist preachers, Schleiermacher believed that his sermons should convey power and humility. Though Schleiermacher never took the steps that Perkins did to identify six different types of audiences, Schleiermacher always assumed that those who attended his churches were Christians.

The Count was a fairly conservative monarchist. He served as an officer in the Prussian army during the Seven Years War and was responsible for finding qualified Reformed preachers for at least four pastorates. He opposed the French and the ideas that emerged from the Revolution, ideas

9. Gerrish, *Prince of the Church,* 26.

that Friedrich was at least a little sympathetic to. It is surprising that it was in Count Dohna's house that Friedrich came to a deeper understanding of Romanticism. While he read Goethe in his youth, under the conservative Count's roof he saw the role piety played in both morality and romantic love.

The two great examples of romantic Christian piety were the family and the Count's daughter. The family was warm and congenial. They maintained a conservative but loving and intelligent Christianity. Equally as impactful was their attractive, charming and sensitive daughter Friederike. Schleiermacher developed a strong and secret affection for her. Social convention and social standings prevented Schleiermacher from expressing his admiration. She was the first in a long line of women that Schleiermacher cherished from afar. Surprisingly Frederick's admiration for Friederike remained a secret from the Count. After three years of employment, a disagreement over the best methods of educating the children resulted in a mutual agreement to terminate their relationship. In keeping with their general tone and demeanor, the separation was a friendly one.

For the next two years, beginning in April 1794, Schleiermacher served as an assistant pastor in Landsberg an der Warthe. While he preached during his time in Schlobitten, Landsberg was Schleiermacher's first employment as an ordained minister. Schleiermacher served as the assistant pastor under a distant relative by the name of Schumann. Both Schumann and Gottlieb Schleiermacher's health were failing. The elder Schleiermacher died in September, and Schumann a few weeks later. At twenty seven, Schleiermacher was still considered too young to become the head pastor when Schumann died. Furthermore, Schleiermacher was Reform and not Lutheran. The middle sized town of about six thousand people was large enough for a Lutheran pastor, but did not have enough Reformed families to support their own fulltime pastor. The young Schleiermacher had to supplement his pastoral duties by catechizing and tutoring more than preaching. Still, the brief two year stay afforded Schleiermacher more opportunities to preach and develop the tools that he needed as a pastor of the larger towns he shepherded, Berlin and Halle.

BERLIN I: ROMANTICISM AND FAME

"For since the Spirit was poured out on all flesh, no age can be without its own originality in Christian thinking."[10]

It was in 1796 that Schleiermacher finally made it to Berlin as a pastor. Most of Schleiermacher's career as a pastor was in Berlin, but it was divided over two different and rather distinct periods. The first stay lasted from 1796 until 1802. Berlin was the sixth largest city in Europe, having 172,122 residents in 1800. The population was also rather young, with more than a third of the population being children. The residents were not very wealthy or modern; a quarter of the population were involved with the manufacturing and sale of textiles.

Schleiermacher's pastorate was in the poor region of the Charité in Berlin, and was attached to a poor house and a hospital. Even in Berlin the population was still overwhelmingly Lutheran, so as in Landsberg, he shared his duties as a pastor with a Lutheran colleague. The joint duties were easily split between the two of them, as the church had two services every Sunday and on feast days. By 1799 Schleiermacher and his Lutheran cohort proposed creating a unified Reform/Lutheran service. Schleiermacher inherited the ecumenical spirit from Zinzendorf. Zinzendorf, in his Berlin Speeches, found little value in externals including confessional identity. This idea brought immediate condemnation from the people, but proved a useful idea for Trinity Church where Schleiermacher served as pastor a decade later.

The hospital ministered to the poorest of Berlin and the population lacked the degree of sophistication that Schleiermacher grew accustomed to working for the Count and at Landsberg. Matters only got worse for the Charité in 1798, when a fire destroyed the insane asylum. Following the fire, Charité hospital absorbed the residents of the asylum. Schleiermacher found himself the minister to both the uncultured poor and the insane. Much like his time in Landsberg, Schleiermacher's time as the Reform pastor was far more than preaching.

While Schleiermacher's vocation was ministering to the poor, his avocation was hobnobbing with the cultured elite. The elites gathered around the salons of Berlin and served as a prime example of Jurgen Habermas's notion of the bourgeois public sphere. According to Habermas, the bourgeois public sphere is best conceived of as the sphere of private people who come together as the public. Following Habermas, this collection of private people, once coalescing around a new collective identity, "debate

10. Schleiermacher, *Christian Faith*, 596.

over the general rules governing relations in the basically privatized but publically relevant sphere of commodity exchange and social labor."[11] In the salons of Berlin, culture became a commodity far more valuable than market goods. Social currency was transforming the German state. Salons as well as related organizations transformed Prussia and the rest of Europe. These associations became the soil from which modernity sprang. Just as the religious impulse behind Pietism and Protestant Scholasticism found secularized expressions, these intimate salons were secularized versions of Spener's *collegia*, with similar transformative results.

Due to the salons secularized character, most devout Protestants viewed them with disdain. They were most certainly not places where you found many ordained clergy. Most parsons viewed the salons as pantheistic dens of Romanticism, filled with pagans and not a fitting place for a real Christian. The stain of association with the salons remained upon Schleiermacher the rest of his life, often with refrains and accusations of being a Spinozist. Accusations of pantheism and associating with the wrong sort of people mattered very little to Schleiermacher, who wanted to be both modern and a Christian. In order to remake Pietism, the older divisions needed to be abandoned and new associations embraced. The salons afforded him this opportunity.

The salon that Schleiermacher found himself in was run by a Jewish woman named Henrietta Herz (d. 1847). Henrietta, and to a lesser extent her husband Marcus, hosted a large circle of poets, artists, and the cultured elites of Berlin. Typifying the Romanticism of the day, notable participants were Friedrich Schlegel, Ludwig Tieck and Novalis. This salon was a perfect fit for the maturing Schleiermacher. Kant and his system of idealism excited Schleiermacher in his youth, but the excitement of Kant faded at the house of Count Dohna, where Romanticism took its place. Schleiermacher used Romanticism to develop his theology of feeling, reinfusing Pietism with the feeling and awareness, and reintroducing Christianity to Romanticism.

As a Reformed Pastor, Schleiermacher never separated his pastoral duties from his current environment and the events and numerous curiosities of his life. While Romanticism occupied his secular attitudes in Prussia, this melded with Calvinism to produces a new definition of religion. For Schleiermacher, religion is the unique heart and source for all that is worthy in humanity; religion becomes the essence of humanity.

With this new theological outlook, Schleiermacher was urged to write something by his friend Schlegel. In response he wrote *On Religion: Speeches to the Cultured Despisers*. Published in December of 1799, here the two

---

11. Habermas, *Structural Transformation*, 27.

trends of Pietism and Romanticism collide. Schleiermacher publishes the work as a corrective to the secularizing impulses of Romanticism and the cultured elites of Berlin. We must keep in mind the relatively small scope of this youthful yet impactful work of Schleiermacher. While Berlin was one of the larger cities in Europe, the 'cultured' consisted of a relatively insignificant percentage of the total population. Only about a thousand Berliners earned their living as academics, writers, or artists. The 'cultured' disparaged religion, and the central aim of the work was to disarm this disdain. Still, for those thousand Berliners, *On Religion* landed its intended blow.

Schleiermacher wrote *On Religion* as a modern apologetic. To serve as a modern apologetic, religion must be personal and not doctrinal. For Schleiermacher, true religion was not submission to doctrines or creeds, rather he argued for an authentic religious experience. Schleiermacher attempted to reargue the Pietist case in nearly the same way it was done in the aftermath of the Reformation, but now Pietism must argue not only against Scholasticism but its demystified form of Enlightenment thought. Just like the earlier Pietists critique of Protestant Orthodoxy, the heart of religion is not found in theological knowledge. The apology was sucessful because it took into account Kant, who advocated in his *Critique of Pure Reason* that one had to "suspend knowledge, in order to make room for belief,"[12] and the Romantics who wanted to deny knowledge to make room for mystery. Schleiermacher also denied that knowledge was antithetical to faith. Faith is not found in knowledge, it remains a mystery, and is only encountered in experience. Schleiermacher explicitly states "I cannot hold religion the highest knowledge, or indeed knowledge at all."[13] If not knowledge, religion is found in the realm of feelings. Schleiermacher's approach to religion is an attempt to infuse Moravian piety into a secularized Romantic ethos. In many ways it is successful.

This early example of Schleiermacher's theology was successful partly because it launched a two pronged attack, criticizing both the static notions of religion and the dynamic cultured elites who despise the status quo and religion. Throughout the five speeches, Schleiermacher weaves one criticism into the other and back again. When he is finished, neither the criticisms of the elites, nor the intractable stale Prussian religious life remains unscathed. Both were forced to react to the new definition of genuine religion that Schleiermacher produces. Schleiermacher's genuine religion resembles the enthusiastic experiential religion that Johann Arndt called for in *True Christianity*, and the message that Zinzendorf echoed. Noticeably absent

---

12. Kant, *Critique of Pure Reason*, 25.
13. Schleiermacher, *On Religion*, 102.

from Schleiermacher's genuine religion is the brutal denial of humanity found in Perkins, Francke, and even Wesley.

Addressing the concerns about religion, Schleiermacher concedes that for too long the trappings of religion have dominated the discussion about religion. Now "the life of cultivated people is far from anything that might have even a resemblance to religion."[14] Schleiermacher argued that the cultured rightfully despise religion because they do not know that what they abhor is not religion; they reject a constraining yet secondary system. Schleiermacher contends that religion should not be a form of coercion, rather a personally freeing endeavor. Schleiermacher exclaims "If you have only given attention to these dogmas and opinions, therefore, you do not yet know religion itself, and what you despise is not it."[15] With this perspective on religion, both the Kantian followers of the *Aufklärer*, and the Goethian Romantics have a place to engage religion, in freedom. Religion, just like Idealism and Romanticism, is an ideology that begins in freedom. Religion is a mode of thought that is expressed in faith, faith that Schleiermacher purports is "a peculiar way of contemplating the world, and of combining what meets us in the world at another, it is a way of acting, a peculiar desire and love, a special kind of conduct and character."[16]

By identifying religion as a competing ideology with Idealism and Romanticism, Schleiermacher simultaneously made religion acceptable, while undercutting the philosophical necessity for the Enlightenment. Schleiermacher lambasted the cultured despisers, contending that "Having made a universe for yourselves, you are above the need of thinking of the universe that made you." Now Schleiermacher sought to replace their secular despair with a Pietist revival. Schleiermacher continued his critique of the cultured despisers by demonstrating that the anti-clericalism which dominated the French Enlightenment was unfounded and logically inconsistent. Schleiermacher inquired, "How then does it come about that, in matters of religion alone, you hold everything the more dubious when it comes from those who are experts, not only according to their own profession, but by recognition from the state, and from the people?"[17] The cultured despisers of religion lacked familiarity with true religion. As a result, Schleiermacher demanded they demonstrate the actual deficiencies of the clergy, rather than simply parroting the false critiques of the French.

14. Schleiermacher, *On Religion*, 1.

15. Schleiermacher, *On Religion*, 15.

16. Schleiermacher, *On Religion*, 27.

17. Schleiermacher, *On Religion*, 2.

Schleiermacher posited that the priests were despised because of a mistaken portrait. In this false image, the priests hold only knowledge of finite trivia, rather than infinite spiritual gnosis. Surprisingly, Schleiermacher partly conceded this point. He separated all clergy, who undoubtedly had members in their ranks lacking understanding, from the higher priesthood, that announces "the inner meaning of all spiritual secrets, and speaks from the kingdom of God." Pure examples of this higher priesthood are indeed rare. They are not only mouth pieces of the kingdom of God, but they are also "the source of all visions and prophecies, of all the sacred works of art and inspired speeches that are scattered abroad, on the chance of finding some receptive heart where they may bring forth fruit."[18]

The higher priesthood, rare as they may be, are prematurely dismissed alongside their weaker counterparts. By discarding all clergy, the cultured despisers illustrate their own ignorance and lack of a special gnosis of the priesthood. "To the man who has not himself experienced it, it would only be annoyance and folly."[19] This is the problem inherent with conflating dogmas with faith and the religious life. Real religion contains some notions of mystery. Religion, as Schleiermacher presents it, "in its own original, characteristic form, is not accustomed to appear openly, but is only seen in secret by those who love it."[20] Schleiermacher's depiction of real religion illustrates his Pietistic conversion in Niesky, echoing Zinzendorf, who argued that "Religion must be a matter which is able to be grasped through experience alone without any concepts."[21] Religion must be experiential or it is not religion at all.

Since religion must be experiential, this experience must be something common to humanity. Schleiermacher concluded "Man is born with the religious capacity as with every other."[22] Since the religious capacity is common to all, "piety cannot be pride, for piety is always full of humility."[23] Religion is therefore also found, not in institutionalized forms, rather in individuals. This then raises the question what area of the individual possesses this religious capacity? Schleiermacher, true to his Pietistic roots, places the religious experience not in reason but in the realm of feelings, not just any feeling but "the essence of the religions emotions consists in the

---

18. Schleiermacher, *On Religion*, 8.
19. Schleiermacher, *On Religion*, 8–9.
20. Schleiermacher, *On Religion*, 26.
21. McGrath, *Christian Theology Reader*, 120.
22. Schleiermacher, *On Religion*, 124.
23. Schleiermacher, *On Religion*, 8.

feeling of an absolute dependence."[24] Not all feelings are religious feelings. When the divine encounters someone, the particular reaction is formulated through a pious feeling. The pious feeling renders one helpless and completely dependent upon the transcendent God. This is the heart of Pietism and Schleiermacher's reconstruction of Pietism, stripping away many of the ecclesiastical trappings is the way that Schleiermacher is the father of modern liberal Protestantism, and reshaped not only nineteenth-century Pietism but also the modern Protestant mindset.

By defining religion as feeling, Schleiermacher's criticism of doctrinal religion, Idealism, and Romanticism is complete. All three are forced to adjust to the work. A new era in theology is birthed with this publication, liberal Protestant theology. This theological trend dominates the nineteenth century, and will be addressed in chapters two and five. Protestant theologians are forced to embrace it or consciously oppose it. It is not until Karl Barth's second *Epistle to the Romans* that this definition of religion begins to wane.

One month after the publication of *On Religion: Speeches to its Cultured Despisers*, Schleiermacher was engaged in a different debate in Berlin. In response to an anonymous Jewish publication in March of 1799, and David Friedländer's *Open Letter* a month later, Schleiermacher wrote *Letters on the Occasion of the Political-Theological Task and the Open Letter of Jewish Householders*. These letters were published in July to address the question of Jewish emancipation in Berlin. Berlin Jews were disenfranchised and unable to fully participate in Berlin social and political life. Many Berlin Jews converted to Christianity to gain voting privileges. These conversions were rarely genuine, and the Christian life of these former Jews consisted primarily in their baptism and continued absence from the Church and its sacramental life.

Schleiermacher's long connection and intimate friendship with Henrietta Herz provided him with an insight to the state of Berlin Jewry. Schleiermacher strongly argued for the emancipation of the Jews and called for an end to these quasi-conversions. According to Schleiermacher, "Reason demands that all should be citizens, but it does not require that all must be Christians, and thus it must be possible in many ways to be a citizen and a non-Christian."[25] Those who maintained a belief that Jewish involvement in civic life corrupted the people were misguided and their reasoning was lazy. Schleiermacher held that Berlin was stronger with devout Jews than it was with false Christians.

24. Schleiermacher, *On Religion*, 106.

25. Frielander et al., *Debate of Jewish Emancipation*, 85.

Schleiermacher believed that trading religion on the public market was dangerous, not only for society, but for Christianity. He rightfully feared that many, if not most, of the new members would be irreligious and even anti-Christian. Without a genuine religious experience, a growing hostility would overcome the baptized Jews. This hostility would likely be directed against the government of Berlin, and the Hohenzollern monarchy, who forced them to abandon their religious identity. Schleiermacher feared that this hostility would grow into a hostility against the Church as well. With these insincere baptized Jews only experience of Christianity being a false one, the church as a whole would be weakened.

The civil rights of Jews were necessary not for their own sake, or even for the sake of Berlin, but for the sake of the Church. To have a large number of inauthentic and impious members of the church would be a cancer to the church, rather than a healthy body on their own contributing to Berlin society. Schleiermacher also believed that Judaism needed its own reform. His knowledge of Judaism came from Henrietta Herz, who held that Judaism "is long since a dead religion, and those who at present still bear its colors are actually sitting and mourning beside the undecaying mummy and weeping over it demise and its sad legacy."[26] Herz called for reform of Judaism and abandoning Halakhic practices to remake and revive Judaism. Schleiermacher encouraged a Jewish reform, just like he desired a Protestant reappraisal.

Later that same year, Schleiermacher published *The Soliloquies*. His tone in this work was rather dismissive of the achievements of Berlin society. Schleiermacher identified the cultured as a "perverse generation (who) loves to talk of how it has improved the world, in order to plume itself and to be considered superior to its ancestors."[27] What made the generation so perverse was the focus on individuality and self-satisfaction. Central to this solipsistic talent is a complete disregard of anything save the material world. The Romantic Pietistic pastor called for a reappraisal of the priorities of Berlin, just as he did for Judaism and the cultural despisers of religion. This examination needed to esteem not only the individual and material world, but embrace community and the spiritual world. Schleiermacher echoed Francke by calling for mutual sacrifice as the mechanism of attaining the highest joy. Communal life must be fostered, and the source for this needed to be the home. Once each home becomes a beautiful embodiment of the unique souls who live therein, all of Berlin and by extension Prussia, and Germany, would be truly free and alive.

26 Frielander et al., *Debate of Jewish Emancipation*, 9.

27. Schleiermacher, *Schleiermacher's Soliloquies*, 50.

If *On Religion* serves as Schleiermacher's Pietist apology to the Romantics, *The Soliloquies* are his attempt to reconnect with the same circle he just decried. In many ways *The Soliloquies* are Schleiermacher's confession. In *The Soliloquies*, Schleiermacher called his audience to accept the unique place humanity has in the cosmos and develop their individuality to the fullest. Schleiermacher cried out "Every home should be the beautiful embodiment, the fine creation of a unique soul; it should have its own stamp and unique characteristics, but with a dumb monotony they are all a desolate grave of freedom and true life."[28] The notion of individuality which embodied the ethos of Romanticism, and at least to Max Weber's reading, Calvinism, is evidenced largely only in this work. Even still, Schleiermacher's individualism that is present in *The Soliloquies* consisted of individuals as household families. These families form larger communities, which in turn form the Prussian state. In *On Religion* and Schleiermacher's subsequent writings, the individual is always coupled with a household. These households consist of multiple people who work in concert with one another. Throughout his sermons, the household is an example for both the uncreated German nation and the Church.

Schleiermacher's brief evaluation of his Berlin contemporaries in the *Soliloquies* fits well as a parallel critique to *On Religion*. Both pieces serve to promote a pious religious life that should be acceptable for the modern Berliner. *On Religion* redefined religion, showing how the priority of religion had drifted towards dogmatism and therefore was losing its grip on the divine. *The Soliloquies* elucidated the errors of modernity and the cold rationalism that strangled humanity in service of the Enlightenment.

One major reason for the fervent call of the Romantic towards individuality in *The Soliloquies* was Schleiermacher's deep love towards Eleanor von Grunow. This illicit love came to a boiling point in 1800 and continued to simmer over the next two years. Eleanor was the wife of a fellow Berlin clergyman. The marriage was childless and by most accounts miserable. It was also an arranged marriage, so not even notions of earlier romantic love could be used to maintain the union. Instead, Friedrich and Eleanor fell in love, with constant discussion of the necessity to dissolve the unhappy Grunow union. While she was unhappy with her marriage, two years into the emotional affair, she chose to remain married. Shortly after her decision, Schleiermacher echoed her sentiment in the indissolubility of marriage. While their relationship cooled some at this point, elements of romantic attraction lasted for years to come. Even though the affair

---

28. Schleiermacher, *Schleiermacher's Soliloquies*, 58.

was never consummated, scandal surrounded the star crossed lovers. This scandal had lasting repercussions for Schleiermacher.

One immediate repercussion surrounded Schleiermacher's relationship with Henriette Herz. Many other salons turned their attention to Schleiermacher and Herz. The gossip produced a query; was their relationship platonic or romantic? Marcus Herz, her husband, found little to be concerned about, believing that their relationship was intellectual rather than physical. The more devastating repercussion of Schleiermacher's torrid yet restrained romance with Eleanor von Grunow came when Bishop Sack exiled Schleiermacher from Berlin.

EXILE, RECONCILIATION, AND REBELLION

"O how deeply I despise this generation, which plumes itself more shamelessly than any previous one ever did, which can scarcely endure the belief in a still better future and reviles everyone."[29]

The exile was to a small parish in Stolpe. Stolpe was on a distant northern coast of Prussia over one hundred miles away from Berlin. Schleiermacher for the last three years had continued to be a liability to the Reformed episcopacy. His association with the salons and Romanticism, as well as the publication of *On Religion*, did not sit easy with the more dogmatically conservative Reformed clergy. Worse still was his involvement with Schlegel who recently published *Lucinde*, the quintessential Romantic description of a "true marriage" and free love. Schleiermacher refused to condemn his friends work and it too closely resembled the worst fears about Schleiermacher and Eleanor.

The Stolpe exile was relatively short, lasting only two years. During this time Schleiermacher served as a court chaplain in the very Lutheran city. Only about fifty Reformed families lived in the small city. His atypical pastoral career took a devotional turn. Schleiermacher characterized this period when he told his friend Georg Reimer in 1802 that he was only able to survive this ordeal because of his Moravian piety. Throughout this exile Schleiermacher remained faithful to Prussia, even turning down a lucrative post in Bavaria.

In August of 1804 Friedrich Wilhelm gave an order concerning worship services at his flagship university at Halle. Every one of the clergy were Lutherans, and the Reform Hohenzollern desired a modicum of denominational diversity. That paved the way for Schleiermacher to return

29. Schleiermacher, *Schleiermacher's Soliloquies*, 50–51.

to Halle, this time as an extra ordinary professor of theology and the university preacher. Once again he delivered his sermons in front of a large congregation. He also found himself the sole Reform professor surrounded by Lutherans both in the faculty and classrooms.

As a theology professor, Schleiermacher came into his own. The love Schleiermacher developed for theology while studying for his ordination exams continued while behind the podium. His lectures, like his sermons, and his personal life, were unconventional. Rather than giving prepared lectures, Schleiermacher used his extensive memory to treat the classroom like a larger salon. His lectures served to process his own theological concepts, with his students serving as sounding boards. At Halle and away from the Berlin salons, Schleiermacher's mature theology developed. In order to advance his theology, Schleiermacher also created a new discipline, hermeneutics. Schleiermacher's conception of hermeneutics will be addressed in chapter two.

A year after his appointment, Schleiermacher wrote what is considered his first mature theological work, a play. Surprisingly the work is penned within a few months of Schleiermacher's romance with Eleanor von Grunow finally ending. To soothe his heartbreak, Schleiermacher sought a number of distractions. A Dillon flute concert served as one of these distractions. After hearing it, Schleiermacher raced home filled with inspiration. The music continued to play in his head for weeks, and while it rung, his heart mended, and he produced *The Christmas Eve Dialogue*. The emotion that a simple piece of music produced highlighted the themes of the incarnation more than his lectures and sermons. To capture the feeling and intimacy of the incarnation was the aim of the piece; words took the place of notes, but the objectives were the same.

The Christmas of 1805 was the opportunity Schleiermacher needed to focus Christianity along Moravian lines. Moving away from the cold notions of dogmatics and sin, he focused instead on Christ. Rather than addressing Christ as the transcendent God who became incarnate in flesh, Schleiermacher's aim was to look at the humanity of Christ, not the fearful judgmental God, but the tender newborn babe. This novel approach is identified as a "Christology from below." Schleiermacher's emphasis on Christ's humanity provided an understanding of religious experience that is common to all. In writing the *Dialogue*, Schleiermacher reintroduced Christology along with Pietism into the theology of the nineteenth century.

Further breaking from convention, Schleiermacher's treatment of Christmas focuses not on the Christmas narratives found in the Gospels of Matthew or Luke. Rather Schleiermacher preferred the mystical description of Christ given in John's Gospel as the source for the *Dialogue*. The *Dialogue* is set as an intimate household get together. The entire play only consists of ten people, six were couples, two were children, and two were single adults. The ten people meet and converse on the meaning of Christmas. Three major themes are present in the work. Not surprisingly, the first is the power and intimacy of music. Schleiermacher's character Edward, who many scholars contend most closely resembles Schleiermacher himself in the piece, proclaims, "In fact, music is most closely related to the religious feeling."[30]

The second theme of the *Dialogue* is the simplicity of childhood. Childlike faith is what is expected. Once again recovering the Pietist priority of experience over doctrine, children become the models of piety. The third and final theme of the piece expands on this point, when Schleiermacher draws a clear contrast between the men and women at the gathering. Since Schleiermacher affirms the child as the model of piety, the contrast between men and women focuses on who can more aptly come to terms with childhood. In the *Dialogue,* men are unable to do so; instead they are too invested in theological disputes. These disputes over the meaning of the incarnation nearly bring the gathering to an end, creating more enemies than friends. Furthermore, none of the men grow closer to Christ through their deliberations. In Schleiermacher's depiction, women on the other hand, have an advantage over the men, partly due to his conception of nature and partly because they care for children. The women move from room to room, reminiscing over previous Christmases. Women, through experience, are growing closer to Christ and the meaning of the incarnation. The work also serves as a veiled political piece. The house that the entire *Dialogue* takes place in serves as a metaphor for Prussia. With the incarnation of Christ Schleiermacher expects that Prussia should adopt a new Christian perspective and each of the characters represent different potentials for the developing nation. Like Francke, whose promethean spirituality developed Prussianism, Schleiermacher attempts to provide a different character to the burdening state, steeped in his conception of pious living.

Schleiermacher also came into his own as a pastor during this period. While during most of his pastoral career Schleiermacher preached in peculiar circumstances and nonconventional settings, this period afforded a degree of normal preaching opportunities. Early in his career Schleiermacher shared his sermons with his father and uncle, but since his father died ten years earlier, Friedrich's tendency to write out his sermons ahead of time slowly dwindled. Friedrich posited that a completely prepared sermon was a wasted effort. If he wrote out the whole sermon and read from it, the sermon

---

30. Schleiermacher, *Christmas Eve*, 29.

lacked power, and the relatively small audiences were isolated and cut off from their pastor if the sermons were read. Whenever Schleiermacher chose to memorize the sermon, he inevitably left something out. Schleiermacher chose instead to only create a framework for the sermons, however within the next five years the frame vanished as well. Schleiermacher's conclusion was to speak the sermons afresh from the power of the moment. While this might not work for every preacher, Schleiermacher's sermons were commanding and informative.

Halle elevated Schleiermacher to a greater prominence than he possessed in Berlin. While he found himself outside of the Romantic salons, he did personally encounter Goethe. Following the chance meeting, Schleiermacher eagerly wrote Henrietta Herz in August of 1805. This brief encounter with one of Schleiermacher's literary heroes was the calm before the coming storm. Exactly one year later, in August of 1806, the tranquil yet energetic mood of Halle came to an end when the alliance between France and Prussia concluded. Berlin learned that Napoleon offered Hanover back to the English. The move was designed to produce a response from Prussia and it did. Napoleon was waiting with his armies. Once the peace was broken, Napoleon quickly defeated Prussian forces at Auerstadt and Jena. Friedrich Wilhelm III fled to the furthest eastern territory of Prussia, Konigsberg. The invasion took nobody by surprise and by October 17 Napoleon conquered Halle.

The conquest of Halle dealt a personal blow for Schleiermacher. Both his house and his church were put into service to the French. When the French troops entered the city, Schleiermacher's house was plundered. Schleiermacher describes the plunder when he and two of his house guests were "obliged to give up our watches, and Gass his money; Steffens was already drained, and in my possession they only found a few dollars; but all my shirts, with the exception of five, and all the silver spoons, with the exception of two, they carried off."[31] After this Schleiermacher was forced to quarter French officers, and his church was used to store grain. These typical wartime atrocities radicalized the thirty-eight year old Schleiermacher.

The French conquest of Halle served to further sever the bonds Schleiermacher once had with the Enlightenment. After all, Napoleon and the French Revolution were consequences of Enlightenment thought, and now French forces looted his house, slept in his beds, and desecrated his church. Worse still, Prussia grew weak because of the Enlightenment. Schleiermacher wanted to see resistance, but everywhere he looked there

31. Schleiermacher, *Life of Schleiermacher*, 53. Schleiermacher to George Reimer. Halle, November 4, 1806.

was not any, at least not from the elites. The *Volk* no longer cared for Prussia, and the Enlightenment leaders viewed the state as a necessary evil. Schleiermacher's political views were at odds with these libertine tendencies. According to Schleiermacher, the state was not a necessary evil, rather it is "the completion (Vollendung) of human life and the maximum of the good."[32] Immediately upon conquest Napoleon closed the university as well. This was a temporary move, intended on preventing the towns youth from mobilizing against him. By November Schleiermacher feared that the temporary closing of the university would become permanent. Schleiermacher could conceive of only two options for Francke's university. The first was its complete ruin, being shut down permanently. The second option was not much better for Schleiermacher. The university, which was founded as a check against Saxony, would be given over to the Saxons. Schleiermacher wished to stay in Halle, but the future at the university was dim. Writing to George Reimer, Schleiermacher bemoans his future prospects, "Should it be handed over to Saxony, perhaps the university will be dissolved, or, at all events, there will be an end to my stay in it, as the Saxons are such very strict Lutherans."[33] The letter concludes with Schleiermacher's view of the Little Corporal. "Napoleon must have a special hatred to Halle."[34]

This reactionary turn from the Enlightenment and the closing of the university also effected Schleiermacher's view of the church and state. Under normal circumstances he was opposed to politics entering into the pulpit. Living under an occupation was not a normal circumstance. If Schleiermacher heard no cries for liberation, he would start them. Since the outbreak of war, Schleiermacher hinted towards Prussian patriotism. In August he delivered a sermon, "How Greatly the Dignity of a Person is Enhanced When One Adheres with All One's Soul to the Civil Union to Which One Belongs." The sermons grew more radical as the occupation grew longer. Of course they were still subtle, as Schleiermacher drew on Biblical stories of oppression and opposition, and on households symbolizing the Prussian house invaded by unruly guests who needed to be put out. There was never any clear line the French censors could hold onto, but the Germans understood the message. The sermons, far more than any earlier writings or activities, made him a national figure almost overnight.

32. Vail, "Schleiermacher and the State," 272.

33. Schleiermacher, *Life of Schleiermacher*, 54. Schleiermacher to George Reimer. Halle, November 4, 1806.

34. Schleiermacher, *Life of Schleiermacher*, 57. Schleiermacher to Henrietta Herz. Halle, November 21, 1806.

Schleiermacher resisted the French occupation in more ways than the pulpit. By 1808 he participated in many secret societies that attempted to undermine the hegemonic forces. That same year Schleiermacher even went so far as to enter into a plot to assassinate Napoleon, however nothing came of it. The next year Napoleon gave Halle over to his brother Jerome and the Kingdom of Westphalia. Napoleon repartitioned the German lands beginning in 1795 when the first treaty was signed with Prussia. By 1815, 112 states of the Holy Roman Empire disappeared, given away to larger neighboring states.

BERLIN II: MARRIAGE, PASTORATE, AND PROFESSOR

"To attribute mercy to God is more appropriate to the language of preaching and poetry than to that of dogmatic theology."[35]

With Napoleon giving away Halle, Schleiermacher chose to remain Prussian. Over the last year he had split his time between Halle and Berlin. Following the transfer of Halle in 1809, Schleiermacher permanently settled in Berlin, where he stayed until his death in 1834. One major reason for remaining in Berlin was his marriage to Henriette von Willich. Schleiermacher had known Henriette from his earlier days in Berlin. He was close friends with her and her then husband Johann Ehrenfried Theodor von Willich. The marriage between Henriette and Johann was a happy one but short. Johann was an army chaplain who died of a typhoid epidemic during the siege of Stralsund in 1807.

Following Johann's death, Schleiermacher wrote many times to comfort Henriette and aid her two children in any way he could. Schleiermacher's concern turned to love and the two were married on May 18, 1809. The age difference was stark, as Friedrich was twenty years older than Henriette (1788–1840), who was only twenty-one. Little exists about the married life of Schleiermacher, but from what does exist, the marriage appeared to be joyous. Schleiermacher wrote to his sister Charlotte, "Except in domestic life, all that we enjoy and all that we attempt, is but vain illusion."[36]

Henriette had two surviving sons, Ehrenfried and Nathanael, from her first husband. Both were rather young at the time of the marriage and Friedrich cared for them as if they were his own. Unfortunately Nathanael died after contracting diphtheria at the age of nine. Ehrenfried survived and wrote in his autobiography that he greatly admired his stepfather "because

35. Schleiermacher, *Christian Faith*, 353.
36. Schleiermacher, *Friedrich Schleiermacher*, 21.

he sincerely cherished and supported his wife even with her weaknesses and faults."[37] In a sermon on marriage, Schleiermacher clarified Paul's decree that husbands love their wives as Christ loved the church (Eph 5:25). He asserted that "we know that this is a love which not only permits but requires love in return," . . . "We know also that it is from another point of view a love that is raised far above all reciprocal love, seeing that the Church cannot in any way repay Christ her Redeemer."[38]

Henriette's weaknesses are largely unknown, but one of them may have been her criticism of Friedrich's sermons. She was a Pietist from Huguenot descent,[39] and she found Friedrich's sermons too complicated and hard to follow. Instead she often went to a neighboring parish. It is unknown if she was present at any of the sermons he delivered about marriage or raising children. Yet in these sermons Schleiermacher's pastoral concerns for both families and communities are evidenced. Affirming "Out of this sacred union are developed all other human relations; on it rests the Christian family, and of such Christian families Christian communities consist."[40] The family is the basic rubric of the Christian community. Furthermore, Schleiermacher pronounced in another sermon that the Christian community is such that the raising of children belongs not only to the family but also to the whole adult community. Now that Friedrich was married, his declarations in the *Christmas Eve Dialogue* about marriage and children were echoed in sermons whose message was extracted from experience of familial love and loss.

Regardless of his other interests and activities, his love of preaching was penultimate. "I consider the position of the preacher as the noblest. . . . I would never of my own will exchange it for another."[41] Schleiermacher served the next twenty five years preaching at Holy Trinity Church, one of the largest churches in Berlin. The church dwarfed its preacher in size. The physically small Schleiermacher grew into the space. The church was noisy, and even overflowing, having a ground floor and three choirs. The doors to the busy street needed to be shut, otherwise no one could hear in any of the three services on Sunday. With such a large and noisy church, Schleiermacher attempted to keep his sermons simple, although his wife did not believe he succeeded in this venture.

37. Redeker, *Schleiermacher*, 210.

38. Schleiermacher, *Selected Sermons*, 139.

39. Clearly, Schleiermacher was not too opposed to the French at this point in his life.

40. Schleiermacher, *Selected Sermons*, 131.

41. Schleiermacher, *Servant of the Word*, 13.

The sermons could not focus on small details, rather large concepts were desirable. Sermons needed to engage the congregation from their shared experiences. Surprisingly, Schleiermacher rarely if ever shared personal experiences in his sermons, only experiences common to all who belonged to the community of faith. Preaching became more than an instructive sermon or an expository lecture, as many of Calvin's sermons are characterized. Rather Schleiermacher viewed the job of the preacher as the model of piety. From the pulpit a voice must ring out and grip the congregation, a voice that is amplified through the expression of personal experiential faith, the faith that Pietists expect of themselves and all Christians.

The majority of Schleiermacher's sermons still resembled the Romantic and Pietistic morality sermons he delivered as the pastor of the Charité. Others are clearly expository, but with a heavy emphasis on application. Many of the sermons written during the French occupation were polemics. Schleiermacher's sermons fall into one of three categories, first a corrective against religious sectarianism, second against particular kinds of religious excitement, and finally those stressing the importance of religious doctrine. It is this third category which places Schleiermacher firmly within the Pietist camp. Schleiermacher uses sermons to prioritize experiential Christianity over and against the other dogmatic forms. Just as the earlier Pietists had done, Schleiermacher chooses to define himself, and by extension true Christianity, as a community that relies on intimacy with God over dogmatic clarity, although Karl Barth points out that Schleiermacher also criticizes the enthusiasts who abandon any church corrective for enthusiasm.

Just like Schleiermacher's post at the University of Halle Church and the Charité, Holy Trinity was a Union church, possessing both Lutheran and Reform clergy. Schleiermacher remained a proponent of a unified church. This attracted criticism from Lutherans, Reform, and even several Unionists. The Unionists criticized Schleiermacher because he maintained that the liturgy should be worked out after union, and the government of the church should be established first. Schleiermacher preferred a synodal-presbyterial form of church government. The thought was that once a church could govern itself, a liturgy could be formulated. As far back as 1804, Schleiermacher believed that most Lutherans and Reformed Prussians could not elucidate the dogmatic reasons that underpinned two separate Protestant churches.

Schleiermacher's social criticism extended into one final realm, specifically the church. Throughout his pastorate, first at the Charité, then at Halle, and finally at Holy Trinity in Berlin, Schleiermacher was the Reformed pastor surrounded by Lutherans. His congregations consisted of Lutherans and Reform and the expectation concerning union was present in all of these churches. This union was at times supported by Friedrich Wilhelm III and at other times opposed. Friedrich Wilhelm III opposed Schleiermacher when the union included ecclesial hierarchical politics that differed from those he desired. Increasingly Schleiermacher represented a bourgeois populace that failed to equate piety with confession. A growing number of Protestants failed to recognize the essential differences between the two dominant confessions. They demanded a personal reception coupled with interpretation of official Church doctrine and a critical attitude towards tradition. Schleiermacher's attempt at unifying Lutheran and Reform confessions increased his popularity amongst a certain percentage of the bourgeois, but it placed him at odds with the monarchy.

By 1817 Schleiermacher received the opportunity to implement his Reform Lutheran union. Friedrich Wilhelm III imposed the union, known as the Union of Prussia. Cynically, many view the reason for this union as a desire of Frederick William III to receive communion with his Lutheran wife Louise. While this undoubtedly played a role in the decree, the rise of Lutheran confessionalism in Prussia at the time necessitated a Hohenzollern response. The Hohenzollerns always remained a Reform minority surrounded by a Lutheran citizenry. It is also at this time that other state reforms were underway.

Schleiermacher found himself in the middle of a new series of debates concerning the issue. His earlier desires remained only vain ambitions. These were either lauded or dismissed depending on who heard them. The practical issues of union dictated an earnest response, as it addressed concrete matters. Schleiermacher's earlier 1804 recommendations for a bi-partisan union were not overly influential in Friedrich Wilhelm III's construction of a unified church. Still, Schleiermacher played a vital role in the events that led to that union. His greater impact on the matter came in 1824 with the publication of his pamphlet "Concerning the Liturgical Rights of a Protestant Prince." In the pamphlet, Schleiermacher accused "Frederick William of breaking the *Allgemeines Landrecht* (General Code) through the forced introduction of his new agenda."[42] In the interim years, Schleiermacher's promotion of union contributed to the confessional conversation.

The greatest opposition was from the Lutherans. Since before the first days of the first Hohenzollern monarch Frederick I (III), the Hohenzollerns sought some way of overcoming the confessional divide. Friedrich Wilhelm III's attempt was simply to declare the two confessions one in his own

42. Clark, "Confessional Policy and Prussian Church Union," 990.

Garrison Church in Potsdam. The Lutherans opposed this monarchical ecclesial fiat for several reasons. First, many Lutheran parishes worried about the financial repercussions of this new union. More substantially, for many Lutherans identified as "Old Lutherans," doctrine still mattered. The idea that their Lutheran identity did not matter concerned them. This led to a large scale departure from the Union Church in the 1830s. This departure resulted in extensive police measures.

Chief among these anti-Unionist Old Lutherans was Christoph Friedrich von Ammon (1766–1850). Ammon and Schleiermacher never met in person, but they corresponded on the issue of church union. Early in the discussion Ammon and Schleiermacher's views coincided, but in 1818 Ammon publically ended his support for union.[43] Another opponent of Schleiermacher's was the Lutheran Karl Gottlieb Bretschneider (1776–1848). Bretschneider opposed Schleiermacher but supported union. Like Schleiermacher, Bretschneider believed that the Lutherans and Reform had overcome most of their theological differences. Bretschneider maintained that the remaining issues needed to be resolved before union could be attempted. Central among the concerns that needed to be addressed was predestination. Schleiermacher alleged that these issues would best be resolved from within the union church.

As the debate between Schleiermacher, Bretschneider and Ammon grew, Schleiermacher found himself increasingly at odds with the state. Friedrich Wilhelm III enthusiastically oversaw the initial legislation and was the sole author of the new liturgy. The proposed union grew to a personal obsession for Friedrich Wilhelm III. Schleiermacher sought to wrench control over the liturgy out of his hands and place it in a synodal-presbyterial form of church government. The monarchical liturgy on the other hand was a significant intervention by the state into the religious sphere.

This division between Schleiermacher and the crown forced a shift in Schleiermacher's views concerning the relationship between the church and the state. Earlier Schleiermacher held that the church was to be in service to the state during the War of Liberation. Now that the state was trying to dictate the practices of the church, Schleiermacher held that the church should be independent. It should not come as a surprise that the Reform pastor who called for union between Reform and Lutherans chose to cite Martin Luther as his source to oppose state involvement. Schleiermacher now took up Luther's doctrine of the two kingdoms.

43. Ammon did so with the publication his book, *Ueber die Hofnung einerfreien Vereinigung beider protestantischer Kirchen: ein Gluckwunschschreiben an den Herrn Antistes Dr. Hess in Zurich* ("On the Hope of a Free Unification of Both Protestant Churches: A Congratulatory Epistle to Antistes Dr. Hess in Zurich").

Luther, in addressing obedience to temporal rulers asserts, "we must divide the children of Adam and all mankind into two classes, the first belonging to the kingdom of God, the second to the kingdom of the world."[44] For Luther these two kingdoms need each other. Luther asserts that true Christians will always remain a minority and need civil protection, but they should not be obliged to do acts which God forbids. The Christian owes allegiance to both kingdoms, though not in the same manner.

Following this Lutheran doctrine, Schleiermacher insists that the church must be independent from the state's involvement. If Prussia interfered with ecclesial politics, any notion of union would ultimately fail. Christianity calls for certain ideas that impact the politics of a state. Still Schleiermacher retorts, "Christianity is neither a political religion nor a religious state or a theocracy."[45] To advance his claim of independence, Schleiermacher even pointed out that civil governments are legal entities which exist everywhere, even where Christianity is not practiced. The creation of civil society emerges from "the corporate life of sinfulness, and everywhere presupposes this, it cannot have the slightest authority in the Kingdom of Christ."[46]

Since the beginning of civil governments are sinful, the leaders of these governments are not bishops, nor ecclesial officers. The best civil authorities can hope for is as guardian of the church. The guardian does not dictate policy, rather they have to guarantee the freedom of the church to have its own independent government. Schleiermacher firmly holds that the two kingdoms are separate, and supports the separation of the two kingdoms by opposing theocracies as well. Schleiermacher's criticism of the state's involvement with the church evolved due to what he perceived to be a princely overstep. His role as an arbiter of social issues extended through any arena that his life encountered.

Schleiermacher's popularity among the elites of Prussia only served to frustrate the monarch. Schleiermacher was a useful tool or an intractable enemy. His patriotism and popularity helped Prussia survive the French. His brand of patriotism eventually placed him at odds with the king, and his popularity only served to limit the monarch's options. Friedrich Wilhelm always had an uneasy relationship with Schleiermacher, but the divide over the church union was greater than any other issue.

Schleiermacher continued to advance his own view of what a unified Lutheran Reform church should look like. Even with different positions

44. Luther, "Temporal Authority," 662.
45. Jungkeit, *Spaces of Modern Theology*, 169.
46. Jungkeit, *Spaces of Modern Theology*, 168.

on the issues of church governance and liturgical dictates, Schleiermacher
supported union. The new union was founded on doctrinal pluralism with
a common liturgical and parish life. This echoes Schleiermacher's own
pastoral positions. While Luther and Ulrich Zwingli vehemently fought over
the issue of the Eucharist, since the time of Calvin, Reformed churches have
expressed a greater degree of openness to this doctrinal matter. As this was
the main dispute at the Marburg Colloquy, and the Reform position relaxed
since Zwingli, this should permit a practical union. Schleiermacher was
convinced that doctrinal discussions had little bearing on daily Christian
life. The effect of this was that doctrine was relegated to scholars.

Schleiermacher's impact during this second Berlin period was greater
than his contributions at Holy Trinity and the efforts to unite the Lutheran
and Reform confessions. Equally as impactful was the founding of the
University of Berlin. In 1809–10 Wilhelm von Humboldt reorganized the
public education system in Prussia and founded the University of Berlin.
Louis Dumont calls the school "the prototype of the modern university."[47]
Before the school was even open, Schleiermacher wrote letters and systems
concerning education. While brief, his time at Halle gave Schleiermacher
the desire to construct the Prussian identity from both the pulpit and the
podium. The Prussian identity is wrapped up in the notion of *Bildung*.
Bildung is the German term surrounding how people relate to their natural
world and God. In a more specific case it concerns culture and the formation
of culture through self-education and self-cultivation. Schleiermacher's
notion of *Bildung* closely resembles Peter Berger's notions concerning the
movements of externalization, objectification, and internalization. Both
view society as "a product of collective human activity."[48] For Schleiermacher,
this social construct resulted in the creation of the University of Berlin.[49]

Since Halle was shut down and given away, Prussia lacked any major
theological schools. While Spener and Francke dictated the theological
aims of Halle, Schleiermacher constructed the new theology department for
Berlin. In 1810 Schleiermacher became first Dean of the theological faculty,
an honor he had four times.[50] Schleiermacher also served as rector of the
university in 1815. The university was commissioned in part by Friedrich
Wilhelm III to ensure that Prussia could make up for the physical loss of
territory through intellectual gain.

47. Dumont, *German Ideology*, 127.

48. Berger, *Sacred Canopy*, 81.

49. The University of Berlin is also known as the Humboldt University of Berlin.

50. Schleiermacher's four terms were from 1810 to 1811, 1813 to 1814, 1817 to
1818, and 1819 to 1820.

Schleiermacher's lecture style closely resembled his preaching. In neither case did he write out his speeches. His lectures were off the cuff, just as they were at Halle. In both cases they were written out only after they were given. The lectures were powerful enough to earn him the nickname the "Plato of Germany." Just as with the pulpit, the temperament of the department was an ecumenical one. Both Lutheran and Reform students found a department they could engage in. Schleiermacher's liberal theological and pedagogical aims of the university found several opponents among the faculty even before the university began. The first series of debates occurred between Schleiermacher and Johann Gottlieb Fichte (d. 1814). Fichte advocated for an authoritarian university that did not need to address practical issues like theology, law, and medicine. Ultimately Wilhelm von Humboldt was the one who reorganized public education in Prussia and sided with Schleiermacher.

The disagreement with Fichte was fairly minor when compared to the outright hostility that grew between Schleiermacher and Georg Wilhelm Friedrich Hegel (d. 1831). Hegel was the prime example of German Idealism following Kant, the same idealism that Schleiermacher rejected for a more experiential and historical philosophy. The theological divide is really the same divide that separated Pietists from the Rationalists, namely the debate between feelings and reason. Hegel criticized Schleiermacher's emphasis on feeling and his definition of religion as the 'feeling of absolute dependence,' quipping "if that were true, 'a dog would be the best Christian, for it possesses this in the highest degree and lives mainly in this feeling.'"[51] This divide was far more than philosophical difference, for Hegel it was personal.

Schleiermacher was one of the founding members of the university and Hegel came along a few years later, in 1818. Hegel believed that Schleiermacher opposed his admission to the university, even though Schleiermacher held no reservations. Before Hegel's arrival, differences in politics resulted in the formation of student movements that coalesced around one of the two figures. By the time Hegel arrived, Schleiermacher excluded Hegel from the Berlin Academy of Sciences. This snub only fueled Hegel's distaste for Schleiermacher. The antipathy and hostility between the two was exactly what the Ministry of Culture, Karl von Alenstein, wanted. Alenstein desired a strong philosophy department to work as a counterbalance to Schleiermacher's theology department. In many ways this was similar to the workings of Halle before it was shut down by Napoleon.

Alenstein's gamble paid off. Both Schleiermacher and Hegel produced great works underlining their theological and philosophical

---

51. Crouter, *Friedrich Schleiermacher*, 11.

positions in light of the oppositions raised by the other. In addition to their philosophical divide, Schleiermacher and Hegel's opinions diverged concerning the relationship between philosophy and religion. Hegel supposed that philosophy and religion were intimately interconnected while Schleiermacher saw the two as mutually exclusive. Schleiermacher understood that the two shared language but philosophy ultimately failed to understand the transcendence of God and religious experience. This conflict of visions strengthened both the philosophy and theology departments. Interestingly though neither Hegel nor Schleiermacher ever directly named or publically debated the other. There are no texts where Schleiermacher even mentions Hegel by name. Each used an exaggerated depiction as a foil in their works throughout the 1820s.

In 1821 Schleiermacher also published his monumental work, *The Christian Faith*. This work further defined Schleiermacher's Pietistic theology, a theology that synthesized Moravian piety with Kantian Idealism, and the Romanticism of the salons. This lays the groundwork for modern liberal Protestantism against the doctrinal orthodoxy of the day. It also delineates Schleiermacher's theological position against Hegel's continued critiques. Through indirect engagement with Hegel and direct engagement with others, the work underwent a revision a decade later. This is Schleiermacher's only complete systematic theology. While it is in no way as long as St. Thomas Aquinas's *Summa Theologica*, Calvin's *Institutes*, or Karl Barth's *Church Dogmatics*, it represents the summation of Schleiermacher's theological mind and it is as important in the development of Western Christian theology as the others are.

LIBERATION

"Everything natural is but a weak shadow of the spiritual."[52]

Schleiermacher spent much of the 1810s fighting multiple battles. In addition to those of the pulpit and the podium, he faced the French. By 1813, the behemoth that was the Napoleonic horde began to show weakness. Napoleon's humiliating defeat in Russia sent waves through Europe. With over half a million French soldiers dead, Prussia joined the fight. Since the devastating losses of Prussian troops in 1807, Friedrich Wilhelm III dismissed his elderly generals and reorganized the Prussian army along the French style. Friedrich Wilhelm called for the Wars of Liberation and the forty-five year old preacher and professor attempted to enlist. Schleiermacher's request to

---

52. Schleiermacher, *Fifteen Sermons*, 146.

become a field preacher was denied. Not discouraged, Schleiermacher continued to drill with the Berlin militia.

Ever since the occupation of Halle, Schleiermacher was a vocal opponent of the French. He was also a critic of Prussia, placing some of the blame for defeat on his homeland. Schleiermacher identified two causes of Prussian defeat. The first cause echoes his criticism found in *The Soliloquies*, that Prussia's hubris grew to its detriment. The pomp and pride was vanity built upon technological advancements, but Prussia was too mechanical. The other cause of its demise grew from the first. Individuals found themselves separated from their families, from communities, from the state. Such isolation existed and this served to rot them from the insides. This decay effected leadership as well as the people's willingness to follow, but there was still hope.

The hope came about in 1813 when the Prussians joined with Russia in defeating the French. The switching allegiance was palpable. Hällesches Tor, the region of Berlin where Holy Trinity was housed, saw French troops marching South and Russians moving in from the North on the same day. Schleiermacher's sermons characterized the war as a holy war and as such Prussia must humble itself before God, expressing gratitude. His characterization of the war was echoed by many Prussians, who called it a holy war of liberation. The notion of a crusade that was so popular during the Wars of Liberation tended towards Francophobia. This was not so with Schleiermacher, who still revered many of the accomplishments of the French, even though he believed they moved to excess. The French excesses were not that different than the Prussians. Schleiermacher's tone was always tempered by this acknowledgement. It was Napoleon and not the French people that was his enemy.

Since the solution for defeating Napoleon lied in a change of Prussian piety as well as practical transformations of society and its leadership, the church and the state had a symbiotic relationship. During the Wars of Liberation, the church was in service to the state. This relationship was natural according to Schleiermacher, as both the church and state originated from the same source, the family. Linguistic bonds, among others, contribute toward affinity. Whenever conflict emerges, it arises only from misunderstanding, and not from an essential conflict. Only later did Schleiermacher come closer to Luther's notion of two kingdoms. During the Wars of Liberation, Luther's two kingdoms were one. Schleiermacher conceived the church and state as two rooms in the same divine dwelling. His notion of nationalism originated from this conflict as well. He argued that while the people called out for a state, the state needed to remember the aspirations of the people and honor God in their actions. While always conscious of the community and collective aspects of humanity, Schleiermacher still maintained a degree of individuality. Those years reading Kant in Barby cemented in him notions of individual freedom.

Schleiermacher's conception of nationalism was one of apparent contradiction, holding opposing poles together. Schleiermacher's idea that people bind themselves together results in many forms. The smallest form is the family, the largest civil form is the nation. The nation must serve to develop the individual. The individual must serve to develop that nation. The nation state should provide freedom for individuality, as long as this individuality does not overtake the collective. Schleiermacher's concept of nationalism is a synthesis of both Kant and Francke. Individuals need to be free, but this freedom should be in service to the neighbor.

While the army had little use for him, Schleiermacher still wanted to serve his neighbor and nation. He found the best way to do this was as a spy for the Prussian monarch. He gathered what information he could for the King in Berlin and traveled to Königsberg to meet with the King and his advisors in 1813. After these meetings, Schleiermacher continued to send secret messages from Berlin. The messages were encrypted with a complicated system of codes, but these did not work very well. Following the failing code, invisible ink was also tried, but with similar results.

Neither his spying nor his drilling with the militia produced much effect in combating the French. Schleiermacher's greatest impact during the Wars of Liberation was found in his preaching. Bishop Eilbert describes Schleiermacher's sermon at the beginning of the war, proclaiming "then in this holy place and this solemn hour, stood the physically so small and insignificant man, his noble countenance beaming with intellect, and his clear sonorous, penetrating voice, ringing to the overflowing church."[53] Schleiermacher urged his congregation to "remember how much happier it is to offer up life as a sacrifice in the noble struggle against this destructive power than in the impotent struggle of medical art against the unknown powers of nature."[54] The message was clear that Prussia was on the eve of a new era.

Schleiermacher's sermons were filled with Christian patriotism that reunited the German state with Pietism along similar lines as Francke. Christian life needed to be placed in service to God and service to the neighbor. In a sermon delivered in March of 1813, entitled "A Nations Duty in War for Freedom," Schleiermacher linked the war to an act of Christian service. "Merciful God and Lord! Thou hast done great things for us in

53. Selbie, *Schleiermacher*, 11.

54. Schleiermacher, *Selected Sermons*, 79.

calling our fatherland to fight for a free and honorable existence, in which we may be able to advance Thy work. Grant us in addition, safety and grace. Victory comes from Thee, and we know well that we do not always know what we are doing in asking of Thee what seems good to us."[55]

In July of 1813 Schleiermacher took over *The Prussian Correspondent*, a political newspaper. Schleiermacher's brief involvement with the paper quickly became a greater detriment than asset. The Prussian censors seized on his criticism of politicians. In his July 14 article, Schleiermacher argued that the Prussian politicians were not decisive enough. This minor and indirect criticism was characterized by Minister Hardenberg as a call for a violent overthrow of the government, and a clear act of treason. The cabinet responded that Schleiermacher needed to resign and leave Berlin and the country within forty-eight hours. In all likelihood Schleiermacher never received the order, and if he did he ignored it. The only thing that emerged from the overblown affair was a reprimand. By September, Schleiermacher abandoned the paper.

When the war concluded in 1815, Schleiermacher tried to use whatever remaining social capital he had to promote liberal ideas. In the last few years Schleiermacher fell out of favor with the monarch and his cabinet, still the masses adored him. Schleiermacher's admiration consisted of two audiences, those who heard him from the pulpit and those who encountered him via the podium. Schleiermacher was considered a dangerous threat. His popularity, combined with his politics, required governmental supervision. Both his activities at the university and church were monitored by the police. Even Schleiermacher's views of church unification that were supported by Friedrich Wilhelm III frightened the aristocratic powers. In January of 1823 he spent three days explaining to the police his sermons and portions of his private correspondence dating from 1813, 1818, 1819, and 1823. While under such strict supervision, it is surprising that Schleiermacher received the medal of the Red Eagle, third class from Friedrich Wilhelm III. What is not surprising is this was the only medal he ever received in his service to the King, while many lesser preachers and professors received greater and more numerous awards.

The censorship and lack of acclaim were due in part to the Prussian monarch's shifting attitude now that the war was over. During the war, the Prussian King Friedrich Wilhelm III encouraged discussions of nationalism. The *Volk* fighting a foreign enemy greatly helped his chances of success. When the war ended, the *Volk* were no longer useful. After all how are the *Volk* defined? Greater political freedom is requested since this freedom was

55. Schleiermacher, *Selected Sermons*, 82.

used to motivate them to begin with. Other questions emerged that caused fear for the monarch. Who shall rule Germany, in what way, and what should the borders be? Likely Prussia would dominate the German lands, but in 1815 this was in no way a guarantee.

Schleiermacher believed that the German states, in whatever form they existed before and after Napoleon, needed to unite. Politics, like religion, needed to be understood from its historical context. History defined a people and its politics. Politics needed to be understood as a hermeneutical field of inquiry, just like theology. With this basic understanding of politics, Schleiermacher expected the future of religion and the German people as unified. Schleiermacher argued that the spirit of German Protestantism was embodied in his notions of Protestant Pietism. Roman Catholics on the other hand have a different spirit to them. They possess a "rigidity which he found antithetical to individuated religious experience."[56]

The division between Catholic Germans and Protestant Germans was not unique to Schleiermacher. Rather this was the central debate surrounding the formulation of Germany through the first half of the nineteenth century. This spirit of authentic German-ness grew in stature because of the nations involved during the Wars of Liberation. Within twenty-five years the events of the war and character of the German nation were redefined. France was not simply a centuries old foe. In the collective memory of Protestant Germans, France became a Catholic foe. The Napoleonic invasion was equated with the Thirty Years War. Notions of *Grosse-Deutch* or *Klein-Deutch*[57] were debated, largely concerning the inclusion or exclusion of Catholic Austria.

Other views of nationalism emerged during this time as well. Fichte proposed his own view that in part was similar to Schleiermacher's. Their opinions differed because they disagreed about what the driving force was behind the German spirit. In his *Addresses to the German People,* Fichte argued "The real destiny of the human race on earth . . . is in freedom to make itself what it really is originally."[58] The German people were preserved through language and education according to Fichte, urging the German people onto the eternal. For Schleiermacher, the freedom exists from the German histories as well, but this is as a result of cooperation with the divine. Regardless of their conceptions of how the state ought to be, both conceived of the rulers as absolute.

56. Raack, "Schleiermacher's Political Thought," 378.

57. "Large" or "Small" Germany.

58. Fichte, *Addresses to the German Nation,* 79.

Schleiermacher's political involvement throughout the entire second Berlin period was closely tied to the reformer Karl Reichsfreiherr vom und zum Stein (d. 1831). Stein's desire to reform Prussia focused on liberating the peasants and municipal reforms, including rationally planning out factories, roads, and canals. He desired self-help and a reworking of hierarchical structures, giving more autonomy to laborers, while transferring accountability of other duties to foremen, all with a hope to become more efficient. For a while Stein's liberal policies were successful. In 1808 King Friedrich Wilhelm III praised and encouraged Stein's reform work and put some changes in effect, such as liberating the peasants in 1811. In 1813 Prussia received a new constitution, one that included a parliament. This promise is credited to Stein. Still Stein's successes were nearly always half measures. While he was praised by Friedrich Wilhelm III in 1808, he was briefly dismissed in 1807. The sweeping reforms and freedoms that Stein desired, and by extension Schleiermacher, were only partial measures.

Schleiermacher's desire for reform eclipsed Stein. The liberal freedoms that Schleiermacher hoped for with the new Prussia only contributed to his role as a thorn in the King's side. Schleiermacher called for a shorter work week for the lower classes, notions of economic equality, and social services. These reforms were grounded in a sense of responsibility that the state has for its constituent members. With these concerns from Schleiermacher, it is of little surprise that he was constantly under government supervision.

Schleiermacher's vision of the state was a liberal yet united German state. The German people were destined to emerge as a single country, a country in service to the state. The state should in turn grant them freedom and individual rights. The Catholic areas of Germany remained an open question. With this vision of a future German state, it is notable the impact Schleiermacher had on the subsequent generation of Berliners. The next generation of German leadership sat in his church on Sunday and many even attended his university. Even without regard to theology, Schleiermacher's liberal nationalism promoted the concept that "We Germans fear God and nothing else in the world."[59] This message was delivered to his confirmands. The most notable of these was none other than Otto von Bismarck.

In February 1824 Schleiermacher contracted pneumonia. Knowing the end was near, the preacher faithfully accepted his death with a firm hope for eternal communion with Christ. In a sermon delivered for Easter, Schleiermacher's words seem fitting for his own death.

If we thus someday look back on the life we have spent, when we have reached its close, we shall thankfully and gladly acknowledge that it has

59. Redeker, *Schleiermacher*, 205.

been the eternally wise kindness and the compassionate love of the heavenly Father towards all who are called His children, which, through errors and weakness, through joys and sufferings, has bound us ever more closely and at last inseparably to Him, whom indeed we cannot let go if the Scripture is to be fulfilled in us, and in fellowship with whom, and comforted as He himself was, we shall be able to cry, "It is finished." Amen.[60]

News of his death spread through the university. His colleagues stopped their lectures to comment on his passing. One faculty member, August Neander remarked that Schleiermacher "is the man from whom a new epoch in theology will be dated."[61] The historian and devout Lutheran Leopold von Ranke commented that Schleiermacher's "whole being, his striving, deeds and life were aimed at reconciliation. . . his life was like his thought: the picture of the most beautiful equanimity. His name is grounded in eternity; no one is apt to be born who is equal to him."[62]

His funeral was a city-wide event. Ranke estimated twenty-thousand people lined the streets of Berlin waiting for the casket to make its way through the city streets. 10 percent of the city and King Friedrich Wilhelm III came out in the winter cold to honor the preacher, professor, political activist, and public theologian. Witnesses said an uncommon sadness gripped the entire city.

Schleiermacher's life and work left behind no direct school of thought, yet no area of nineteenth-century Protestant theology exists without his influence somehow touching it. Schleiermacher learned Pietism from his Father and his school years at Niesky and Barby. It was also at Barby that Schleiermacher learned Enlightenment thought and his lifelong journey to unite the two began. This journey reinvigorated and reinterpreted Pietism, bringing in elements of Romanticism, but always redirecting his attention towards experiential Christianity. He remained an outsider even while holding many positions of power. Like Spener, anytime he advocated for a new theological perspective he faced challenges from both the civil power and his church. Beyond his contributions to social construction, pedagogy, and nationalism, Schleiermacher's legacy is his Pietistic theology, where he set the standard for all Protestant theology in the nineteenth century.

60. Schleiermacher, *Selected Sermons*, 249.

61. Schleiermacher, *Servant of the Word*, 12.

62. Crouter, *Friedrich Schleiermacher*, 29.

II

Theology of Schleiermacher

"Only through Jesus, and thus only in Christianity, has redemption become the central point of religion."[1]

SCHLEIERMACHER'S THEOLOGY IS A synthesis of his formation in Pietism, and his uneasy yet sympathetic relationship to modernity. The theological constructs of modernity posed a challenge to rational and experiential Christianity. The orthodox rationalist Christian Wolff was the first to reach a compromise. While the Pietist Francke founded the theology department at Halle, it was Wolff who founded the philosophy department. The two departments radically diverged on the course and shape of Prussia. In many ways Francke, won but Wolff's philosophy shaped the early centuries of the German *Aufklärung*.

Wolff, a follower of Gottfried Wilhelm Leibniz, was particularly attracted to Leibniz's *Theodicy*. In the *Theodicy*, Leibniz argued "it is sufficient to show that a world with evil might be better than a world without evil."[2] Continuing this course of reasoning, Leibniz maintains that this world with evil present in it still contains more goodness than evil and this is the best of all possible worlds. Wolff expands this in his essay "All is Right." Wolff's expansion of Leibniz's conclusions takes the line of reasoning to a nearly absurdist level. Wolff's contemporaries thought differently and the essay received an award at the 1755 Berlin Academy of Science. In "All is Right," Wolff claims that perfection in the world means reflecting on God's love for the world rather than the world's imperfections. This became the

1. Schleiermacher, *Christian Faith*, 57.
2. Leibniz, "Selections from *The Theodicy*," 1890.

compromise between rationalism and scholastic Protestant Christianity for the German *Aufklärung*. Many of the rationalists resisted the lure of compromise as unsatisfactory. Wolff's system still possessed a theological rather than rational eschatology. In this rational eschatology, God, or humanity working with God, tended towards perfection, a position not all rationalists could hold.

A generation after Wolff, Voltaire shattered the uneasy Wolffian compromise. His satire against Wolff in *Candide* landed a deadly blow to the German philosopher. Voltaire's Enlightenment was French as opposed to the German *Aufklärung;* and while the two held some concepts in common there was a noticeable difference, especially when it came to the church. The rationalists who supported Voltaire were thoroughly entrenched in the anti-clericalism of the French Enlightenment. Voltaire went so far as to sign himself "Mocker of Christ."[3] Deism was the furthest the French Enlightenment thinkers could go. Wolff, Leibniz, and the Germans following him maintained a relationship with Enlightenment rationalism and Protestant, usually Lutheran, Christianity. Luther's reform of the church was interpreted as a rational reform and the beginnings of the Protestant led Enlightenment, away from the medieval Catholic Dark Ages. The ultimate belief that God is a God of reason allowed for an uneasy relationship between rationalism and German religion. Following Voltaire the French anti-clericalism briefly dominated German Enlightenment thought. The same thing was mirrored within the Hohenzollern monarchy. No longer was Wolff's student Friedrich Wilhelm I the king, rather Voltaire's student Frederick II. Frederick II, while personally anti-clerical, feared that openly supporting such a position may lead towards antiestablishmentarianism. His successor Friedrich Wilhelm II is best known for his Edict on Religion of 1788, which forbade heterodox academic discussions about God, the church, and religious speculation. Furthermore part of the Edict stated "No one should despise, deride, or disparage the clerical order."[4] Not surprisingly, the Edict was unpopular amongst the Enlightenment supporting elites who followed in Frederick II's skepticism.

Following Voltaire, the Wolffian position was rehabilitated by Kant. For Kant, religion was not simply theological knowledge as his sixteenth-century progenitors believed, but theoretical knowledge. Reason and religion cooperate. In this new venture, religion and rationalism are not enemies as Voltaire supposed, nor is reason subordinate to religion as Wolff assumed. Under Kant, religion necessarily operates by the rules of logic and reason.

---

3. Delumeau, *Catholicism between Luther and Voltaire*, 204.

4. Sauter, *Vision of the Enlightenment*, 44.

This result is Kantian metaphysics. If this was a victory for the rationalists, it was empty, as religion still existed. Religion survives Kant in two ways. First, reason has natural limits. The mind can only know phenomena rather than the *nomina*, or thing in itself. This denial of knowledge makes room for faith. Religion is also maintained by Kant since religion is equated with morality. This apparent demotion of religion did not sit easy with many Protestant scholastics, but it preserved religion and their dogmatic teachings from the assault launched by Montesquieu and Voltaire. Kant's position, while not perfect, changed the direction of the relationship of modernity and the Protestant Churches to a greater extent than Wolff. This pivot provides a separate sphere for religion that is largely immune to French Enlightenment critiques. This does not mean that Kant emerged unscathed from Friedrich Wilhelm II's Edicts, as even this position was viewed as radical.

Still the relationship between Christianity and modernity was not firmly established. Over the next generation two strands of Kantian modernity emerged, the first belonging to Schleiermacher. Schleiermacher understood Kant, but rejected the compromise. The other followed Hegel, who upheld Kant. Hegel's contributions supported a theological and metaphysical compromise. Religion is a part of a larger philosophical world. The Wolffian perfection was re-categorized as progress under Hegel. Underneath Hegelian philosophy, there remained the beating heart of a God who was involved in the world. Hegel declared in his lecture on the consummate religion, "The nature of spirit itself is to manifest itself, make itself objective; this is its activity and vitality, its sole action, and its action is all that spirit is."[5]

GEFÜHL AND CHRIST

"The Piety which forms the basis of all ecclesiastical communions is, considered purely in itself, neither a Knowing nor a Doing, but a modification of Feeling, or of immediate self-consciousness."[6]

This is the theological and metaphysical challenge that Schleiermacher faced. It was from this point that even Schleiermacher's early theology, found in *On Religion*, takes its stand. It is from this challenge that *The Christian Faith* ultimately supports and bolsters his earlier claims. In *On Religion* Schleiermacher asserts, "belief must be something different from a mixture of opinions about God and the world, and of precepts for one life or for two.

---

5. Hegel, *Consummate Religion*, 63.
6. Schleiermacher, *Christian Faith*, 5.

Piety cannot be an instinct craving for a mess of metaphysical and ethical crumbs."[7] It is from here that Schleiermacher creates a larger space for theology in the modern world. Religion does not exist in the corners and limits of reason, but is itself supra-rational, and natural. Religion is experiential. Proper religion belongs not to the rationalist, or the scholastic, but to the Pietist.

To begin, Schleiermacher deconstructed the uneasy alliance that existed between rationalists and Protestant scholastics. Both the younger Schleiermacher, as evidenced in *On Religion*, and his more mature theology with his work *The Christian Faith*, participated in this dismantling. The first step illustrates the flaws inherent in the alliance. The rationalists elevate science while the Protestant scholastics elevate dogma. Schleiermacher asserts that "the process of defining a science cannot belong to the science itself," therefore none of these propositions "can themselves have a dogmatic character."[8] The dogmatic affirmations can exist only in the realm of theology and not from a science of theology.

Proceeding from this point, Schleiermacher proclaims "I cannot hold religion the highest knowledge, or indeed knowledge at all."[9] Religion not only does not belong to the realm of science, it exists in its own realm. To support his claim that religion cannot simply be a type of knowledge, Schleiermacher points out that "Quantity of knowledge is not quantity of piety. Piety can gloriously display itself, both with originality and individuality, in those to whom this kind of knowledge is not original."[10] Even the layman who lacks the doctrinal expertise of the theologian may be more religious.

To further divide these two camps, Schleiermacher addresses the existence of miracles. Brilliantly, Schleiermacher addresses an issue that the rationalist deists and doctrinal orthodox subordinated in their alliance. After all, if God is simply the divine clock maker and left the universe to continue on its own mechanical operations, then a miracle which grounds theological knowledge cannot occur. One may expect that Schleiermacher, the pastor and theologian, would side with the Protestant scholastics. Rather he seemingly sides with the rationalists by denying the existence of miracles in the conventional sense. In doing so Schleiermacher defines a miracle as the religions name for an event. The event remains within the mechanical world but is enchanted by the perceptions of the pious. By permitting the

7. Schleiermacher, *On Religion*, 31.

8. Schleiermacher, *Christian Faith*, 2.

9. Schleiermacher, *On Religion*, 102.

10. Schleiermacher, *On Religion*, 35.

miraculous a space in the rational world, Schleiermacher also affirms the experience for the devout. Schleiermacher offers up a new synthesis of religion and reason but bases this not in doctrine or science, rather in the realm of Pietism, in experience.

Feeling of Absolute Dependence

"Your feeling is piety in so far as it is the result of the operation of God in you by means of the operation of the world upon you."[11]

The Kantian compromise was to place religion into the camp of ethics. Schleiermacher rejects this idea as well. Ethics, while a part of one larger system or another, ultimately resides in actions, in doing. If religion is not concerned with knowledge, nor in actions, Schleiermacher posits that religion can fall into only two possible areas. The first is *Anschauung* or intuition, the other is *Gefühl* or feeling. Both knowledge and ethics serve as objects of study, as rational facts that are easily partitioned and positioned far from the lives of people. While information may be powerful, its power is only when it draws someone into itself, and this internalization is done through *Anschauung*. Once the knowledge is drawn in, it does not remain a sterile fact, rather it becomes *Gefühl*. Religion is not a fact, as earlier demonstrated, rather religion is only religion when it is internalized. Intuition helps this, but the real domain of religion must be in feeling.

What feeling is not is simple emotions. Schleiermacher is not advocating for universal emotional mysticism, but still emotions play a role. Max Weber argued that "Pietism from Francke and Spener to Zinzendorf moved in the direction of an *increasing* emphasis on the emotional."[12] Schleiermacher's Pietism and defnition of religion places him one step beyond Zinzendorf in this emotional Pietist continuum. Schleiermacher supports emotions, but feeling is also something outside the self.

Schleiermacher characterizes feeling as both inside and outside the person. Feeling is based in reality and individuality. Two feelings emerge as aspects of the self. The first is a feeling of freedom. This first feeling of freedom dominates when the object of the feeling is wrapped up in the self. While Kant and Hegel assert that everything must be done in freedom, this freedom taken to its natural conclusion remains only within the individual and is isolating. In this isolation the consciousness is only individual

---

11. Schleiermacher, *On Religion,* 45.
12. Weber, *Protestant Ethic,* 94.

consciousness. With its source only in the individual, feeling is free, but this is not religious feeling.

Religious feeling must then be a feeling from outside the self rather than inside. If the source of the feeling is outside the individual, the feeling is one of dependence rather than a feeling of freedom. Religious feelings must present itself to the other. As such feeling is in association with society and the world and not just the individual. Emile Durkheim echoes this when he defines religion as "a unified system of beliefs and practices relative to sacred things, that is to say, things set apart and forbidden—beliefs and practices which unite into one single moral community called a Church."[13] The moral community is the religious because it is outside and therefore greater than the individual. While Schleiermacher and Durkheim differ concerning the ultimate cause of the outside object which brings forth the religious, both maintain that religion, while internalized, must be greater than the self.

Schleiermacher unequivocally identifies the source of religious feelings by stating "our being and living is a being and living in and through God."[14] Since the source for religious feelings ultimately lies within God, Schleiermacher continues, not all feelings of dependence are religious, and religious feelings must be a particular type of dependence. For a feeling to be religious, it must be a pious feeling, that is, the object which intuition internalized to produce the feeling must have at its source God. As such, pious feelings cannot be equated with simple emotionalism. Emotions remain a part of feeling, but pious feelings are of a separate character.

The pious feeling must be primarily a source of dependence, and this dependence is not partial but complete. Simply stated, Schleiermacher declares "the essence of the religions emotions consists in the feeling of an absolute dependence."[15] Since the dependence that is required for a religious feeling is absolute, the subject must possess a degree of freedom in their dependence. While religion is not an operation of a feeling of freedom, freedom must still remain for religious feeling, and otherwise it is not a feeling of dependence but a feeling of servitude. Religious feelings consist in the feeling of dependence, because there must be an other to which religion is directed towards. Yet the feeling of dependence is not a feeling of coercion either. A degree of freedom must be present to afford the feeling

---

13. Durkheim, *Elementary Forms of Religious Life*, 62.

14. Schleiermacher, *On Religion*, 49.

15 Schleiermacher, *On Religion,* 106.

of dependence to be a religious feeling of dependence. Schleiermacher pointedly states "there is no will without freedom."[16]

Schleiermacher clarifies this later in his work *On the Glaubenslehre,* especially when applied to Christianity. In the work he states "I deduce Christianity from the feeling of the need for redemption, which is indeed a particular form of the feeling of dependence."[17] Christianity exemplifes the feeling of absolute depenence because humanity is in need of redemption. The pious feeling of absolute dependence reshapes the individual as it is itself a mechanism for uniting with God. Schleiermacher describes, "The immediate feeling of absolute dependence is presupposed and actually contained in every religious and Christian self-consciousness as the only way in which, in general, our own being and the infinite being of God can be one in self-conciseness."[18]

The feeling of absolute dependence produces a consciousness of God. The first thing this God consciousness shows is the need for redemption, which in effect produces greater dependence and fuels the growth in this God consciousness. This is the purpose of redemption and the Christian message. The Christian message is understood therefore not through knowledge and gaining insight, rather through experience. Rationalism and Protestant orthodoxy, rather than piloting the ship of modernity, crash into the third strand of Protestantism. The Pietists, as embodied not in their recently formed schools and ideological movements, rather in Schleiermacher who embodied the experiential strain of Protestantism, modeled this third strand.

Pietism provided Schleiermacher the victory over Enlightenment critics of religion. The victory of Schleiermacher did not come in denying the Enlightenment but in overcoming it. While Kant synthesized reason and doctrine, Schleiermacher combined reason with piety. Schleiermacher was educated in both Moravian schools and the Enlightenment circles. Throughout *On Religion* and *The Christian Faith,* Schleiermacher develops a dogmatic system that references classical Protestant orthodoxy, then Pietist and Enlightenment critiques, before synthesizing them under a new yet familiar experience.

In light of this move towards philosophy, it is not surprising that Schleiermacher prefigures the assertions of later American Pragmatists such as John Dewey and William James. When James states "In the religious life the control is felt as 'higher'; but since on our hypothesis it is primarily

16. Schleiermacher, *Christian Faith,* 519.

17. Schleiermacher, *On the Glaubenslehre,* 70.

18. Schleiermacher, *Christian Faith,* 131.

the higher faculties of our own hidden mind which are controlling, the sense of union with the power beyond us is a sense of something, not merely apparently, but literally true."[19] He incorporates psychology and theology. Elsewhere in *Pragmatism* Lecture II, James also tries to mediate between empiricism and religion, this time with his notions of pragmatic truth. Truth for James and the pragmatists "becomes a class-name for all sorts of definite working-values in experience."[20] These claims come even closer to Schleiermacher's words that "in religion, error only exists by truth and not merely so, but it can be said that every man's religion is his highest truth. Error therein would not only be error, it would be hypocrisy. In religion then everything is immediately true, as nothing is expressed at any moment of it, except the state of mind of the religious person."[21] Both James the Pragmatist and Schleiermacher the Pietist hold notions of truth as psychological and relative to the experiences of the pious individual. Both create a space where religious experience confronts and overcomes the rational and dogmatic world.

Christology

"The sole source of this life is Christ, and the former human being does not oneself actually live in that source but rather bears the living Christ in oneself."[22]

Schleiermacher's second key theological development grows from the first. This is his treatment of Christology. Schleiermacher's Christology progresses as his theology matures. His first mature work, *The Christmas Eve Dialogue*, was a reappraisal of the person of Christ and the impact that Christ has as the source of experience and the embodiment of complete God consciousness. From this point on Christ is the central figure in his mature theology.

Today this message appears almost comically unnecessary as Christ is essential to Christianity and one would expect a Christian preacher, especially one who emphasizes experiential theology, to ground their work in the Christ's humanity as it relates to his divinity. Yet at the beginning of the nineteenth-century Christology was widely neglected by Protestants and the doctrine of the incarnation was denied by new forms of Gnosticism. Schleiermacher's emphasis on Christ was a departure from the trends in

19. James, "Varieties of Religious Experience," 458.
20. James, "Pragmatism," 516.
21. Schleiermacher, *On Religion*, 108.
22. Schleiermacher, *On the Doctrine of Election*, 64.

Protestant Christianity as dictated by the Protestant scholastics. Instead Schleiermacher remained true to his Moravian teachings and the fervent Christology of Zinzendorf.

This message may also surprise some who have read *The Christian Faith*. A typical misreading of the texts exists due to the construction of the treatise, a fact that Schleiermacher even acknowledges. "I see quite clearly how the present outline has been misunderstood."[23] *The Christian Faith* begins by addressing dogmatics and religious self-consciousness, rather than specific Christian doctrines and practices. While a brief reading of Schleiermacher's only systematic text often leaves readers with the impression that the God-consciousness is more important than Schleiermacher's Christology, those who are more familiar with the text see past this. Schleiermacher's desire to re-engage Protestantism with Christ shaped both his theology and his pastoral life.

Schleiermacher's Christological beginnings start with looking at the historical Jesus. This produced a minor uproar, but nothing compared to D.F. Strauss and his work *The Life of Jesus, Critically Examined*, or Ludwig Feuerbach and his work *The Essence of Christianity*, who both cast doubt on the existence or nature of the historical Jesus. Schleiermacher constructed his own understanding of who the historical Jesus was. In a series of lectures called "The Life of Jesus," Schleiermacher elevates the Johannine Gospel over the synoptic Gospels. He believed that personal testimony of John related a historically accurate depiction of Christ. Schleiermacher also used the historical evidence that existed at the time in determining his preference for John. In the lectures, Schleiermacher still admits that complete knowledge of the historical Christ is unknowable given the limited number of primary sources.

While determining facts and aspects of Jesus's life as it truly existed in history was an essential first step, the value of the step comes from what it can tell us. The first and most important conclusion from John's Gospel is understanding the humanity of Christ. John's phrase "'the Word become flesh" becomes the appropriate way to regard to Jesus, since following the incarnation the phrase takes on a double meaning when the word "word" becomes incarnate in the believer as well. Only from the perspective of the incarnation does the rest of the Christian life and theology take shape for Schleiermacher.

Since this is the fount of Schleiermacher's mature theology, he is quick to point out that the historic Christian faith never assumes sin as an essential element in man's essence. Rather sin, and the necessary grace that is created

---

23. Schleiermacher, *On the Glaubenslehre*, 56.

by sin, are secondary characteristics to the psychology and anthropology of man. Christ, being man, in no way needed to sin to be man. Rather since Christ became man, man can then be formed in the image of Christ. This image is the image of a perfect God-consciousness. Schleiermacher marvels at the ability of Christ the man to "take into itself such an absolute potency of the God-consciousness."[24] This God-consciousness that Christ knows fully is only partially known by Christians. This fragmental knowledge is the limited God-consciousness that is experienced by sinful humanity. Christ's redemption provides greater access and clarity in this God-consciousness, as it can now be shared from Christ to the inner life of the believer.

Christ the man possesses a perfect God-consciousness. It is only Christ who has this perfect consciousness, and as such he remakes humanity. Schleiermacher proclaims, "For, the entrance of Christ into humanity being its second creation, humanity thus becomes a new creature, and one may regard this entrance as also the regeneration of the human race, which to be sure only actually comes to pass in the form of the regeneration of individuals."[25] In this He is the second Adam, and the new creation, model and template that every other Christian, through the feeling of absolute dependence is able to resemble. Through Christ's perfect God-consciousness, humanity can be born anew.

Christ possessing a perfect God-consciousness and becoming the first of the new creation through the incarnation is His redemptive act for Schleiermacher. Christ's redemption of humanity is found not in a sacrificial atonement. This, after all, was the issue which caused a dramatic though brief break with his father and his expulsion from Barby. Rather it is the incarnation that redeems humanity. The incarnation re-makes men and women, now along the image of a person with a perfect God-consciousness who can truly have fellowship with God's creation. Christ assumes humanity into fellowship with him, by first entering into fellowship with humanity in the incarnation.

Schleiermacher's mature theology was shaped by his Christology, and no aspect of Schleiermacher's later theological works can be understood without first taking up his understanding of Christ. Still for Barth, Schleiermacher's Christology, "is the point where the system involuntarily breaks up."[26] Barth views Schleiermacher's Christology not as the beginning of Schleiermacher's larger system, but as the end of Schleiermacher's engagement in rational theology. Not surprisingly,

24. Schleiermacher, *Christian Faith*, 368.

25. Schleiermacher, *Christian Faith*, 477.

26. Barth, *Theology of Schleiermacher*, 107.

Barth links Schleiermacher's Christological turn to Zinzendorf and his Moravian upbringing. "To his particular piety with its background of a gentle waft of Zinzendorf, I would rather ascribe the erroneous content of Schleiermacher's Christology. . . I believe that the intolerable humanizing of Christ that triumphed under the aegis of Schleiermacher in the nineteenth century was very closely related to pietism, especially in the form that it had been given by Zinzendorf."[27]

While Barth's condemnation falls on Schleiermacher's Christ, viewing him only as a mere exemplar of human nature, a similar criticism exists from others who believe that Schleiermacher did not go far enough. Schleiermacher began his Christology from below, where all aspects of theology must originate in the knowledge of the incarnation, but this theological system is left incomplete. The further discussion of a Christology from below is left to Schleiermacher's followers and those engaged in a reexamination of Christology in the nineteenth century. The incomplete ideology still served to combat the public controversies of pantheism and atheism that grew in the eighteenth and nineteenth centuries. Schleiermacher's humanizing of God through the incarnation of Christ, within a rationalist system, grounded in the historical figure of Christ, silenced these two blaring trumpets, at least for a time.

GOD, SIN, AND REDEMPTION

"God, at the thought of whom all wishes become prayers, might all these wishes also refer to what is in accordance with your good pleasure, to what we are able gladly to consider jointly with our thought of you."[28]

With Schleiermacher's Christology as his theological lens, his notion of God begins to develop. God as the source of man's dependence can only be apprehended as pure activity. God as pure activity is not knowable to humanity, as God is in God's self, rather God is only known through his activity in the world, specifically the activity initiated by Christ. Humanity related to God through our passive nature, in utter dependence upon God and through this developed God consciousness.

The developed God consciousness is not dependent upon a knowledge of Trinitarian theology, nor a conception of the God-head. While Schleiermacher matures his theology through the incarnation, the

27. Barth, *Theology of Schleiermacher,* 106.
28. Schleiermacher, *Fifteen Sermons,* 83.

role that Pentecost has, and the Holy Spirit as a distinct person of God, is underdeveloped. Schleiermacher did not deny Trinitarian theology, but he did subordinate it to a secondary status. Schleiermacher's discussion of the trinity is not found in the doctrines of God, rather in secondary theological issues that are delineated through church history and tradition.

In a similar fashion, much of the early part of *The Christian Faith* addresses religion apart from specific Christian claims. Unlike other scholars of religion, especially those coming from England in the eighteenth century, Schleiermacher opposes any notions of natural religion. For the eighteenth-century English scholars, the notion of *noesis* that could be discovered in nature grew to a point of an amorphous god who largely resided as a moral governor. Like Schleiermacher's other critiques of limiting religion to morality, this notion of *noesis* falls flat. Schleiermacher appeals to history and historical developments, not only in his understanding of the person of Christ, but also in how religions grow and are differentiated.

While Schleiermacher discusses religion as a natural phenomenon, and relegates essential Christian doctrine to secondary status, he remains fervently a Christian theologian. Again this springs from his Christology. Christ as the incarnation of God is a historical event that Schleiermacher clings to. This construction above all others places Christianity at the apex of religious ideologies and provides the solution of how humanity is to encounter the transcendent God. It is from Christ that the God-consciousness is manifest in nature.

Sin is also a part of this theological construction. The God-consciousness that humanity inherits from Christ is often disrupted. This disruption is sin, both in its cause and in its effect. Sin creates a greater distance between man and God, therefore weakening the God-consciousness. The act of committing a sin and the impulses towards this result in a distancing from God. Sin is a disturbance of the religious God-consciousness.

For Schleiermacher, "the character of sin is the self-centered activity of the flesh."[29] The desire of sin is for its own sake. Just as when feelings of freedom continue to grow to the point of complete freedom, which is isolation, the character of sin continues to grow as its focus is on the individual rather than the outsider. As sin is for its own self, it is not for the other. God is always active. The complete God-consciousness, as formed in the incarnation, is not found within God, but only humanity. Schleiermacher says it this way, "The ground for this assertion is best expressed in the formula that evil cannot be a creative thought of God. It follows that the term redemption is not so suitable to describe the divine decree as it is to

29. Schleiermacher, *Christian Faith*, 307.

describe the effect of the decree, for the Almighty cannot ordain one thing for the sake of another which He has not ordained."[30]

Just as Christ, the second Adam, initiates a new creation, sin is primarily a corporate rather than individual act. Sin can best be understood through its effects on the corporate consciousness rather than the individual. While sins affect humanity as a corporate body, Schleiermacher's theology does not credit notions of original sin or an Adamic fall from grace as the cause of sin's character.

The source of sin is not a part of human nature, rather individuals themselves are the cause of their own sin and in the act of sinning evils are produced. These evils produce effects outside the self and produce a world with evil. Sin may have origins in the individual but its effects are on the collective. In *The Christian Faith*, Schleiermacher states "all evil is to be regarded as punishment of sin, but only social evil as directly, such, and natural evil as only indirectly."[31] Sins natural and otherwise beget more sins, and require some form of justice. Sin creates its own form of justice as it weakens the God-consciousness, and distances man from God. Schleiermacher conceives of sin, like Augustine does, primarily as a disorder. Sin confuses our loves and our love is then in the self and this world rather than God and the eternal.

With the existence of sin in the world, Schleiermacher, like all theologians, must develop doctrines concerning justification and sanctification. Christianity is the pinnacle of the world religions for Schleiermacher because it contains the clearest description of salvation. This salvation, like all other key theology, grows out of Schleiermacher's Christology. Salvation for Schleiermacher is the persistence and growth of the God-consciousness in humanity. One may assume that other than his Christological spin, the remaining theology concerning the atonement and salvation would lie close to his fellow Calvinists. William Perkins outlined his Calvinist notions of the atonement and justification in *A Golden Chain*. This interpretation dominated Calvinist views at the Synod of Dort, and by the time of Schleiermacher these Calvinist views are reflexively accepted as convention.

Still Schleiermacher's theology is anything but conventional. As we have already mentioned, Schleiermacher's view of the atonement takes place not on Calvary but in Bethlehem. The incarnation becomes the atoning work of God. Schleiermacher states "Christ certainly made *satisfaction* for

---

30. Schleiermacher, *Christian Faith*, 366.
31. Schleiermacher, *Christian Faith*, 317.

us by becoming."[32] Schleiermacher also rejects the Calvinist doctrine of the limited atonement. Just as sin is a corporate act, so too is redemption. "Election cannot be understood as a human credit because this would undermine the clearest expression of the grace of God as evidenced in the incarnation."[33] Schleiermacher's notion of election was not the selection of a few souls who are saved from a well-deserved damnation, rather the occasion for election was the human need.

Since the atonement took place at Christ's birth, there is no need to address Christ's death as a vicarious suffering. Plainly stated "this satisfaction is in no sense 'vicarious;' it could not have been expected of us that we should be able to begin this life for ourselves, nor does the act of Christ set us free from the necessity of pursuing this spiritual life by our own endeavor in fellowship with Him."[34] There can be no atonement through a vicarious suffering because the atonement preceded the suffering of Christ. Furthermore for God to then choose to punish a section of mankind and withhold the possibility of atonement would be antithetical to God's nature. Schleiermacher clearly separates himself from the blood and wounds theology of Zinzendorf, but still focuses on the experiential relationship inherent to the incarnate God.

Still God's nature does include a cosmic drama to be played out. This drama includes creation and redemption. This creation includes sin and a fall of humanity away from perfect God-consciousness. This failure to possess a clear God-consciousness creates a void wherein God may engage with creation through the redemptive act of becoming man. Humanity still needs to be converted following redemption but this conversion is defined as a "transformation, the right-about-turn to better things, makes evident that it is the beginning of a new page, a new order in contrast to the old."[35] The opportunity for sin helps to produce a greater humanity. Schleiermacher does not hold Wolff's notion that 'all is right,' nor Leibniz's conclusion from *The Theodicy*. Rather Schleiermacher upholds St. Irenaeus's view that God created an immature humanity. This immaturity provides the development of a God-consciousness.

Schleiermacher contrasts his notion of election from both the Calvinist and Lutheran doctrines. Schleiermacher depicts the Calvinist interpretation as "the fact that not all persons will actually be restored through Christ but

32. Schleiermacher, *Christian Faith*, 461.

33. Schleiermacher, *On the Doctrine of Election*, 9.

34. Schleiermacher, *Christian Faith*, 461.

35. Schleiermacher, *Christian Faith*, 480.

that some are pardoned and others lost."[36] The Lutheran position is not much different, proclaiming "God has intended redemption for all but that those who did not accept it became lost on account of their resistance."[37] The essential difference between the classical interpretations of these two doctrines is the size of the net cast by the fisherman. For the Calvinist viewpoint the net is small, and it intentionally only targets a few fish, but the skill of the fisherman is such that those selected fish are caught. The Lutheran fisherman has a much larger net, but the net has wide holes in it that many fish, even possibly those that the fisherman desires, escape. In both cases many are excluded, either by design or accident. Schleiermacher finds little satisfaction in either of these models.

These models rely on Christ's atonement, costing either God or humanity something. Schleiermacher's conception of the atonement costs God nothing. Furthermore Schleiermacher's treatment of humanity is that humanity must always be viewed as a collective rather than a collection of individuals. Schleiermacher reworks Perkins's *Golden Chain*, by reinterpreting the first link as the predestination of humanity. From here Schleiermacher simply follows Perkins's theological outcomes. With his view of humanity and the atonement, Schleiermacher posits that God predestined humanity and all its members. From this position Schleiermacher comes close to the view held by Origen of Alexandria. Origen argued that at some point a universal restoration of humanity will occur. He reasoned that "We think that the goodness of God, through the mediation of Christ, will bring all creatures to one and the same end."[38] This notion of universal salvation resulted in the discrediting of the bulk of Origen's work, and a condemnation of this theology at the Fifth Ecumenical Council in Constantinople in 553.[39]

Following Origen, the doctrines connected with universal salvation fell out of favor. These views were regarded as heresy, or at least as heterodox and dangerous. Still, notions of universalism persist within Christianity, though in different forms. Universalists argue that the doctrine of universal salvation is heterodox rather than heretical. Universalists generally hold two theological assumptions to validate their claim to heterodoxy. The first is the rejection of God as vengeful and desiring to punish sinners though eternal torment, generally identified as hell. The second is the assertion that death

---

36. Schleiermacher, *On the Doctrine of Election*, 43.

37. Schleiermacher, *On the Doctrine of Election*, 43.

38. Origen, *Sacred Writings of Origen*, xxviii.

39. Some Origen scholars hold that he was not himself condemned at this council, rather only these teachings and many of his followers who applied these principles of Origen in a way beyond their original scope. If this is the case, then it opens the door for reexamination of Origen and possibly the doctrine of universal salvation.

is not the decisive line that separates the redeemed from the unredeemed. From this point it is possible that one may die unregenerate but then postmortem convert and accept God's grace. Damnation may occur, but it would be self-imposed and only temporary. Ultimately all humanity will choose grace and salvation rather than self-imposed isolation.

Some Universalists also presuppose that no one can be in a state of blessedness if anyone is damned. This dictum becomes popular in the late nineteenth and twentieth century, such language is absent from any discussions Schleiermacher has on the subject.

Schleiermacher is the first major Christian theologian since the time of the Patristics to seriously consider universalism. While this may appear to be a rejection of his Reform teachings and Calvin, Schleiermacher's doctrine of universal salvation is developed from the Calvinist perspective. The notion of the elect remains. The difference is who the elect are. For Calvin, the elect are individual men and women. For Schleiermacher, the elect is humanity in the singular rather than singular humans. Schleiermacher does abandon Calvin's notion of the reprobate. Calvin believed that the reprobate along with the elect were created for the same purpose, to bring glory to God.

For Schleiermacher, God becoming man through the incarnation changes the teleology of creation. Schleiermacher rejected Perkin's golden chain, but could still uphold Francke's view of redemption. Francke argued, in his work *On Christian Perfection,* that "Just as God looks upon the Lord, Christ as sin, so he sees the sinner as just and completely perfect because he gives to the sinner as the sinner's own the innocence and righteousness of Christ."[40] While Francke did not advocate universal salvation, Francke's depiction of imputed righteousness is echoed and amplified with Schleiermacher.

Schleiermacher's universalism grows from his new interpretation of predestination in the singular along with Francke's and others view of imputed righteousness. God's will remains ultimate as Calvin demands. Schleiermacher rejects Luther, who believes that people themselves determine their own fate. "Rather, only in this way is it to become clear how the election and rejection of individuals are simply the two contrasted yet in each instance correlated aspects of one and the same decree, whereby through divine power, yet in a natural way, the human race is to be transformed into the spiritual body of Christ."[41] This transformation becomes complete and universal.

---

40. Erb, *Pietists,* 114.

41. Schleiermacher, *On the Doctrine of Election,* 75.

The transformation of humanity and ultimate universal salvation of creation grows from these theological tenets as well as Schleiermacher's belief that death is not final. Death is a transformation, but this transformation does not preclude the possibility for repentance and ultimate salvation. Death cannot be the determining factor because if it was then God would be limited. Schleiermacher is still close enough to Calvin that anything that limits God's sovereignty results in a dismantling of the nature of God. Neither death nor any other thing can restrict the activity of God through Christ's operation in humanities God-consciousness. Schleiermacher concludes that "Whichever road is taken, the difference at the point of death, then, between the person of faith and the person not of faith is simply the difference between being taken up into the reign of Christ earlier and later."[42] The reprobate, if we choose to use that term, are nothing other than the not yet redeemed.

If one can choose to remain reprobate, even with this modified definition, past the point of death, this naturally leads to the question of an individual's salvation, or the conversion of an individual. Schleiermacher still holds to the notion of individual justification and conversion. While humanity is redeemed through the incarnation, individuals can convert to God and this new creation, which we are all destined for. Individual conversion therefore includes "forgiving of his sins, and the recognizing of him as a child of God."[43] Schleiermacher still refers to this point as regeneration and a new beginning.

For Schleiermacher, it is true for regeneration as well as the various synonyms for regeneration such as repentance, regret, change of heart, etc. that this occurs at a distinct point, but also throughout the course of the new life.[44] Even though humanity has been redeemed by Christ, regeneration is still an appropriate term when addressing the individual. "Individuals, then, submit voluntarily to the lordship of Christ; but in so doing they at the same time enter a society to which they did not previously belong."[45] As far as the debate which existed among our earlier Pietists as to whether or not a conversion experience is needed, Schleiermacher affirms that multiple conversion experiences are needed. There is not a single conversion that does not then produce further conversions and a deepening of the God-consciousness.

42. Schleiermacher, *On the Doctrine of Election*, 78.
43. Schleiermacher, *Christian Faith*, 496.
44. Schleiermacher, *Christian Faith*, 482.
45. Schleiermacher, *Christian Faith*, 465.

Schleiermacher does hold that an initial moment of faith is still necessary. This initial faith creates a new and permanently enduring state of mind. This new state of mind becomes the basis of the new life in Christ. An individual's conversion is therefore in no way superfluous. The initial conversion provides the basis for the entire Christian life that reaches into eternity. Justification, conversion, and the new creation become practically identical, the difference only lies in temporality and not in effect. One is justified through Christ's incarnation. Christ therefore becomes the first of the new creation. Each individual will then at some point convert to Christ. Conversion is therefore the gift of repentance. This conversion marks the point where the individual becomes a part of this new creation, partaking of an ever increasing level of God-consciousness.

Schleiermacher remains a bit vague as to the nature of the increasing level of God-consciousness. Two interpretations remain possible. The first is that the level of God-consciousness for the believer can increase *ad infinitum*, as God is infinite. Along this line of infinite God-consciousness there is a point where the believer crosses some threshold and is in a state of blessedness for the rest of eternity. The state of blessedness is produced by the directional attitude of the God-consciousness. The individual now only chooses to remain conscious of God, rather than sinning, or turning away from God. As God is infinite, the nature of man's finitude precludes complete consciousness of God, but God-consciousness is all that is eternally desired. This first view largely focuses on God's nature and humanities ability to fully grasp the ungraspable.

The second interpretation of this growing God-consciousness is focused on the state of grace for the believer. For this view the Christian's finite existence does not need to grasp eternity, rather only be consumed by it. Humanity is like a water vessel; it is full, empty, or somewhere in between. The discussion of a complete God-consciousness needs to only address how full the vessel is and not the quantity of the liquid. As the vessel is a fixed size, there is an upper limit where it is completely filled with God-consciousness. The opposite can also exist, the vessel can be emptied, as it is prior to regeneration. This is the state of God-forgetfulness.

Both views address an expanding and contracting God-consciousness, the exact state of which is still undefined. The default term for the ever increasing level of God-consciousness is faith. The increasing level of God-consciousness correlates with an increasing feeling of absolute dependence on God, therefore faith is essentially a level of dependence upon God. Schleiermacher states that "faith is nothing other than the consequence of something given."[46] Though it is given, Schleiermacher still maintains the Protestant notion of salvation through faith. The doctrine of *Sola Fida* is interpreted as "man is justified as soon as faith has been wrought in him."[47] This faith is always a given faith, wherein the regenerate cooperate in their blessedness.

This new life of faith is humanities share of the new creation, first initiated in Christ. According to Schleiermacher, when one becomes redeemed they are quantifiably different. "Life thus becomes under a different formula, making it a life that is new; hence the phrases 'a new man,' 'a new creature,' which bear the same sense as our phrase 'a new personality.'"[48] This new creation is new not only because of the personality that it takes on, a personality that is marked by faith, but is new in its associations. "The result is, not only that there arises among them a new corporate life, in complete contrast to the old, but also that each of them becomes in himself a new person—that is to say, a citizen."[49] The citizenship and association is with God. Therefore the new creation is marked by faith and this faith produces real communion with God. As such, the purpose of creation and the new creation are made complete through this redemptive model. In many ways this echoes the mysticism of Johannes Tauler and his doctrine of the inner man. Schleiermacher's theology of the new creation echoes Tauler's claim that "Man is created for time and for eternity for time in his body, for eternity according to his spirit."[50]

Schleiermacher affirms that faith lends itself to greater faith, and a greater cooperation in blessedness. He is unwilling to follow John Wesley down the road of ascribing perfection to anyone except for Christ. Any degree of faith for the Christian can never be anything but the act of Christ's "sinlessness and perfection as conditioned by the being of God in Him."[51] To Christ alone belongs perfection. For only Christ began as God and therefore has a complete God-consciousness. The Christian, even one who has attained a state of blessedness, still only shares in this Christ's blessedness. When the Christian becomes a new creation, they do not become perfect, rather the "New life can only, as it were be grafted on to the old."[52] The imperfections of the old natures still persist, though life continues from the

---

46. Schleiermacher, *On the Doctrine of Election*, 67.

47. Schleiermacher, *Christian Faith*, 503.

48. Schleiermacher, *Christian Faith*, 476.

49. Schleiermacher, *Christian Faith*, 429.

50. Tauler, *Following of Christ*, 97.

51. Schleiermacher, *Christian Faith*, 425.

52. Schleiermacher, *Christian Faith*, 476.

new. Christ was born with a completed God-consciousness and this granted humanity the ability to share in divinity. Christ "bears within Himself the whole new creation which contains and develops the potency of the God-consciousness."[53]

As stated earlier, once redeemed the Christian still can sin. What marks the Christian as different in their converted state is a knowledge that their sin is forgiven, even during the sin. With knowledge of sin, repentance and forgiveness are offered and ultimately received. This life of sin is the old nature which is not deadened, only overcome. "The actual sin of those who have been brought into permanent connection with the power of redemption is no longer 'originating' in themselves, or, through their ill-doing, in others. It has been vanquished by the energy of the God-consciousness implanted in them personally and spontaneously, so that where it still shows itself it is seen to be on the wane, and has no further contaminating power."[54]

The sin is reckoned to the existence of the old nature that is still present in the life of the believer. "He still has something in him of the old common life of sin."[55] This old nature is the originator of the sin. The connection with God in the new creation is a permanent connection with God's power of redemption. "In every case where sin appears to have entered we must say either that the sin is not really new, but belongs to a former period and has simply been revived; or else that regeneration has not been of a right and true kind, inasmuch as sinfulness has borne new fruit."[56]

THE CHURCH AND ITS PEOPLE

"Let us still note how our services of worship have also been blessed for the quickening and elevation of our religious feelings."[57]

The power of sin is disrupting the God-consciousness not only of an individual but of the community. The community, along with the individual is therefore an agent who combats sin. Sin is combated through faith. The corporate body that engages in this life of faith is known as the church. For Schleiermacher the church is the communal form of faith. This is why Schleiermacher continues beyond a description of religion as it applies to an individual and addresses its corporate character. From Schleiermacher's

---

53. Schleiermacher, *Christian Faith*, 388.

54. Schleiermacher, *Christian Faith*, 313.

55. Schleiermacher, *Christian Faith*, 515.

56. Schleiermacher, *Christian Faith*, 511.

57. Schleiermacher, *Fifteen Sermons*, 56.

earliest works he attempted to draw the cultured despisers of religion into accepting religion as a communal activity. In *On Religion* he exclaims, "The essence of the church is fellowship."[58]

The church is the form of faith. Schleiermacher expands on this idea in his later lectures on religion. "The essence of the church lies in the organic unification of a mass of people of the same type for the purposes of subjective activity of the cognitive function under the opposition of clergy and laity."[59] The unification is the key element of the church. In Schleiermacher's view, once there is religion, it must necessarily be social. For Schleiermacher, the social aspect of religion is something engrained in humanity. It "is the nature of man, and it is quite peculiarly the nature of religion."[60]

The church as the social expression of the God-consciousness is found not only in anthropology, but also in history. The origins of the church came about as events unfolded in history. This historic event began with the life and preaching of Jesus. The Christian experience is one of a historic community with its origins in a person, Jesus Christ, who is also the model of faith. At this point it should not surprise anyone that Schleiermacher's ecclesiology comes directly from his Christology. Since Schleiermacher's Christology begins from addressing a historical Christ, the beginnings of the church must likewise come from this historic event. The new creation, which has its source in the incarnation, immediately manifests itself in a historic community. In *The Christian Faith*, Schleiermacher describes the transition from the incarnation to a community. This community takes on the God-consciousness of the incarnate Christ, as a logical and natural progression. "The new corporate life is no miracle, but simply the supernatural becoming natural."[61]

Since the church is the social expression of faith, it is natural that the Holy Spirit would guide the church, increasing faith in those who hear the gospel message. Schleiermacher states "the Holy Spirit makes itself felt through the Christian Church as the ultimate world-shaping power."[62] The mechanism for this world shaping power is through preaching. Schleiermacher remains thoroughly Calvinist with this proclamation. Preaching conveys the image of Christ to the community and from the community to the world. The church becomes the agent of salvation. Contrary to the Catholic notion, the Church is not the agent of salvation because it administrates the sacraments.

---

58. Schleiermacher, *On Religion*, 213.

59. Dole, *Schleiermacher on Religion*, 123.

60. Schleiermacher, *On Religion*, 148.

61. Schleiermacher, *Christian Faith*, 365.

62. Schleiermacher, *Christian Faith*, 737.

Rather the church is the agent of salvation because it is the collective social unit that proclaims and expounds on scripture. Schleiermacher exalts the role of the church, but from a Calvinist Pietist perspective. The influence of Christ, therefore, consists solely in the human communication of the Word, insofar as that communication embodies Christ's word and continues the indwelling divine power of Christ Himself.

Schleiermacher continues within the Reform vein of Zwingli when he continues in his denial of the efficacy of sacraments in the process of regeneration. The specific claim Schleiermacher makes is removing the link between baptism and regeneration. In *The Christian Faith*, he asserts "baptism of itself produces no inward result, but is only an external sign of entrance into the Church."[63] Schleiermacher, elsewhere in the *Glaubenslehre*, claims that "If, therefore, in spite of infant baptism, sin thus shows its power in them, they need conversion as much as anyone born outside the Church." He precedes this statement by arguing that some are "baptized in heart alone."[64] The actual baptism performed by a priest becomes secondary. Schleiermacher is not becoming an Anabaptist, nor a Baptist with these claims. Rather he contends that if the act of baptism itself produced this change then Christianity would degenerate into the realm of magic.

The sacrament is not eliminated from his church and Schleiermacher still does find meaning in the practice of baptism, including baptism of infants. Baptism is still described as "the seal of regeneration,"[65] it is just that this seal is only valid when actual regeneration occurs. Since Schleiermacher believes all will eventually be saved, the act of baptism becomes regeneration only when this is coupled by faith. Baptism does not save, apart from the connection of faith, which will eventually be common to all.

He is equally as skeptical of identifying regeneration with culture, even if this is a Christian culture. Simply because one is born within a culture that has to one degree or another accepted Christianity as a guiding principle, this does not somehow transmute righteousness. Schleiermacher asserts "Less obvious perhaps is this, that the state of grace cannot be inborn, but that even Christian children at birth essentially resemble all other sons of Adam."[66] Everyone, regardless of their nationality or confession, still needs redemption, and to accept that redemption. Christian children possess an advantage because they should have greater ease in hearing the gospel preached than those who are outside the church.

63. Schleiermacher, *Christian Faith*, 624.

64. Schleiermacher, *Christian Faith*, 489.

65. Schleiermacher, *Christian Faith*, 652.

66. Schleiermacher, *Christian Faith*, 537.

Schleiermacher asserts that the state has a duty to the Church and vice versa. Of course the view of the state for Schleiermacher comes directly from his Christological presuppositions. Christ did not set up a kingdom, rather he established a network of preachers. The Church owes the state and its people this message. The state, in turn, owes the church the freedom to proclaim the gospel. Other than that no real union exists. Unfortunately a link exists where the church in service to the state becomes little more than bureaucracy. Baptism, instead of a consecration of children to God, becomes the occasion when the state receives them from the church's hands into their own. Similarly confirmation is not an ecclesial training of Christian, but becomes a beacon to the state advancing the individual towards civil independence. The state co-opts the rites of the church and transforms them into civil obligations. In doing so, neither the church nor the state are properly served.

With this view of the church and sacraments, it may come as a bit of a surprise that Schleiermacher also affirms that salvation can only come in and through the church. "No one, therefore, can be surprised to find at this point the proposition that salvation or blessedness is in the Church alone, and that, since blessedness cannot enter from without, but can be found within the Church only by being brought into existence there, the Church alone saves."[67] The church saves because the church is the global expression of Christianity. The church is the community that is founded upon the uniquely formed God-consciousness. The church also maintains the message of Christ. Explicitly, Schleiermacher affirms that the church is "the fellowship though the influence of which his regeneration was conditioned, and out of which, by preaching in the widest sense of the word, this new life was transmitted to him."[68]

The church as it is currently constructed often fails to be the fellowship of the regenerate. To explain this failing, Schleiermacher develops the concept of a visible and invisible church. Elements of this idea exist to one extent or another before Schleiermacher. Wesley believed that there was an invisible church that all Christians belonged to. For Schleiermacher the division is more precise and spelled out. The visible church is the one that is institutionalized and recognizable on earth. The invisible church contains those who are redeemed but may or may not be a part of the earthly institution known as a church. "The invisible Church is everywhere

---

67. Schleiermacher, *Christian Faith*, 527.
68. Schleiermacher, *Christian Faith*, 574.

essentially one, while the visible is always involved in separation and division."[69] Schleiermacher defines the invisible church as the true church.

The visible church has numerous failings, including exclusion of the members of the true church from the visible church. The visible church also has many members who are not themselves pious, but desire to appear pious. The invisible church cannot be extracted from the visible church, for even if the pious leave and establish their own church, the impious may be attracted to them. With this obvious failing of established churches, Schleiermacher returns to the long standing treatment of Pietists as a church within a church. The true Christians cannot become institutionalized as they did in the eighteenth century, rather the true Christianity as expressed by Arndt and Spener must be lived as a part of this world.

There is a second benefit for the regenerate to remain within the established and corrupted visible church. Schleiermacher asserts that "as long as the unregenerate live here in company with the pious, they too experience gleams of blessedness though the God-consciousness latent in them; and these make their presence felt powerfully as preparatory workings of grace."[70]

The invisible church is the church that saves according to Schleiermacher. While the outward trappings of the visible church may help facilitate regeneration, true regeneration occurs from the community, and the true community is the invisible church. The invisible church remains the same, while always adding members, regardless of the epoch or location it is found in. The visible church exists and serves God, not because it is the source of redemption, but because it makes visible Christ's reconciliation. The visible church is the historic body of Christ, even though this body does not always belong to Christ, as the members exist at the time they claim to represent Christ. The visible church for Schleiermacher serves a very similar function as Wesley's "almost Christians"[71] did for him. They perform the acts of Christianity but still need regeneration.

The visible church contributes to the redemption of individuals in more ways than existing as a corporate body and through the use of sermons, but also in the historic development that occurs within the visible church. As stated earlier, Schleiermacher's ecclesiology is based on his Christology. This Christology is developed through the experiences of the apostles and from them and their teachings the church as it exists today. Doctrine and theology cannot be the starting point for regeneration. Still

---

69. Schleiermacher, *Christian Faith*, 680.

70. Schleiermacher, *Christian Faith*, 735.

71. See Wesley, "Almost Christian."

the use of doctrines, creeds, and dogmas have value within the church, as an expression of the story of redemption. The creeds, doctrines, and theology are developed from the experience of members in the visible church. Again Schleiermacher grounds his theology in Pietism as it is this experience, rather than secular reason or scholasticism that develops correct theology.

This experience, as codified in doctrines and creeds, is the language of piety as understood within the social matrix of the church and the confluence of historic events and challenges. Doctrines, dogmas, and creeds are useful for the invisible church as they relate the experiences of the visible church and the expressions of faith of its earlier members. Doctrines, dogmas, and creeds are even more useful because they are an expression not only of individual scholars, theologians, and mystics, but they are collective representations of what the church shared as common.

The doxa that is always produced through any doctrine is exclusionary in its attempt to vocalize an experience. Those who do not possess this experience are excluded, often within the attempt at drawing them into this expression of Christianity. The critics of the church are serving the same function as the clerics who canonize dogmas, the difference is the expression of experience. The heretics experience may be a genuine experience of the God-consciousness, but it cannot be a replicated experience by the rest of the visible church, therefore it is excluded. Redemption, while believed to be extant in the heretic, is perceived as absent. The heretics "regeneration has been only apparent."[72]

Interestingly, some heterodox theology becomes mainstream and even preferential when the experiences of the surrounding culture change. The distinction between heretic and saint, heterodox and hero of the faith, illustrates the division that exists between the visible and invisible church. Schleiermacher maintains the "Visible and the invisible Church. . . the former is a divided church while the latter is an undivided unity. . . the latter is infallible."[73] The infallibility of the invisible church can accept the clarification and expression of all who will become and are in the process of becoming the redeemed. As Schleiermacher proclaims, "through the unfolding of Christ's own God-consciousness, this one God, the creator and preserver of all things, is deemed to be actual among us in the church and thereby in each individual."[74]

The division between the visible and invisible church is also the basis for Schleiermacher's attempt at creating a Protestant church union.

72. Schleiermacher, *Christian Faith*, 514.
73. Schleiermacher, *Christian Faith*, 678.
74. Tice, *Schleiermacher*, 32.

As mentioned in his biography in the previous chapter, Schleiermacher spent most of his pastoral life as the Reformed clergy to a mixed audience consisting of both Lutheran and Reform communicants. The congregation was divided and the practice of communion was still divided; more often than not the services were divided. The only thing truly held in common was the church building. While at Charité and Halle, he proposed an actual union of the Lutheran and Reform congregations into a single united confession. The desire was to overcome the doctrinal differences between Lutheran and Reform and create a single Protestantism. Schleiermacher believed that if these two confessions joined, Anglicanism would follow suit, and he generally did not regard the Radical Reformation as a strand of Protestantism to contend with. Undergirding this opinion held by Schleiermacher was his connection with Pietism. Andrew Stephen Damick expresses a common concern that "Pietism ultimately led to a general feeling that doctrine didn't matter very much and that the concrete life of the church as a community is of only secondary importance."[75] Schleiermacher still maintained that doctrine holds value, but nowhere near the same extent as Protestants did at the eve of the Reformation.

Schleiermacher endorsed any attempt at further reforming the visible church, hoping that these reforms could bring the visible church closer to the invisible church. Many of his reforms placed him at odds with Friedrich Wilhelm III. Schleiermacher's disagreement with his monarch concerning ecclesial matters and political liberty persuaded the Calvinist to abandon any notions of a theocracy and magisterial involvement in the life of the *ecclesia*. For most of medieval Europe the three estates performed specific roles in the life of the church. Schleiermacher applied his liberal social politics to the relations that existed in the church. The clergy, the nobility, and the laity each represent different aspects of society, but all are equal within Christ. In his *On Religion* speeches, Schleiermacher admits that these divisions of society exist and even permeate the church, even though they should not. Schleiermacher contends that "When one stands out before the others he is neither justified by office nor by compact; nor is it pride or ignorance that inspires him with assurance. It is the free impulse of his spirit, the feeling of heart-felt unanimity and completest equality, the common abolition of all first and last, of all earthly order."[76]

Schleiermacher quickly dismantles the theological justification for the second estate's involvement in the life of the Church. While he maintained a belief in a monarchy, the monarch of the church remains Christ. Since Christ

75. Damick, *Orthodoxy and Heterodoxy*, 85.

76. Schleiermacher, *On Religion*, 151.

is the true king, the earthly political monarch has no divine calling. Once again this Reform clergyman used Luther's doctrine of the two kingdoms to further dismantle one of his chief ecclesial-political adversaries. The kingly office can be found in the history of the church, but there always remained a primacy of community, where Christ's kingly power outweighed the prince. Schleiermacher, in affirming the kingly office of Christ, sets His majesty against earthly kings. As a result of the Christian's rightful obedience belonging only to Christ, "among believers there is nowhere any lordship other than His alone."[77] All kings may require a degree of obedience by their subjects, but Christ's lordship is supreme above all.

The notion of Christ's lordship superseding the king's authority does not mean that Schleiermacher believes that the priest supersedes the King. Schleiermacher turns his attention towards the first estate, showing it to be as problematic as the second. Schleiermacher believes the origins of the priesthood have an accidental beginning in history. Early in *The Christian Faith*, Schleiermacher supposes that in early societies a few individuals were marked off as more religious or pious than others. Their extraordinary involvement in spiritual affairs separated them from the larger community as they took on these religious duties for the rest of the community. While this began as an individual assuming these responsibilities, Schleiermacher surmises that the family of the pious became equally involved, thus creating a hereditary priestly class.

Once this class exists in any real form, Schleiermacher doubts that societies could function without a continued distinction between the priests and the laity as two different religious orders. In *On Religion*, Schleiermacher argues that any individual who discovered a talent for piety must "allow himself to be sent back by the true church to lead as a priest."[78] In both cases societies and individuals create the priestly class and perceive it to be a necessary portion of society.

As an ordained clergyman, Schleiermacher is not entirely opposed to the view that the priests provide a service to the community. Even in his younger theology, as expressed in *On Religion*, Schleiermacher identifies the priestly art as a trade, which like other trades must be cultivated and shared from one craftsman to another. "Wherefore, what the Christian layman has in less perfection than the theologian and which manifestly is a knowledge is not religion itself, but something appended to it."[79]

77. Schleiermacher, *Christian Faith*, 468.

78. Schleiermacher, *On Religion*, 163.

79. Schleiermacher, *On Religion*, 102.

At the same time Schleiermacher transforms the priesthood from a hereditary position or a private calling by the Almighty into a skilled trade like any other, just like the carpenter does not have a special calling to his craft, but only a developed skill that they may train others in. In this way Schleiermacher works to dismantle the priesthood, or at least to bring it down from the pulpit and place it within the congregation. He professes, "According to the principles of the true church, the mission of a priest in the world is a private business, and the temple should also be a private chamber where he lifts up his voice to give utterance to religion. Let there be an assembly before him and not a congregation. Let him be a speaker for all who will hear, but not a shepherd for a definite flock."[80]

In this way the priest is necessary, but not the priesthood as it existed at the time. The divisions between the priest and the laity began to erode. The priest shared from his understanding of the gospel and his experiences of the divine. The content of Schleiermacher's sermons only partly express this same perspective. While Schleiermacher's sermons connected the congregation to experiences of God, rarely were they his private experiences. Rather they were nearly exclusively experiences common to the congregation. Schleiermacher valued the preacher more than the priest. Just like Calvin, the sermon remained the pinnacle of the Church service. It was in the sermon that the congregation grew closer to God. It was from the sermon that Schleiermacher expected his congregation to experience God, and his Pietism was manifest.

Contrary to modern revival sermons, Schleiermacher never intended to spark a conversion. Rather he assumed that a conversion had already occurred. The job of the preacher is not to reduce the sermon to the level that is only of any benefit to the unbeliever, rather the sermon should edify and grow the Christians in the congregation, or at least to "approximate to the ideal."[81] The gospel must be clear, and if it is, then the believer is edified and the unbeliever will hear the sermon as a call to repentance, even though one is not explicitly given. In a New Year's sermon, Schleiermacher affirms that "Belief comes through preaching; that is the natural way, and so it was natural that initial belief in Jesus came from John's preaching."[82]

Schleiermacher's notion of ecclesiology is also present in his sermons. Upholding the priesthood of all believers, the preacher is both a minister and ministered to by the congregation. "All Christians offer the Word of

---

80. Schleiermacher, *On Religion,* 174.

81. Schleiermacher, *Servant of the Word,* 6.

82. Schleiermacher, *Fifteen Sermons,* 144.

God to one another."[83] As such, even in a large overflowing church the congregation is intimate, members are "friends" and "beloved" and the relationship is personal rather than formal.

Schleiermacher believed that the sermon itself was the embodiment of a Christian art form. The sermon needed to be sufficiently long, but not too long. Schleiermacher believed that half an hour was too short, and an hour too long. With this in mind it is not surprising to find that most of his sermons when read aloud take about forty to fifty minuets. Schleiermacher continued his practice of preaching without writing them out in advance. By the time he began preaching in Berlin, not even the introduction was penned. Schleiermacher's extemporaneous preaching astonished his audience. Schleiermacher wrote out several sermons after he delivered them, and many others are reconstructed from the notes of his audience. Due to his popularity, the sermons were gathered and published, often without his knowledge or consent.

Following Schleiermacher's developed ecclesiology, the priest is only a preacher. For Schleiermacher there is only one king and only one priest, Christ. He simply states, Christ "is also the end of all priesthood."[84] Schleiermacher couches this discussion of the priesthood in his reading of early church history. He argues that "Even the Apostles never claim for themselves anything that can properly be called priestly, so that the revival of the priesthood in the Church must be viewed as one of the greatest misapprehensions."[85]

Schleiermacher eliminates any salvific power on the actions of the Apostles or any clergy. Christ's appearance in the world signaled an end to the distinction between the holy and human. Humanity is saved, not through the intercession or acts of a priest as a special class of people, rather humanity is saved through "the priestly intercession of Christ."[86]

Following Christ's incarnation, no distinction can remain that separates the clergy from the laity. In this Schleiermacher echoes Zinzendorf and Wesley and promotes the laity within nineteenth-century Pietism. Schleiermacher proclaimed, "Every man is a priest, in so far as he draws others to himself in the field he has made his own and can show himself master in; every man is a layman, in so far as he follows the skill and direction of another in the religious matters with which he is less familiar."[87]

83. Schleiermacher, *Servant of the Word*, 7.

84. Schleiermacher, *Christian Faith*, 465.

85. Schleiermacher, *Christian Faith*, 465.

86. Schleiermacher, *Christian Faith*, 491.

87. Schleiermacher, *On Religion*, 153.

Going back to his anthropology of the early priesthood, Schleiermacher identified the priest as a member of the laity whose vocation is piety. The pious experiences of the clergy serve as the reason for their position. Once these experiences are transformed from the individual to the collective, the distinction between priests and laity fades. To this extent Schleiermacher argued, "the distinction between priests and laity is only to serve the occasion and cannot be permanent."[88]

The key mechanism for increasing the piety of the laity to the level of piety found in the priest is to support the reading of scripture. Once society advanced to the point of universal literacy, the privileged God-consciousness as it exists among the ordained class evaporated, and it spread among the entire community like a refreshing rain. From this position, the laity are "simply those who by them have been formed to piety, and who therefore stand under continual spiritual guidance, while the highest triumph is for some to become capable of reception into that closer sphere of the religious life."[89] The guidance of priests is not an authority, other than the authority a craftsman has over the tools of the trade.

Following Schleiermacher's contribution to the Pietists tradition of Zinzendorf, the laity are equal in all respects to the clergy, except training. The laity share in the same essential responsibility as the clergy. This responsibility is in sharing their experience of the divine with the community that surrounds them. The communal sharing of personal experience of God is not only the duty of the priest, but of every Christian. It is also the essence of religion as the transformative power that brings people together.

No discussion of Schleiermacher's view of the church and the laity would be complete without an examination of his views of women. While Zinzendorf and Wesley both initiated practices that promoted the possibility of female ordination, Schleiermacher does not take any real steps in that direction. Schleiermacher believed that Christian women needed to exercise their control in the public sphere through their husbands.

Yet the role of women and religion for Schleiermacher is not so clear cut as to assume that women possess no spiritual vocation. The spiritual vocation of women in Schleiermacher's theology begins with his *Christmas Eve Dialogue*. In the *Dialogue*, he proclaims very few doctrines, nor does he speak on dogmatic issues in a direct fashion as he does in *The Christian Faith*. Instead the work serves as a discussion which provides for multiple interpretations, depending on which of the characters are held up as examples. One of the characters in the *Dialogue*, Edward, states essentially

---

88. Schleiermacher, *On Religion*, 206.
89. Schleiermacher, *On Religion*, 194.

this, saying "Particular events are only the passing notes for music. Its true content is the great chords of our mind and heart, which marvelously and with the most varied voices ever resolve themselves into the same harmony, in which only the major and minor keys are to be distinguished, only the masculine and the feminine."[90] Schleiermacher further promotes the idea that women's predominant religious personality is feeling rather than cognition. While this is often used to denigrate women, Schleiermacher intends no offense. Since his definition of religion is a feeling of absolute dependence, women's natural inclination towards feeling only lends to a greater ease for women to experience the life of faith that Schleiermacher calls for.

The work also serves to illustrate the irony of typical gender roles. One of the few children included, Sophie, rejects the common female activities and is still characterized as angelic and good. Schleiermacher maintains a distinction between male and female vocations and temperaments, but the purpose behind the work is not to subordinate the male nor the female, rather to express different modes of experience. Still, Schleiermacher's ecclesiology recognizes only men as priests, even in their diminished role. Women's primary contribution in religion is to take place at home, once again characterizing men and women's modes of religious expression as two distinct voices. Religion largely remains rooted in the family. Schleiermacher maintains that women's expression of their religious feelings rightly belongs at home because of the methods of expression. The feminine voice is loudest when internalizing these feelings, and men need to express them externally to process and share before the experience can be properly internalized.

Schleiermacher also valued women's contribution to the religious life at home. As exemplified by his own marriage and family life, Schleiermacher assumes that "The feeling of being the housewife, who takes care of the whole household, and who may arrange everything according to her own will and pleasure, is, I think, always precious to a woman, and I also value it very much, and am proud of the dignity."[91] Schleiermacher found dignity and not denigration in the vocation he assigned to women. Reading his letters presents a Schleiermacher who is a great admirer of women. His admiration extended far beyond his wife. From his childhood, his sister Lotte was his primary confidant. Following this, Schleiermacher's doomed romantic desires for Count Dohna's daughter Frederike and Eleanor Grunow were both born out of admiration rather than carnal lust. Schleiermacher also

---

90. Schleiermacher, *Christmas Eve*, 32.

91. Schleiermacher, *Life of Schleiermacher*, 11. Henriette von Willich to Schleiermacher, November 25.

retained a lifelong friendship with Henriette Herz, whose salon he was engaged with during his earlier stay in Berlin.

This fondness toward women extended to the point that in a letter to his sister Schleiermacher proclaimed, "Therefore if I ever find myself sportively indulging in an impossible wish, it is, that I were a woman."[92] He believed that women's intuition was a religious intuition. In a separate letter to his sister he states "It lies very deep in my nature, dear Lottie, that I am always more closely attached to women than to men, for there is so much in my soul that men seldom understand."[93] Schleiermacher's view of women is greatly influenced by the early Romantic circles he was a part of. It is rather easy to read Goethe's influence when he elevates the feminine as the redeemer in *Faust*. "Virgin, beautifully pure, Venerable mother, our chosen queen through art, Peer of gods, no other! Clouds form a garland around her splendor Penitent women, People so tender, Her knees embrace, Drinking the ether, Asking her grace."[94]

SCHLEIERMACHER AS A MODEL OF NINETEENTH-CENTURY PIETISM

"The thought that nothing new happens under the sun is the most natural expression of how the world appears to the eye of one who is looking for the Lord everywhere in the world."[95]

Pietism, like any other movement, is one that is always in a state of flux. Throughout the eighteenth century, the institutionalized forms of Pietism robbed the movement of its true identity. Throughout the nineteenth century, there were many Pietist schools founded by Francke, Zinzendorf, Wesley, and others, but each of these schools outgrew their initial purpose. That purpose was to emphasize experiential Protestant Christianity over its rationalist and orthodox expressions. These schools each created their own systems of orthodoxy and reacted to the different strands of rationalism, incorporating some aspects and rejecting others. In their institutionalized forms, these schools increasingly sought to preserve their privileged system rather than the mission.

At the beginning of the nineteenth century, Schleiermacher found himself competing with many other voices arguing for the future of Pietism.

---

92. Schleiermacher, *Life of Schleiermacher*, 1:382.

93. de Vries, "Schleiermacher's 'Christmas Eve Dialogue,'" 171.

94. Goethe, *Goethe's Faust*, 497.

95. Schleiermacher, *Fifteen Sermons*, 65.

Most of these voices sought the preservation of their newly formed and codified systems of theology rather than the promotion of experiential Protestantism. This is why Schleiermacher called himself a Moravian of a higher order. The rank and file Moravians lost what it meant to be Pietists. Their systems promoted new schools in order to combat Frederick II and the Enlightenment on the terms of the Enlightenment without truly understanding their opponent.

Most of these schools and their graduates could not be defined as Pietists by my definition. They were no longer a quasi-mystical experiential revivalist movement, found within Lutheran, Reform, and Anglican Protestantism of every age, which seeks to understand and rework their world, both inside and outside of themselves along lines of personally meaningful relationship between themselves as individuals and God, while maintaining a general antipathy or outright hostility to the greater Christian culture and religious formalism which dictates that culture's norms and practices. It is of little wonder why some believe that Pietism was dead by the conclusion of the eighteenth century.

It is from this ossified structure once called Pietism that Schleiermacher emerged. While Schleiermacher did not set out to mold Pietism in a new direction, this is what he did. It should come as no surprise that Schleiermacher did not concern himself with the standard Pietist critiques of the later eighteenth and early nineteenth-century Pietists. Prussian Pietists, as well as English Puritans had long attacked the use of novels. Reading them was described as time "wasted and lost for eternity."[96] Schleiermacher took a rather different tact towards popular literature and even stood up for Schlegel's *Lucinde*, a work that his contemporaries characterized as pornography.

Schleiermacher also spent no time protesting the theater. The theater was just as bad as novels, or worse in the eyes of many Pietists, including Phoebe Palmer who will be addressed in the next chapter. Like novels, they stirred the passions, and distracted the faithful from their task of salvation. In Halle, the anti-stage crowd was so successful that they suppressed performances in the city between 1700 and 1745. In no work does Schleiermacher condemn actors. Schleiermacher was rather libertine with his treatment of these "perverse" social practices. Likely his time at the Moravian schools of Niesky and Barby led to a softening of views rather than reinforcing the Pietist morality. Since he lacked the freedom to read Goethe and Kant, Schleiermacher undoubtedly viewed these other restrictions as equally capricious.

96. Melton, *Rise of the Public*, 95.

When Schleiermacher had his opportunity to directly found a university, he did not place the sort of restrictive demands on his students like he had at Niesky. Francke and Wesley likely would have disapproved of Schleiermacher, since their pedagogical programs reduced leisure time for students, including the elimination of playing and laughter. Schleiermacher's contribution to the Pietist edifice required the removal of these ethical burrs that appeared so very important to his predecessors.

A greater divide between the institutional Pietists and Schleiermacher is evidenced with the events surrounding the Berlin Awakening of 1817. The Awakening was started by Pietists in Berlin and spread across northern Germany. These "awakened Christians" emphasized the emotional character of their faith and the transition from a nominal Christianity to a new awakened awareness akin to the born again experience of Francke and the revivals of Wesley and later Holiness movement. The Berlin Awakening was the greatest success of the institutionalized Pietists in nineteenth-century Europe. Many social and political elites participated in the revival, but it is conspicuously absent from Schleiermacher's letters. The only possible mention was in a letter to his sister that he and "an old fellow student from Barby. . . intended to go to a meeting"[97] It is also quite possible and even likely that this meeting had nothing to do with the Awakening. Many of the figures connected to the Awakening were colleagues of Schleiermacher's at the university, including Friedrich Karl von Savigny (d. 1861). Since his colleagues were involved to some degree or another with the Awakening, Schleiermacher was surely aware of it.

It is possible that Schleiermacher remained an outsider to the unfolding events in Berlin since his theological approach to piety was not the same as many of its participants. von Savigny, along with another figure in the Awakening, Moritz August von Bethmann-Hollweg (d. 1877), preferred other Pietist preachers synthesis of Pietism and Enlightenment rationalism. They both favored Justus Gottfried Hermes (d. 1818). Bethmann-Hollweg described Hermes as "a more convincing man of prayer than Schleiermacher."[98] von Savigny also had Hermes baptize his children, instead of Schleiermacher.

Other depictions of the Awakening characterize the movement as more conservative, or at least a conservative Pietism. It's possible the revival was simply reviving the Pietism that Schleiermacher rejected, therefore his liberal theology and their conservative theology were at odds, but not to the point that a direct confrontation was forthcoming. Schleiermacher

---

97. Schleiermacher, *Life of Schleiermacher*, 205. August 1817.
98. Hope, *German and Scandinavian Protestantism*, 389.

also made no mention of the German Catholic revivals that took place during his later years. The absence of these revivals from Schleiermacher's autobiography and letters has a few potential causes. It is possible that the reports of the wide spread Awakening are exaggerated in later accounts. It is also possible that these events were a flash in the pan. They were important enough for some to notice, but the impact was not lasting enough for someone like Schleiermacher to generate a response. David Blackbourn points out that throughout the nineteenth century, "Pietism was socially as well as geographically limited in its appeal."[99]

It is likely that Schleiermacher chose not to engage in movements other than his own. Schleiermacher's entire career, both as a pastor and as a theologian, was focused on separating himself from established Pietism. In separating himself from Pietism, Schleiermacher once again reinforces the habitus of Pietism. The habitus of Pietism was that as an experiential outsider. The only way to remain an outsider is to reject the institution. Just as early modern religious studies scholars Zakiya Hanafi and Randall Styers point out, the nineteenth century witnessed the creation of communal identity. Styers illustrated that "A condition of modernity presupposes an act of self-conscious distancing."[100] To engage in modernity while simultaneously reaffirming his religious identity, Schleiermacher creates a modern Pietism. This is not simply an updated version of Pietism. Schleiermacher rejects much of what is called Pietism during his day. He, like many others, characterizes the aim of nineteenth-century Pietism to be on the state and society rather than the divine. Instead, Schleiermacher created a new system, one that at its core is thoroughly Pietist, because it emphasizes experience over rationalism and dogmatic orthodoxy.

In his rejection of institutional Pietism, Schleiermacher founded a new movement, often called modern liberal Protestantism. Schleiermacher himself was never a part of this movement. It is accurate to say, as many have, "Schleiermacher had no children only grandchildren." He didn't pass a movement off to any direct set of followers. There is not a recognizable school of theology that bears his name, but the impact Schleiermacher had upon Protestant theology is unmistakable. In his attempt to remake Pietism, Schleiermacher's theology produced modern liberal Protestantism. While I will get more into detail about modern liberal Protestantism in chapter five, a definition is still fitting here. Modern liberal Protestantism grew out of Schleiermacher's *The Christian Faith*. There are two essential pillars to this ideological movement. The first addresses the origins of Christianity. The

99. Blackbourn, *Long Nineteenth Century*, 292.

100. Styers, *Making Magic*, 4.

second redefines what essential Christian doctrine is. It is a reevaluation of standard Christian theology.

The Christian Faith, and the system it created, drew heavy fire for its theological assumptions. So much so that Schleiermacher chose to write his own defense of the work. The defense was in two letters to a friend of his, Dr. Lücke. Today it is commonly known as *On The Glaubenslehre*. Very early on, in his first letter, Schleiermacher tells Dr. Lücke "If I had written my book with the intention of founding a sect or school, then I could have opponents. But I know that I had no such thing in mind"[101] Unfortunately for Schleiermacher the criticism from opponents of modern liberal Protestantism still came. They directed their criticism not at the movement, but at Schleiermacher, its unintentional founder. Throughout the work Schleiermacher characterizes their critiques as mischaracterizations. Schleiermacher was troubled by what he believed were falsehoods about his beliefs, just like the critics were troubled by Schleiermacher.

Throughout all of his theology, Schleiermacher could still be identified with the phrase he penned to his father. Schleiermacher remained "a Moravian of a higher order." At the heart of Schleiermacher's claim was his insistence that religion is essentially experiential. Furthermore this experience was found in the realm of feeling. By locating the experience of the Christian in the realm of feeling, Schleiermacher reinterpreted or contradicted many earlier Pietists. Earlier Pietists, while grounding religion in experience, did not agree as to the relationship of feelings to these divine experiences.

William Perkins warned "that feeling must not be made the touchstone of religious experience, for in the last analysis 'religion doth not stand in feeling but in faith.'"[102] While Perkins influence within English Pietism is unmistakable, Schleiermacher rejects his interpretation of faith and feeling. Following his engagement with the Enlightenment and Romanticism, Schleiermacher's understanding of thought and feeling adjusted. While Perkins warned against feeling, Schleiermacher elevated it to the very heart of religion. Perkins understood feeling and faith as two separate impulses, Schleiermacher saw them as one and the same.

Contrary to Perkins belief that feeling and faith were two separate things entirely, Spener believed that one could have a feeling of faith. Still, Spener's view of faith and feeling is a lot closer to Perkins than it is to Schleiermacher. Spener never wanted to "make faith itself dependent on

---

101 Schleiermacher, *On the Glaubenslehre*, 34.

102. Stoeffler, *Rise of Evangelical Pietism*, 58.

the feeling of faith."[103] Francke prioritized assurances of salvation more than Spener. As a result, Franke prioritized feelings more than Spener. Feelings of intimacy with God assured the Christian of their salvation. Ultimately for Francke, the assurance of salvation came in part from experience and in part from the feelings that they imparted.

Zinzendorf, while engaged in the very feeling oriented Herrnhutters, still retained a degree of unease concerning feelings. In his 1738 speeches in Berlin, Zinzendorf characterized feeling as itself "something questionable, so that if one cannot deny it immediately the very same minute, and something even remains behind I suppose, doubtless the actual influence of the truth is often over and done in less than half an hour, until something comes anew, which also strikes only a few minutes, and rushes away again in its turn."[104] Wesley called for conversion experiences, and was equally attracted to the experiences of Moravian piety, but was always unsure as to the role and scope of any feelings.

The Pietists that emphasized feelings the most were indeed the Moravians, both before they encountered Zinzendorf and afterwards. It is rather clear to see the impact of Niesky and Barby upon Schleiermacher. His exclamation was not a rejection of the feelings of piety, rather only the dogmatic additions. To eliminate what Schleiermacher perceived was bad doctrine, he created his own. This is why Schleiermacher is a Moravian of a higher order and Barth can state "Schleiermacher's theology is the theology of feeling, or to put it more exactly, the theology of pious feeling."[105]

If we look at Schleiermacher's life and theology against my definition of Pietism we can see that Schleiermacher remains at his heart a Pietist, and he establishes a new Pietist theology. It is easy enough to equate a quasi-mystical experiential religion to Schleiermacher's emphasis on personal religious experience and his definition of religion as a feeling. Schleiermacher also challenged the concept of religion in his work *On Religion*, in order to make the work of the mystic more palatable to the cultured elites. This new treatment of religion is grounded in experience rather than theological or philosophical systems. Any theology that develops is developed out of this experience.

While Schleiermacher did not participate in the revivals of Berlin later in his life, his earlier treatment of religion permitted the once cultured despisers of religion to embrace a revival, even if it is not the one that Schleiermacher had in mind. Historically Pietism is found within the three

103. Gawthrop, *Pietism and the Making of Prussia*, 142.

104. Zinzendorf, *Christian Life and Witness*, 76.

105. Barth, *Protestant Theology*, 440.

major mainline Protestant denominations. Schleiermacher's message was grounded in the Reform, but through his pastoral life, the message he spread was equally applied to Lutheranism. Schleiermacher held out hopes that the Protestant union would eventually include Anglicanism as well. Schleiermacher's theology indeed sought to understand and rework the world he was a part of. Similarly, Schleiermacher's theology was at its essence a theology of relationships. Schleiermacher's construction of the God-consciousness was a measure of intimacy of the Christians relationship with God. In like manner the historical manifestation of this God-consciousness was not only on an individual level but was found within a community, known as the church.

The only area where Schleiermacher's theological system is not clearly a Pietistic theology is the maintenance of antipathy towards the greater Christian culture and religious formalism, which dictates that cultures norms and practices. Schleiermacher spent most of his life as a culture critic and less of it criticizing the churches around him. Schleiermacher did believe that Christianity in its current forms in Berlin was flawed, but his efforts to revive the Christian life were not founded in the same level of antipathy towards the larger Christian community as we see with Perkins, Arndt, Francke, and Wesley. Schleiermacher remained a Moravian at heart and his contempt for the established church was much closer to the attitude of Zinzendorf. Both Zinzendorf and Schleiermacher chose to promote a new church or way of doing church that was contrary to the established churches. The churches/movements they initiated served as the criticism and antipathy to the greater Christian culture. It can also be of no doubt that both Zinzendorf and Schleiermacher opposed the religious formalism that dictated the cultures norms and practices. Additionally, it is clearly seen that throughout his life and theology, Schleiermacher always emphasized experience over rationalism and orthodoxy.

In many ways Schleiermacher's emphasis on experience incorporated elements of rationalism and orthodoxy. As Barth argues, "All the so-to-speak official impulses and movements of the centuries since the Reformation find a center of unity in him: orthodoxy, pietism, the Enlightenment. All the official tendencies of the Christian present emanate from him like rays: church life, experiential piety, historicism, psychologism, and ethicism."[106] Within the first twenty years of his life Schleiermacher was thoroughly immersed in all the major trends that produced modernity. His childhood was spent in a Moravian household and later Moravian schools. In his late adolescence he was equally submerged in Kant and the Enlightenment, only

---

106. Barth, *Theology of Schleiermacher*, xv.

to later reject it when he began to tutor for Count Dohna and then spend times in the Romantic salons of Berlin. Throughout all of these periods, Schleiermacher faced challenges from the orthodox elements of both Reform and Lutheran churches in Prussia.

The legacy of Schleiermacher has gone through various cycles following his death. Not being the explicit teacher of a single movement, his theology was accepted and rejected in whole and in parts by different people and different theologians within decades of his death. Schleiermacherian systems were created and then destroyed, often with little involvement of Schleiermacher's actual written corpus. Schleiermacher was a progenitor and prototype of the new liberal Protestantism with all of its successes and failures. F. Naumann wrote in 1910, "The collapse of Protestantism would not have been so great had it eaten more of the bread of Schleiermacher."[107] This is the legacy of a figure that was only tangentially connected with the developing theological systems that emerged in the nineteenth century. Schleiermacher's theology directly impacted and contributed to the theology of some of the nineteenth and early twentieth century's most influential theologians and theorists including Søren Kierkegaard, Albert Ritschl, Adolf von Harnack, Erast Troeltsch, Rudolf Bultmann, Rudolf Otto, Emil Brunner, and Karl Barth.

Whatever faults lie within the system that Schleiermacher initiated are credited to his life and work, rightly and wrongly. This is the fitting legacy of a pioneer of modern theology, the father of modern Protestantism, and the most important Protestant theologian between John Calvin and Karl Barth. Schleiermacher receives the credit and blame because he was the turning point in Protestant theology, just as Kant was in the realm of philosophy. Following Schleiermacher, the impact of feelings as a religious expression, and not just something tangential to religion needed to be addressed, and either accepted or rejected. Schleiermacher made religion about experience even for the rationalist and the orthodox. Schleiermacher also forced Christ back into Christianity. For too long, the gospel lacked an image of Christ as the God-man, focusing only on Christ the redeemer or substitute for sins of the elect. Schleiermacher not only added another layer to the edifice of Pietism, he reconstructed most of the theologians whom he came in contact with, re-contextualizing and reprioritizing their accomplishments in light of his own. He made experiential Christianity accessible, knowledgeable, rational, theological, and personal.

107. Naumann, *Zur Einführung*, 8.

III

Phoebe Palmer (1807–1874)

METHODISM: AMERICAN PIETISM

"There's a spirit below, and a spirit above; The spirit of hate, and the spirit of love; The spirit above is the spirit divine; The spirit below is the spirit of wine."[1]

WITH SO MUCH SAID of Schleiermacher and his impact on Protestantism in the nineteenth century, we must now turn our attention to the other side of the Atlantic. Schleiermacher's direct impact primarily affected the continent of Europe and those ecclesial advancements. It is really not until the end of the nineteenth and the beginning of the twentieth century when modern liberal Protestantism comes to America. Yet this should not imply that no theological change or reworking of Protestant Christianity along Pietist grounds occurred. We must first remember that Anglicanism had its own history of experiential Christianity both from the Puritans and later the Methodists following Wesley, whose reinterpretation of Anglicanism along Moravian lines is clearly established. It was from this crucible that nineteenth-century American religiosity grew and matured. It was from this time, both along the Western frontier and the established cities in New York and New England, that experiential Christianity was shaped along a Holiness model, well before Pentecostalism took root in America. While Schleiermacher is undoubtedly the father of modern Protestantism, there existed a mother as well, and she grew up not in Germany, or England, but in America.

---

1. White, *Beauty of Holiness*, 80–81.

COMMOTION

"Everything in religion is exceedingly simple."[2]

Between Aldersgate and Azusa Street lies the parlor of Phoebe Palmer. Her Tuesday afternoon meetings for the promotion of Holiness serve as the crucial link between Wesley's conversion and the rise of Pentecostalism and fundamentalism at the dawn of the twentieth century. Palmer's contribution to experiential Protestantism built upon the institutional forms of the nineteenth century rather than directly opposing it as Schleiermacher did. While Schleiermacher opposed the rigid Pietism in Prussia, Palmer reinterpreted Pietism in America. The political and cultural challenges in Prussia were significant and should not be discounted. The resulting Germany at the beginning of Schleiermacher's life still largely resembled the German state which outlasted him. This was not the case for Phoebe Palmer. She was born during the presidency of Thomas Jefferson and died during Ulysses S. Grant's term. Palmer's America was not a singular society undergoing one or even a few changes. She lived through foreign invasion with the War of 1812, Manifest Destiny, and the Mexican American War, as well as the Civil War, Reconstruction, and the Gilded Age of Antebellum America. One cannot even speak of America in the singular in the political sense, as during the Civil War there existed the United States and the Confederate States of America. This was the chaos that Palmer's Methodism thrived in. This is the context of Palmer declaring *"Names and sects and parties fall, and Christ alone is All in All."*[3]

Within nineteenth-century America, Palmer supported and ignored the Methodist institution which dominated her religious landscape. Methodism protruded out of the edifice of Pietism, providing its own ledge and divergent development, while firmly remaining a part of the Pietist structure. While Schleiermacher confronted the political and philosophical conclusions of the Enlightenment, Palmer's Pietism disregarded philosophical discussions in favor of direct challenges to American culture. Palmer, and the resulting theological movements, are distinct from her nineteenth-century European counterparts in part due to the distinct history, culture, and religious climate of America. Palmer's country shaped Palmer's Pietism as much as her Pietism shaped America. What is remarkable is that Palmer's message not only thrived in America, but was successfully imported into the United Kingdom as well, including her insistence that living a holy life included abstention from alcohol, an

2. Palmer, *Full Salvation*, 46.
3. White, *Beauty of Holiness*, 40.

unfavorable opinion in nineteenth-century Europe, even among many of her fellow Pietists. Palmer's brand of Pietism developed from the Methodist lineage and produced the Holiness movement. For her, the terms Methodist and Holiness are more fitting and appropriate, but they all convey the same appeal towards defining their Protestant Christianity as experience, rather than scholasticism or rationalism.

TRAINING IN METHODISM

"Thou Great Eternal One in Three! With grateful hearts we come to dedicate our all to Thee, Ourselves, our babes, our home."[4]

Just as was the case for Schleiermacher, Palmer's preparation to become a Pietist leader began with the conversion story of her father. Phoebe's father was Henry Worrall. In 1785, at the age of fourteen the adolescent Henry grew tired of his families Anglican Church. Hearing stories of a dynamic preacher, one morning he awoke earlier than his parents and snuck out of his home before 5:00 a.m. His parents were devoted members of the Church of England and occasionally housed curates in their Yorkshire home; they would have disapproved of their adolescent son's curiosity. Henry arrived at the grounds to hear John Wesley's sermon on John 3:7, "Ye must be born again." The sermon was common to Wesley. He delivered it or a version of this same sermon scores of times, but to the young Henry it was innovative and novel. While Wesley did not even record the day in his journal, it was a day that forever changed Henry's life.

Henry was now on to road to becoming a Methodist. He attended other meetings with Wesley and even received his membership ticket into Methodism from the hands of Wesley himself. This personal contact with the founder of Methodism was always a point of pride for Henry. Having separated himself from the church of his parents within seven years, the now young man Henry Worrall broke from his parent's country, and made his way to America. Once in America he settled in New York and joined the Methodist Episcopal Church. He also met Dorothea Wade, another pious Methodist, and the two quickly married. Their union was a fruitful one. They produce sixteen children, ten boys and six girls. Phoebe was their fourth child. Only half of the children reached maturity.

The Worrall home was a prosperous and pious one. Henry was involved in manufacturing large industrial items, such as steam engines. He was also involved in other large construction projects. These endeavors

4. Palmer, *Selected Writings*, 304.

afforded the Worrall home a degree of prosperity. Their financial wealth was rivaled by their personal devotion. Phoebe later wrote "My parents, prior to my being entrusted to them, were rather devotedly pious. I was therefore early instructed in experimental religion."[5] Phoebe received her parent's Methodist education rather well. She was tortured by the idea of telling her parents a lie. This followed her seeing the intense anguish on her parents' faces after she was found in telling an untruth at three and a half years of age. Following this point, her fear of misspeaking grew. The family joked about her penitence towards precise prose, jesting "Phoebe knows nothing, she only thinks." If the statement could not be verified, Phoebe never declared it to be so. Following her one major infraction at three, Phoebe maintained "I do not remember ever to have been willfully disobedient to any parental command."[6]

With such a personal emphasis on piety, Phoebe missed out on an evangelical rite of passage. She never had a conversion experience as a youth. Just like Zinzendorf, Phoebe never had an obvious break, or a period of youthful revelry in sin. Moments of repentance undoubtedly occurred, but no decisive moment where she abandoned her previous life. Just as was the case for Zinzendorf, this isolated Phoebe from many of her Methodist contemporaries. For the Methodists, as with Puritans, Presbyterians, Baptists, and Calvinists, the conversion experience was an emotional experience that grounded the child or adolescent in the faith. It assured them of their salvation and it marked their entrance into the church, more than any sacrament. Phoebe, and many children who chose not to rebel against their pious parents, are stuck in a limbo, feeling connected to the church but lacking the decisive moment that assured them of their place inside.

These conversion experiences were also very emotional moments. Phoebe struggled with emotions. A rather stoic child, like Francke and Wesley, she found very little value in the role of emotions in religious life. For Phoebe a feeling was not something definitive. While Schleiermacher defined religion as the feeling of absolute dependence, Palmer wanted to arrive at religion through cold calculated reason and the eruption of divine intervention. Phoebe did have a few emotional religious moments as a child though. When she was fifteen, her Methodist class-leader gave her a gift of Wesley's *Plain Account of Christian Perfection*. Upon receiving the work Phoebe had intense and powerful temptations, followed by a sweet feeling that Jesus was her refuge like a babe safe in its mother's arms. Later that year

---

5. Palmer, *Selected Writings*, 57.
6. White, *Beauty of Holiness*, 2.

she opened her Bible in the middle of the night and after reading Hebrews 10:36[7] she felt encouraged in her Christian struggle and resolved to live by faith.

MARRIED WITH CHILDREN

"Our love is still in youthful mood, As when, in manhood's pride, You at the nuptial altar stood, And called me first your bride."[8]

The young Phoebe Worrall was as dutiful with her suitors as she was with her speech. Many boys, even good Methodist boys, sought her hand in marriage, but she rebuffed them. Phoebe was not one to accept flattery and thus be moved to an impious or irrational decision. The Worralls were a wealthy and pious family. Anyone who sought their daughters needed to prove themselves not only by being good Methodists, but they likely needed to secure a level of financial potential as well. The financial barrier was never directly mentioned, but since most of Phoebe's suitors likely came from the same church and her sisters married into equally wealthy families, it was likely an unspoken but understood threshold. Phoebe's discouragement of her suitors was not based on an active opposition by her parents, but they did not explicitly approve of them either. The message was loud enough for her to understand their desires. As such Phoebe avoided contact with them, personally resolving "not to favor attentions I could not return."[9]

The favors she could return were those of Walter Clark Palmer. Both were members of the Allen Street Methodist Church, and Walter's piety matched his promising pecunious prospects. Walter graduated from Rutgers Medical College at twenty two years of age. Walter was born in New Jersey on February 9, 1804, but his parents Miles and Deborah moved to New York shortly thereafter. As Methodists themselves, they likely were familiar with the Worralls for a while before Walter's affections towards Phoebe blossomed. The Palmer's piety was unrivaled. Walter even considered a career as a clergyman instead of in medicine. He eventually decided that being a pious physician afforded him greater ministry opportunities than being a clergyman. His assumptions proved correct, but he needed

---

7. "For you have need of patience, that, after you have done the will of God, you might receive the promise. For yet a little while, and he that shall come will come, and will not tarry. We Are Not of Them Who Draw Back. Now the just shall live by faith" (Heb 10:36).

8. Wheatley, *Life and Letters of Palmer*, 141.

9. White, *Beauty of Holiness*, 4.

Phoebe to ensure that. It was only in July of 1826 after he graduated that his attentions could turn to romance.

Walter first began by pursuing a focused friendship with Phoebe. The two found success and the courtship grew beginning in September. One year later on September 28 the two were married. A month before her marriage Phoebe recorded. "The most eventful period of my life is approaching. During the past eleven months, friendship has been ripening into a mature affection between myself and a kindred spirt, who, I have reason to believe, is in every respect, worthy of my love. I have not approached this crisis, without careful circumspection and prayer. I have ever felt that it was a step too momentous to be hastily taken, fixing as it does, life's destiny."[10] Phoebe concludes this segment of journal declaring that God would not permit her affections had it not been ordered by divine providence. Under divine providence the two wed. Apparently providence approved of Palmer-Worrall marriages, as Walter's brother Miles married Phoebe's sister Hannah a little while later as well.

In September of 1827 Walter was more pious than Phoebe. It was either around this time or five years later when he experienced his second conversion. The concept of a second conversion, not a subsequent conversion, is a conversion to a higher level of holiness and one where the Christian would receive a second blessing. What this second blessing was varied depending on the particular group, but for Walter Palmer this was a further step in sanctification. In the early years of the Palmer marriage Phoebe mocked this idea. Walter also spoke of becoming a missionary and heading off to China. Phoebe did not want to become a missionary, but equally did not want to dissuade her new husband from following the Lord's calling. It was quite fortuitous for Phoebe when Walter interpreted her lack of enthusiasm for the idea as a tacit rejection and chose not to pursue the venture further. Years later when Phoebe experienced her second conversion and proposed missional stirrings as well as ministerial salacity, Walter reinforced her drive towards Holiness. Walter championed her without coercion or pride, often remaining silent, letting Phoebe preach, as both recognized her as the stronger orator. They even moved houses twice to accommodate her growing ministry on Tuesday evenings. Despite the travels and tragedies, their marriage was one of mutual support and undying love for one another and for their God.

By most measures the couple were content with one another, and the marriage could be identified as a happy one. Phoebe's journals are filled with pronouncements about her love for Walter. The measure that diminished

10. Wheatley, *Life and Letters of Palmer*, 22.

their joy was the death of three of their six children. Their first child was a boy named Alexander. He was born on September 28, 1828 on their first wedding anniversary, but he would not live to see their second. Alexander became Phoebe's whole world. She spent hours embroidering his baby clothes. Phoebe wondered if God approved of her spending so much time on mere decorations. Alexander was sickly, but Phoebe never considered the possibility of his death. She refused to have him baptized for most of his life, believing that baptizing Alexander was the same as giving him over to God. Alexander was her boy, not God's. She was not willing to share her child with her God. When he died on July 2, 1829 Phoebe believed that his death was due to her reluctance to share her affections. Phoebe's God was a jealous God and if she was not willing to share than God had to take him. A while after Alexander's death Phoebe surmised that "God takes our treasure to heaven that our hearts may be there also."[11] She saw the error of her ways and accepted that she must offer her children to God.

The next spring Phoebe gave birth to another boy. Samuel was born on April 29. Phoebe believed that God granted Samuel as a replacement for Alexander. Phoebe believed she needed to offer Samuel to God, since Alexander was taken without a free offering. Just like with Zinzendorf, whose first child was taken at the moment of his dedication to God, Phoebe's God accepted the offer and Samuel lived for less than two months. He died on June 19, 1830. She recorded that Samuel "was lent but seven short weeks and was then recalled; giving us two angel children in heaven, and leaving us childless on earth. I will not attempt to describe the pressure of the last crashing trial. Surely I needed it, or it would not have been given."[12] Now Phoebe needed to learn that she spent too much time on her children to the neglect of her religious activities.

Phoebe was about to be surrounded by religious activities. Less than a year after Samuel's passing, Allen Street Methodist Church began a revival. The Allen Street Revival, as it soon became known, occupied most of Walter's time. If he did not experience his second conversion before now, it most assuredly was underway within this revival. Walter attended so many services that Phoebe believed that he too would be taken from her, passing away due to overwork and exhaustion. This was the first of many revivals on Allen Street; most remained fairly small compared to this first one.

Walter survived the revival and shortly afterwards Phoebe became pregnant again. She gave birth to her first daughter, Sarah on April 11, 1833. The child was named after Phoebe's older and favorite sister. Sarah Worrall

---

11. Palmer, *Selected Writings*, 239.

12. Palmer, *Selected Writings*, 78.

was energetic and full of life and so was the child Sarah Palmer. Unlike her two sons, Phoebe's daughter was healthy. Sarah was the first of Phoebe's children to reach maturity and her life was a pious one. Sometime in 1847 Sarah Palmer professed conversion. She then graduated from Rutgers like her father and married a Reverend named Elron Foster. Sarah lived until 1918.

A month before Walter and Phoebe's eighth anniversary, Phoebe gave birth to another daughter, Eliza. In the summer of 1835 Phoebe was rather ill and it was believed that she might die. This was not an opportune time to give birth. Many believed that both Phoebe and Eliza may die, but miraculously they both recovered. This brush with her own mortality gave Phoebe a new perspective. While she was a devout child, she struggled to be a devout mother. Phoebe was also still uncertain about the idea of entire sanctification. Phoebe's sister Sarah had recently professed her second conversion, being entirely sanctified on May 21 of that year. While Phoebe still dismissed the idea, her sister and her husband's piety was attractive. Phoebe still believed the notion to be foolish, but sought out additional prayer meetings. This added level of prayer continued through the year. In February of 1836 Sarah and her husband Thomas Lankford moved in with Phoebe and Walter. The two couples encouraged one another with their spiritual lives. Phoebe continued to go to prayer meetings, many not in her own home, but refused the idea of entire sanctification.

After returning from one of these meetings on the evening of July 29, 1836 Phoebe checked in on her two daughters. She paid extra attention to Eliza. Though she was not ill Phoebe believed that Eliza was not long for this world. She looked at her all tucked into her bassinet which was draped with gauze, and exclaimed that she was an angel, holding her close before laying her to bed. Shortly thereafter a visitor came by and Phoebe left Eliza in the care of a nursemaid until after her visitor left. The lamp which lit the room began to flicker and the nurse decided to fill it with alcohol. Instead of blowing out the sputtering flame she began to refill the lamp while it was still lit. The foolish nurse spilled some of the fuel on her hands, which quickly ignited. Reflexively she threw the lamp away which caught Eliza's crib on fire. After hearing a shriek from the room Phoebe ran in to the room to see it ablaze. She grabbed Eliza out of her burning crib. Eliza was alive but she was so badly burned that she lived only a few hours, dying in her mother's arms. Phoebe records that Eliza "darted one inexpressible look of amazement and pity, on her agonized mother, and then closed her eyes forever on the scenes of earth." This tragedy broke Phoebe. She isolated herself from her loved ones. Phoebe records that "turning away from human comforters, I coveted to be alone with God."[13] In reality she simply could not cope with the horror of the event.

Phoebe, who eschewed emotions for most of her life, now had too many to count. She was perplexed and bewildered concerning how easily and carelessly her children could be taken from her. Understandably she was filled with shock and grief. Phoebe was also filled with anger directed towards her foolish nurse. The only thing she could do was to walk the floor, wringing her hands and crying out "O Lord, Help! Help!" She then opened her Bible to Romans 11:33.[14] She found help in the scriptures and had a mystical experience. She felt the Holy Spirit whisper to her. The whisper told her to stop blaming herself, the stupid maid, the innocent visitor, and the freakish circumstances for her daughter's death. Her mystical encounter also included a glimpse into heaven where she saw her departed child now in the presence of Jesus. What is surprising is that this mystical experience still predated her sanctification by nearly a year. Reflecting on her children's death, Phoebe wrote the following February, "I have often felt as though God had called me peculiarly to a life of holiness. I have also felt that in order to be led in this way, the path of self-denial must be mine."[15]

Her next two children survived past infancy and both outlived her. On March 9, 1839 Phoebe gave birth to another daughter. She named her after herself. In 1855 Phoebe Palmer, the daughter, wed Joseph Fairchild Knapp. Knapp was one of the founders of the Metropolitan Life Insurance Company of New York. The Knapp's hosted three US presidents in their home, Grant, Cleveland, and Harrison. Beyond her husband's fame Phoebe Palmer Knapp was well known for writing music and lyrics for many hymns. She died July 10, 1908.

On November 20, 1842 Phoebe gave birth to her sixth and last child, a boy they decided to name after Walter. Walter Clarke Palmer, Jr. was the only one of the Palmer children to accompany their parents on their missionary journey to England and spent most of his life continuing his parents work after their death, including running their publishing empire. He died in 1885.

Walter and Phoebe were also involved in foster care and once adopted a boy who needed their aid. Leopold Soloman was a poor Jewish lad who shortly before encountering Phoebe embraced Christianity. His conversion isolated him from his family who disowned him. Living on the streets he was

13. Palmer, *Selected Writings*, 99.

14. "O the depth of the wisdom and knowledge of God, how unsearchable are His judgments and His ways past finding out" (Rom 11:33).

15. Palmer, *Selected Writings*, 109.

jailed as a vagrant and forced to spend a short time in prison, aptly named the tombs. It was here that he encountered Phoebe. The Palmers took him in, first planning on fostering him. They chose to adopt him and even sent him to a boarding school. During the vacation from school, Leopold's birth parents sought him out and he returned to live with them. He returned to Judaism and never contacted the Palmers again.

While the case of Leopold Soloman is an isolated case, it serves as an example of the generosity of the Palmers. Walter often gave his medical care free of charge for those too poor to pay him. Like Francke, medicine was used to advance ministry goals, especially with the poor. Phoebe spent most of her efforts in benevolence both inside and outside of her home. For most wealthy, American women in the nineteenth century, their sphere of influence was their home. Phoebe Palmer accepted the domestic sphere as well as expanded it. She believed that the home did not imprison women, rather it nurtured their spirit and granted freedom of activities fulfilling their divine office. Most of her control in the domestic sphere occurred after her sanctification on July 26, 1837, especially considering that Phoebe and Walter the youngers were not even born until 1839 and 1842 respectively.

The divine office was fulfilled in a number of ways. First she ensured family devotions. These devotions occurred twice daily, once in the morning and the second in the evening. This encompassed the entire household, including servants and houseguests. During the devotions they sang Methodist hymns, read the Bible, and prayed. Every meal also was preceded by a sung prayer. In addition to the communal devotions, Phoebe Palmer encouraged personal Bible reading. She recommended that everyone rise at five and read the Bible for an hour. Every day would also conclude with reading the Bible to ensure that it was the first book in the morning and last one at night. These were counted as "holy times," and to be unwilling to offer a sacrifice of time which was granted by God was foolish, after all it is a sacrifice which costs nothing. The afternoon also held some time dedicated to the reading of scripture, but it was not as crucial as the morning and evening devotions. Phoebe herself woke and read the Old Testament, she then read the Gospels midday, and the Epistles before going to bed. Along with scripture reading, Palmer believed that Christians should keep a journal. To not keep a journal was almost a sin. The practice of spiritual autobiographies moved from a word of encouragement in the eighteenth century to a requisite in the nineteenth. Palmer like Schleiermacher, and many Pietist leaders, all kept personal journals that relayed their spiritual progress.

ENTIRE SANCTIFICATION AND TUESDAY MEETING FOR THE PROMOTION OF HOLINESS

"I cannot wash my heart, but by believing Thee."[16]

Like Francke, Phoebe used her home as a vehicle to convert the masses. It was a place for those who sought financial aid in addition to spiritual aid. It was her home that gave Phoebe her first real ministry leadership role, one that was in front of both men and women. Palmer believed that her household should be a place to sanctify all those who sought refuge. It was the place to experience the blessedness of peace. Her salon was the foretaste of glory. It was also a place that she controlled. Unlike most church classes, her house was not under the purview of Allen Street or any other parish. Her home allowed her to preach to Methodists as well as anyone else who desired holiness. It was the residence shared by her sister and the place of her personal entire sanctification and the Tuesday meetings for the Promotion of Holiness.

Phoebe Palmer's conversion to entire sanctification was deeply dependent upon her older sister Sarah Lankford. Sarah was nineteen months older than Phoebe but the two of them spent most of their life together, even living together after they were both married. As adults, people even joked that they were twins because their lives were so interconnected. In an odd twist of fate, after both Phoebe and Thomas died, Sarah and Walter married each other in March 1876. So as it turns out, Sarah and Phoebe also shared a husband, though not concurrently. Phoebe was younger, but she married Walter four years before Sarah married Thomas Lankford. Thomas A. Lankford was an architect from Virginia. He moved to New York and won the hand of Sarah Worrall. Thomas died in March 1871.

In May of 1835, four years after Sarah's marriage to Thomas, she experienced her second conversion experience. Sarah, while closely identified with Phoebe, possessed many of the churchly qualities her sister did not. While Phoebe was never able to point to a conversion experience as an adolescent, Sarah could. Sarah's first conversion took place as a thirteen year old. When she read Wesley's *Plain Account of Christian Perfection*, two years later in 1821 she tried to figure out how to attain this level of piety. Sarah proclaimed "Lord I will believe, help Thou my unbelief: . . . Yea, Lord from this hour, half-past two p.m., the 21st of May, 1835, I dare reckon myself dead, indeed unto sin."[17] Her second conversion was now underway, even though she experienced no feeling to that effect for an entire week.

---

16. Palmer, *Full Salvation*, 34.
17. White, *Beauty of Holiness*, 9.

It took the Allen Street Revival in 1835 to show her the way. This was the same revival that Walter was so tirelessly involved in. Following the revival and the experiences of Walter and Sarah, Phoebe was constantly urged to experience it on her own.

Sarah was also the one who began the Tuesday Meeting for the Promotion of Holiness, not Phoebe. Sarah was involved in women's prayer meetings at Allen Street in August 1835. She also led the First Tuesday Meeting at 54 Rivington Street on February ninth the following year, over a year before Phoebe was sanctified. Both the earlier prayer meeting and the Tuesday meeting in Rivington were outgrowths of Sarah's own piety. She was always interested in encouraging others to "perfect love." Her sister was no exception.

On July 26th, 1827, Sarah felt a special burden in her heart concerning her sister. That morning, Sarah pled with Phoebe before breakfast to spend the day in fasting and prayer for her salvation and the second blessing. Sarah announced she was planning on doing the same. Phoebe replied that she must have her breakfast but would pray. The lighthearted response was intended to wound, and it succeeded. In Phoebe's journal she voices her doubts concerning this Wesleyan doctrine. "Though I have ever been a firm believer in the doctrine of Christian holiness, embracing the entire sanctification of body, soul, and spirit, as taught from the Scriptures by the apostolic Wesleys, and their contemporaries; yet the terms made use of, in speaking of this attainment, were objectionable to my mind, in a manner which I cannot now take time to explain."[18] This Methodist doctrine which became so central to her teaching began as a foolish notion. She continued to argue that the blessing could only be comprehended by those who experienced it. The notion of a second blessing will be fully addressed in the next chapter.

With Sarah praying and fasting and Phoebe spending some time in prayer, Phoebe's thoughts turned to her three departed children. This was just three days shy of the one year anniversary of Eliza's horrible death. At nine in the evening Phoebe experienced her second conversion, still absent of the first conversion experience. Phoebe describes the experience in two different accounts. In the first she states that it was during her last prayer of the evening when she was overwhelmed by the power of God. "I felt an inexpressible change in the depths of my heart, and, from that hour, I have felt no anger, no pride, no wrong temper, of any kind; nothing contrary to the pure love of God which I feel continually. I desire nothing but Christ, and I have Christ always reigning in my heart. I want nothing; He is my

18. Palmer, *Faith and Its Effects*, 39.

sufficient portion in time and in eternity."[19] In another account she styles her conversion as a faithful servant off in the kitchen to one who was taken by her father into the parlor. "But now it is my Father—my own dear Father!"[20]

The vehicle for this conversion was an act of faith. For too long she believed that faith was a difficult task. After all, she was generally averse to emotional decisions and relying upon emotions to dictate her actions. Most of her fellow churchgoers linked faith with feeling, in much of the same way Schleiermacher did. It was only when Phoebe separated the two that she could come to faith. Now she understood faith to be believing what she professed. Resolving "Whatever my feelings may be, I will believe God's immutable Word unwaveringly, irrespective of emotion."[21] With this new understanding of faith she heard God speak to her like she was Moses on Mount Sinai. She then resolved to follow Wesley's example and become a Bible Christian.

Phoebe understood the concept of a Bible Christian to be a Christian who has unshakable faith in the Bible. The Bible was the sole source of authority in her life and it was the fountainhead of her doctrine and worldview. Of course the lens she interpreted scripture through was as an American Methodist, so just as Perkins, Arndt, Spener, and others, there was already a preexisting conception of what the scripture is, how certain verses are to be read, and what concepts should be prioritized. Like Wesley, Palmer had little knowledge of primitive Christianity and simply followed Wesley's pronouncements as the starting point. For Palmer, Wesley's commentaries dominated her understanding, but she also went beyond Wesley. Palmer read the Bible as the written word of a living God who spoke directly to her through the sacred texts. Faith is then interpreted as believing the Bible and believing that its claims were directed to her personally. Therefore when a moment of doubt entered her mind, saying "'How do you know that God will receive you?' and. . . 'How may I know that the Lord does receive me?' To this, in gentle whispers, the Spirit replied, 'It is written, I will receive you.'"[22] Following this experience, Phoebe told her sister of her conversion and the two then shared in the ministry of the Tuesday Meeting.

The Lankford/Palmer Tuesday Meeting is the best example of a Methodist conclave. These small groups resembled Spener's *collegias* at first, usually having a small number of members who shared accountable discipleship with one another. Wesley, following Spener and Francke,

19. Palmer, *Full Salvation*, 41.
20. Hughes, *Fragrant*, 28.
21. White, *Beauty of Holiness*, 12.
22. Palmer, *Selected Writings*, 119.

instituted the practice as well and the goal was to have their co-religionists pray for one another and exhort them in scripture readings. While the Tuesday meetings began with this small intimate setting, they quickly grew beyond this. The actual workings of the Tuesday meetings were not intimate like Spener's groups, rather it was a symposium on Holiness, much larger than most classrooms. It was not unheard of for smaller groups to break off of the larger gathering. Furthermore, visitors were always welcome, so the intimacy that Spener and Francke encouraged with their groups and even with the salons that Schleiermacher was a part of could not be attained.

Every Tuesday at 2:30 in the afternoon the session began. It began with the reading of sections from the Bible. From here the congregation sung and prayed. After this someone chose to speak on the scripture reading, but the speaker varied, and their exposition was rather short. Following this people gave testimonies about their conversion experience or their encounters with God since the last time they gathered. In many ways this resembled Methodist church services. Two noticeable distinctions were obvious. First, it took place at a home rather than a church. Second, while clergy were often present, they did not run the meeting. George Hughes wrote a contemporary account where he states that most meetings had six to ten ministers present, and often even more. Their rank and position was inconsequential and it was only mentioned if it served a larger purpose to the gathering or they served as an example to someone else. While there was a general structure to the meeting, it was far more social than other religious gatherings and one person might pray, then another, without following a strict liturgical formula. In many ways it resembled a Quaker meeting more than a Methodist service. Freedom permeated the service, from who prayed to what songs were sung, to what topic would be addressed.

Not long after her total sanctification, Phoebe took the leadership reins from her older sister. Once involved, Phoebe ensured that the meetings included an evangelical climax usually following the testimonies. In this moment Phoebe gave those who attended an opportunity to repent, convert, or accept total sanctification. In this altar call there was no altar, nor a large crowd present who pressed the uninitiated towards entire sanctification. Palmer or others also used this time to answer any questions from the doubting visitors and guests, sometimes taking the form of an inquiry meeting. They often concluded with one or more receiving sanctification and someone praying for them. Those who attended claimed that the meetings were opportunities to lay their burdens down, dispel doubts, and obtain pardon. They maintained that no controversy occurred, or very rarely for the over 2,500 Tuesday Meetings. Each meeting averaged two hundred participants.

With two hundred or more guests showing up in the Palmer home, space became quite the concern. When the Tuesday Meeting began with Sarah Lankford she used Dr. Palmer's back office on 54 Rivington St. Then they utilized the second floor parlors. Still the meetings grew and according to Hughes the meeting had three locations, the first on 54 Rivington, then St. Mark's Place, then finally 316 East Fifteenth Street. This final location was much larger than the previous locations but the spacious parlor still grew cramped with more and more visitors. The halls, staircase, and adjoining rooms began to be filled. In order to accommodate without moving yet again, the Palmers decided to expand the parlor in their home. This cost them two thousand dollars in 1857, and by most estimations this is well over $50,000 today. Beyond the new locations and size, the meetings had two other significant changes. The first was to allow men at the meetings led by the two sisters. The second was the interdenominational atmosphere that was created.

The first man to attend the meeting was Thomas Cogswell Upham. Upham's wife invited him to the meeting in 1839. Upham was a professor at Bowdoin College in Maine, and he was a Congregationalist, but was rather interested in the concept of Holiness. He was permitted to attend the smaller meeting at the time and following him, many more men began to seek instruction on Holiness from Phoebe and Sarah. The next man to attend the meeting was their longtime friend Timothy Merritt who edited the *Christian Advocate* and later founded *The Guide to Christian Perfection*, subsequently titled *the Guide to Holiness*, a publication that the Palmers purchased after the Civil War. Other prominent Methodists attended the meeting including Nathan Bangs and two Methodist Episcopal Bishops, Janes and Hamline.

Since Upham was a Congregationalist, his arrival also opened the door to non-Methodists as well. Palmer wrote that in addition to Methodists, her home was visited by lay and clergy members that were Baptists, Congregationalists, Dutch Reformed, German Reformed, Presbyterians, Protestant Episcopalians, Quakers, Minted Brethren, and Jews in Christ. All met without splitting theological hairs or party distinctions. Since the meeting took place in her home rather than at a church, this ecumenical meeting had a greater chance of success than nearly any other in nineteenth-century America. She credited her success to the focus of the meetings. "Not Wesley, not Fletcher, not Finney, not Mahan, not Upham, but the Bible, the holy Bible, is the first and last, and in the midst always. The Bible is the standard, the groundwork, the platform, the creed. Here we stand on common ground, and nothing but the spirit of this blessed book will finally eradicate and extirpate a sectarian spirit."[23] Additionally no favoritism was given to the testimony of anyone based upon their denominational affiliation. Just like with Zinzendorf, the appeal to denomination to validate experience seemed laughable and each denomination brought their own *tropus* to the Pietist meetings. Prayers were given and praises sung for any Protestant who arrived. We must say Protestant since she never records Catholics or Orthodox in her meetings and her attitudes towards them are anything but charitable.

Overall the Tuesday Meetings lasted weekly for over fifty years. They began without Phoebe, led by her sister, and they continued even when Phoebe was unavailable, including when she was out of the country, or on missionary journeys outside of New York. The structure of the meetings were such that someone else could lead them fairly easily. They even continued for thirty years after Phoebe's death. Apart from Phoebe's occasional absence until her death, the meetings suffered another loss when the Lankfords moved fifty miles away to Caldwell-on-the-Hudson in 1840. Sarah spent most of her life down the hall from her sister, but then she and her husband decided to aid Henry Worrall in a business venture. The company he was building a steam engine for went bankrupt and the Lankfords decided to take over the business, believing they could be missionaries in Caldwell. The Lankfords began a new congregation, but Sarah regularly still took the long trek to New York in order to attend the Tuesday afternoon meetings.

In addition to the Tuesday Meetings, Phoebe was asked to lead a young convert's class at Allen Street in 1839. She accepted this, becoming the first woman in New York appointed to permanently lead a mixed class meeting. This occurred a few months before Dr. Upham attended the Tuesday Meeting, and likely provided justification for her accepting him at that meeting. Phoebe's convert class met on Friday evenings in her home. Walter taught one on Thursday afternoons. As his medical practice grew, Phoebe instructed his class as well on numerous occasions. They each led these classes until 1848 when they were called to assist another Methodist Church.

BEYOND TUESDAY AFTERNOONS

"Labor is rest, and pain is sweet."[24]

If all Phoebe Palmer managed to do in her life was to host and grow a parachurch meeting that lasted over half a century with men and women

23. Hughes, *Fragrant Memories*, 38.
24. Wheatley, *Life and Letters of Palmer*, 156.

of various denominations, and be the first woman to be appointed to permanently lead a mixed Methodist class in New York, her accomplishments would have been worthy of mention. In many ways these accomplishments are only the preamble to Palmer's impact on nineteenth-century experiential Protestantism. Her calling was to reach the world beyond a few blocks in New York, both directly and indirectly. The first way she did this was to take her show on the road.

At the same time as she was teaching a mixed class of converts at Allen Street, Phoebe Palmer began to travel to other churches, spreading her message of entire sanctification. Both Phoebe and Walter Palmer became full-time Methodist evangelists. Walter continued his medical practice, often linking the two together. The Palmers were two of four noteworthy Methodist evangelists before the mid-1850s. The other two were ordained and foreign born John Newland Maffitt[25] (d. 1850) and James Caughey (d. 1891). The Palmer's message focused on entire sanctification as well as the idea that everyone, including college presidents, elders, bishops, pastors, and the laity were responsible for saving souls. Instead of relying upon ordination as the qualification one required to proselytize, their faith was the only qualification they needed.

Phoebe's perfectionist message was simple, and simply done. She took what was happening on Tuesday afternoons and did the same thing elsewhere. This was a basic pattern of evangelism and it emphasized experience over creeds, so most Protestant denominations accepted her. Often her sermons consisted of stories of conversion experiences rather than much, if any, theological prose. This allowed for accessibility as well as relating local people to the idea of sanctification. Like Zinzendorf and the Moravians, Palmer's message was simple and easy to deliver and receive. This message not only attracted Protestants of various denominations, but opened the pulpits of other denominations to Phoebe and Walter as well. Baptists, Presbyterians, and Congregationalists all welcomed the preaching Palmers inside their churches. Everyone agreed that Phoebe was the better speaker and she was the headliner rather than Walter.

The Holiness message existed outside of the Methodist church. At the same time Phoebe and Walter were delivering their message, Charles Finney was conveying his. Finney's message found a larger home with the Presbyterians and he was eventually named the president of Oberlin College. The Palmer's message of perfection lined up with those of Finney and Oberlin. Together they launched the Holiness movement. Most reports say that while Finney began his emphasis on perfectionism before Phoebe,

---

25. Not the famous privateer of the same name.

he eventually was influenced more by her than vice versa. For a brief period in 1842 Oberlin and Methodist Holiness were inseparable. They held Holiness conventions in New York City, Buffalo, Rochester, Newark, and other towns in and around New York State.

The Holiness movement grew beyond the Palmers and Oberlin and before long other denominations began spreading the message of Holiness. The most significant occurred in 1858 when a revival connected to the Businessman Revival broke out and was called a modern Pentecost. Like Zinzendorf's Pentecost the previous century, this one included long prayer meetings and repentance. Unlike Zinzendorf's Pentecost, this one focused on the "gift of power" and the power was expected to be used to combat sins of this world.

With such success preaching, Phoebe desired to reach an even greater audience. The press was the perfect place for this. She began publishing accounts of her views of salvation in the *Christian Advocate and Journal* in 1842. Through the Journal she constructed her first published work, *The Way of Holiness* in 1843. This book quickly became a best seller among devotional works. The work underwent several editions and was translated into French, where it sold 1,600 copies. It was also translated into German, and versions existed in Liberia and Siam, but not with as much success. The work's greatest success was in English speaking countries, the United States, Canada, and England. Worldwide it sold more than a hundred thousand copies during her lifetime. More remarkable than its success was her choice to let her name appear on the title page. Many women used pseudonyms, especially when writing devotional or theological works. Her choice not to do this adds significant weight to the argument that she was an early feminist. It was also a good move for her evangelical career. The success of her work only made her more popular and opened new areas for her to speak and advocate entire sanctification.

The Way of Holiness was followed by *Entire Devotion to God* in 1845, and *Faith and Its Effects* in 1848. These works make up the core of her theological notion of Altar Theology, which the next chapter will address. These three books are also modeled after her sermons. They are filled with stories of conversion and accounts of her own life and her own struggles with faith. None of these works are a systematic theology of the Christian faith. They are primarily devotional aids that reveal her theology and are not overtly theological. Palmer's most theological work, *Promise of the Father*, published in 1859, was also her most controversial. In this work Palmer sets out her justification as a woman to speak in church. This is the only work where Phoebe moves beyond personal testimonies and Bible quotes and uses arguments from history and biblical criticism. She published many more works than these four and throughout all of her works Palmer is rather comfortable with utilizing new technology to advance her message. She utilized inexpensive books and magazines, as well as the railroads and steamboats to reach audiences impossible for preachers just a generation before.

Throughout the 1830s, most of Phoebe's preaching circuit was in New York State, with occasional journeys into New Jersey. As her name grew in prominence, so too did requests from other locales. The first real journey outside of the New York area came by a request from Miss Frederica Kohler. Frederica Kohler was the granddaughter of the Moravian Peter Bohler, who helped Wesley convert. Frederica told Phoebe that many in the Moravian community in Pennsylvania were backslidden. Phoebe left Walter to care for their children and went to preach amongst the Moravians. The trip was a success. Shortly after returning, other denominations made similar requests.

One of the more memorable events for Phoebe came when they were returning from a trip to Boston. The boiler on their steamship exploded. Smoke and steam filled the boat and everyone assumed the ship was going to sink, likely resulting in a massive death toll. Phoebe, who was accompanied by Walter and her sister Sarah, heard someone singing. They were singing two Methodist hymns "We're Going Home to Die No More" and "How Do Thy Mercies Close Me Round." They immediately joined in the chorus, excited that there were other Methodists on board, and those who found solace in their hymns more than they feared death. The boat did not sink and she records no deaths. Phoebe took this moment as a badge of pride that her husband, sister, and herself all gave clear testimony of their faith in the face of death. This is rather humorous considering John Wesley's own encounter with a ship that appeared it was going to sink. Wesley heard the hymns of the Moravians and he was gripped with fear of his own death. Now Wesley's hymns brought comfort to those on a boat that did not sink.

As an odd twist of fate the Palmers considered becoming missionaries to China during this period as well. While the idea frightened Phoebe earlier in her marriage, the idea now intrigued her. They were determined to go to China as missionaries, but then felt called by the spirit to remain in America a little longer. Instead they decided to pledge five hundred dollars towards the establishment of a mission in China if they could get twenty others to do so as well. They gathered others and structured the payment over ten years. Five missionaries were sent in 1847. Phoebe also decided that she would work just as hard in New York as she would have if sent to China herself.

1848 was a turning point for Palmer, just as it was for most of Europe. As revolutions swept through Europe, challenging and toppling established power structures, Palmer encountered her first real opposition to her

Holiness message. The first rumblings of trouble came from the success the Holiness movement had. Too many young and less pious ministers saw the movement as an opportunity to court applause rather than urge them onto spiritual growth. As such, clergy both inside and outside of Methodism began to criticize the movement as a whole. As expected, the greatest opponents were those who never held Wesley's notion of Holiness to begin with. Protestants of every stripe began to question the notion of a second blessing. To combat this and defend her ministry, Phoebe Palmer wrote *Incidental Illustrations*, in 1855.

The greatest onslaught of attacks took place in the 1850s and occurred in *The Christian Advocate and Journal*. These disputes were played out in print for all to see. Amidst the critiques Palmer had a prophetic dream concerning the brewing controversy over Holiness. During her dream she was chased by several terrifying wild beasts, bears, and lions. Some beasts attacked one another, but most were headed towards her. Then suddenly a fierce lion, much larger than the other beasts, attacked her in great fury. She lost focus on the other beasts who now seemed so small and insignificant compared to this fierce lion. She then grabbed the lion's mouth and managed through supernatural assistance to hold its jaws closed. Palmer was convinced that if the lion could open its mouth she would be lost. The lion turned out to be Hiram Mattison. The other beasts were a host of other contributors to the controversy played out in *The Advocate*. Most of these authors were clergy and some even sided with Palmer. In addition to Mattison, the list includes Spicer, Woodriff, Bangs, Perry, and a whole host of anonymous contributors.

Mattison was a Methodist elder and professor of astronomy and natural philosophy at Fahey Seminary in upstate New York. His first criticism of Palmer's theology came out in December of 1851, with a work titled "Professing Holiness." This was followed by other articles in *the Advocate*, in total at least a dozen spanning from December of 1851 to January 1856. Eventually *the Advocate* ended the argument by choosing to no longer publish works concerning the Holiness controversy. Palmer responded in kind, not only with *Incidental Illustrations*, but also with five articles, with titles such as "False Statement Corrected," and "A Voice from the Laity." Only three of her articles were aimed directly at Mattison, and some others even came to her defense against him.

Mattison believed that Palmer's teachings were divisive and filled with errors. He spelled out eight propositions which he believed illustrated the errors of Palmer's theology. The first criticism was that sanctification was nothing more than consecration, that it was not a second blessing, but a mere dedication to God. The next few critiques centered on the relationship between faith and what it is to be sanctified according to Palmer. Mattison also did not like how Palmer viewed this doctrine as something extra and separate from church life, including meetings such as her Tuesday Afternoon Meeting. Mattison believed that Palmer was constructing a new and different church than the one that the Apostles or Wesley delivered them. While Palmer refused this notion, Mattison's criticism has merits, especially in light of the divisions in the Methodist Episcopal Church at the turn of the twentieth century that resulted in Holiness churches as separate denominations and the launch of both fundamentalism and Pentecostalism, which will be addressed in chapters five and six.

Mattison's judgment of Holiness had some lasting repercussions, though Palmer and the doctrine survived the 1850s. Few were willing to criticize the wildly popular Palmer or the foundation of Oberlin theology. As the century continued, anti-Holiness sentiment grew and eventually Methodist evangelists were subjected to ecclesiastical oversight if they held meetings without approval of a list of clergy, who often disapproved of Holiness teachings. By the 1880s those who supported the doctrine of Holiness created an independent National Holiness Association. This loosened the reins of those who advocated for Palmer's position, but it also placed them outside of the Methodist fold. The largest effect was in the South and West, the very places where Pentecostalism had its greatest success at the beginning of the twentieth century.

During the controversial years, Phoebe, along with Walter, took their first trips outside of the United States to spread the Holiness message. From 1853 to 1857, the Palmers went to Canada on several occasions and held camp meetings. In 1854 she engaged in eight meetings in Canada alone. At one meeting in Brighton, Ontario she witnessed two hundred conversions. Another convention lasted ten days in Quebec. This was an especially proud moment for the Palmers, since Quebec was filled with Catholics, and Phoebe was not sure how they would receive the message. She was proud to report that one hundred fifty claimed salvation, followed by one hundred more in Spencertown. After this, Phoebe encountered even greater success, recording "never before have we witnessed such effusions of the Spirit on believers. Hundreds on hundreds have received the tongue of fire, and have returned to the cities and villages round about, filled with faith and the Holy Ghost to spread the Pentecostal flame."[26]

The Palmers also spoke in the United States, mostly at camp meetings, over twenty in 1855 and 1856. It was in 1857 that she predicted that over 800,000 new converts would enter the Methodist churches the following

26. Palmer, *Promise of the Father*, 208.

year. This was a remarkable claim since the membership was only increasing by a little more than 20,000 a year. Phoebe stressed that the task of converting the masses was not on her shoulders, nor those of her husband, or even the ordained clergy, rather the task was laid upon every sanctified Christian. Since everyone should be sanctified, everyone should be evangelizing. With a new focus for the laity to win the lost to Christ, 800,327 new converts was the anticipated growth. In actuality the northern Methodists only gained by 136,036 members in 1858. More than two thousand of those converts came from the Palmer's camp meetings. This was a far cry from the goal, but still a significant growth. The growth was enough for contemporaries to call it the *annus mirabilis*, the year of miracles.

During the 1850s Phoebe became involved in church planting and building new ministries outside of Allen Street in New York. The Palmers foray into church planting actually came two years earlier in 1848. The Norfolk Street Methodist Episcopal Church was poorly run and decided they needed help. They sent a delegation to Allen Street to ask for help. Phoebe was not sure exactly how to help their feeble sister church until she had a dream. In this dream she found herself in a large glass house at noon. The brightly filled room was blinding and she was holding an oil lamp. She was asked if her lamp was shining. It was lit, but it was difficult to see it in the bright light from the sun. When she awoke she realized that she must change churches. Allen Street was thriving, it had multiple revivals and it did not need her light, while Norfolk Street did. The Palmers moved churches and the first Sunday they attended Norfolk a revival broke out there as well. They remained at Norfolk for eight years until Allen Street's light began to fade and they returned.

In addition to reviving Norfolk, Phoebe recognized a need for the poor on Seventeenth Street. She decided that they needed a church. Phoebe used her wealth and the wealth of other affluent women to financially support this struggling church. She donated a hundred dollars in 1850 to this endeavor. She pledged to continue this support as long as it was needed. Others joined in the cause and within six months they began construction of the church and were holding meetings in the basement. Within five years the Redding, or Seventeenth Street Methodist Episcopal Church, was large enough that it was self-supporting.

After this Palmer believed that the Jews would be converted in the end times, and she believed that living in the second Pentecost, the end was nigh. To this end she set out to build a Jewish-Christian synagogue to call the Jews to faith in Jesus as their messiah. In 1855 the Palmers donated five hundred dollars to this end. At first she was encouraged as several converted

Jews attended. Their number did not increase though, and at the end of ten months the project failed.

In 1850 Phoebe also began the first inner city mission in the United States. While Finney and others intentionally planted churches in gritty inner city neighborhoods, these churches were used as a lamp to attract the denizens of the borough and did not actively proselytize as missionaries in the cities. Palmer's inner city mission closely resembles Francke and his involvement in the slums of Halle in Glaucha. Most respectable Americans ignored the downtrodden in their cities, especially the gritty Five Points area of New York. It was filled with poor, violent, immigrants who drank alcohol, were largely Catholic and came from Germany and Ireland. The Five Points were also the flash point of a cholera epidemic. The gangs and violence could be overlooked, but cholera was something that the respectable New Yorkers could not ignore. Unsure as to what to do, a group of Methodist women began addressing the topic. The group was the Ladies' Home Missionary Society, of which Phoebe was a founding member of their New York branch. One woman said she would be willing to give ten dollars towards a German mission, but not one dollar towards Five Points. There was no point in spending money on a lost cause. Phoebe surmised that their problem was not simply their intemperance or poverty, but their religion. If only they could be converted, they would overcome the power of alcohol and they would then become thrifty and nonviolent. She then burst out that she would give one hundred dollars towards a mission at Five Points. This silenced all objection. Thus the Five Points mission was born. Other women rallied to her cause and the matter carried. They hired a missionary to begin work that very year. The Five Point Mission was very successful and overshadowed any other projects to the point that the Ladies' Home Missionary Society and the Five Point Mission were nearly synonymous. Surprisingly, women were also deeply involved in the Five Point Mission, going down to the rough part of town, battling urban poverty, and spreading the gospel. Most women involved with the Five Point Mission believed that the best way to win others to Christ was to improve the lot of the poor, who when converting also aided their own lives and the neighborhood.

The following year, after her father's death, Phoebe seriously began her involvement with the Tombs. The Tombs were one of the worst prisons in America and they were located in lower Manhattan. Palmer, like Perkins and Wesley, took Christ's words "I was in prison, and you visited me" (Matt 25:37) to be a directive. Just as with Five Points, she spent a good portion of her time distributing Bibles and working with alcoholics. In her journal entry on March 30, 1851 she mentions that she and others "Went out this morning at an early hour, to do something toward reclaiming an inebriate,

Mr. B. Begged him, on my knees, to lay his hand on the Bible, and promise the God of the Bible that he would neither 'Touch, taste, nor handle' spirituous liquors. This afternoon, on his knees, he solemnly pledged himself. Thank the Lord!"[27]

THERE AND BACK AGAIN

"With me, no melancholy void, No moment lingers unemployed, Or unimproved below."[28]

While the Palmers did not go to China, they did feel called to go abroad on a missionary journey. Instead of heading to the Far East, they traveled East of New York—to England—in 1859. Tensions were high in the States and the pending outbreak of the Civil War likely contributed to this decision. If nothing else, it likely extended their stay in England, as preaching at camp meetings in the war torn Union or Confederacy was a dangerous if not impossible task. The Palmers left for their voyage to England on June 4, 1859 onboard the Steamer City of Baltimore. The steamship made the twelve day journey far less treacherous than the voyage Wesley took to America. At the time of their departure Phoebe and Walter were not sure how long they would be gone for.

As things worked out, the Palmers spent four years in the British Isles from 1859 to 1863. While most of their time was spent in England itself, they did take a few trips to Ireland, Scotland, The Isle of Wight, and Wales. There was not a definitive plan to the trek, and their stay varied depending on the local need and how well their message was received. On numerous occasions they stayed longer than they initially planned and later in their trip they threatened to leave the city if certain conditions were not met. These conditions usually involved the elimination of alcohol from the church grounds or the refusal of a parishioner to give up their sale of liquor. The durations of each revival meeting naturally varied but over the four years they took part in nearly sixty recorded revival meetings.[29]

By the time of their journey to England, both of their daughters were already married and gone from their home. Only their son Walter was still living with them. They decided it was best to take the sixteen-year-old Walter Jr. with them. The trip to England came with mixed blessings. Naturally the wealthy Palmers traveled in first-class. Still these accommodations did not

---

27. Palmer, *Selected Writings*, 227.

28. Wheatley, *Life and Letters of Palmer*, 264.

29. Nine in 1859, sixteen in 1860, thirteen in 1861, twelve in 1862, and nine in 1863.

really suit them well. The amenities were nice, but the company they kept treated the voyage across the sea like a vacation. For the Palmers, this was a mission, not a sabbatical from their ordinary lives. Phoebe often made her way down to steerage and was overjoyed to find some "disciples of Jesus" there. She then decided that it was fitting to hold a worship service among the second class. Phoebe was shocked and horrified to find so many ministers on board who failed to live up to her own personal standards. None of them organized prayer meetings. That was left to her, and she even found some of them gambling, playing cards, chess, dice, or board games. Worst of all some were even drinking. One of her fellow travelers was a professor from Union Theological Seminary who she engaged in conversation about such vices. He granted that many were in error, but thought that some games were harmless, although cards were dangerous as they led to gambling. Phoebe wondered how anyone could possibly play a board game to the glory of God. Phoebe does not mention the name of the well-known professor, but was shocked that he too was playing dice and doing so in the presence of others. Palmer echoed the moralism that grew to dominate Pietism with Francke and Wesley, the moralism that Schleiermacher believed to be disruptive and dangerous to the future of Protestantism.

When the boat docked in Liverpool, the Palmers did not know exactly what their plan was to be. To their surprise a Reverend Thomelow met them. He had read of their journey across the sea in the paper. Having followed the Palmers and read Phoebe's works, he thought it best to meet them and offer them a place to stay and a ride to wherever they planned on going. Phoebe's first impressions along the drive toward their lodgings were "Surely this looks like the Old World! Everything appears so ancient and somber, as though grown hoary with age."[30]

Within a few months of their stay in England they decided to travel to Ireland, arriving there on July nineteenth. Once there, Phoebe and Walter put on a prayer meeting like they had done countless times in America and like they did over the previous weeks in England. There initial views of the Irish were not that high. She believed that so many of them were illiterate poor who had little opportunity to hear the gospel or gain any religious knowledge. Phoebe recorded that the Lord was good to remember those in this low estate, where thanks to her arrival "Thousands are yielding to be saved. Ireland, so long bowed down beneath the oppression of the Man of Sin, is now being rescued. The Deliverer is come out of Zion; and, by the brightness of his appearing, Popery is unmasked, and its very form seems

---

30. Palmer, *Four Years*, 20.

destined to be consumed speedily."[31] Her mission in Ireland was similar to her mission with the Irish in Five Points, to save them from poverty, popery, and potation. Her tools for this were the same as elsewhere. She confronted those in attendance, declaring that to touch strong drink was the work of Satan, and only through Christ could they hate swill and sin.

Palmer's accounts in Ireland are often the same battles over and over. She calls for them to give up intoxicants, illicit acts, as well as indoctrinations they had accepted from Rome. One account of a newly converted man she felt especially excited about, saying that he was like a man pulled by four horses in different directions, now converted he needed to give up his lucrative business. Palmer proclaimed that "a Christian, and a distiller or whiskey-selling Christian, are not compatible terms."[32] That same passage she records that "the Man of Sin," by which she means both the devil and the Pope, was losing ground. "Those who are stricken are at once done with Romanism, whether the subject be young or old. A Roman-Catholic girl was stricken, and thoroughly converted. Among her first exclamations was, 'No Virgin Mary for me!'"[33]

The Bible was to replace their previous lives. She urged them to put aside all that hindered them. For some, this was family who she said laid threats against the new converts. For others, this was done by burning their Catholic manuals, rosary beads, or what she called amulets. She lauded the cries of "No priest but Jesus, no mediator but Jesus; no purgatory but the fountain opened for sin and for uncleanness."[34] She laughed at the Catholic priests, who in her words were confounded after they first scoffed at her mission, then blustered and now lost their tempers, at her revival.

Upon her return to England, she marveled at the relics she encountered of Wesley and other early Methodists. The irony of her veneration was lost on her, but Palmer was as enamored by encountering Mary Fletcher's New Testament, or an "ancient" copy of Wesley's hymns, as any Catholic was of their own saints and relics. A few passages later she mocks the church that was under repair, but the walls stood since the time of William the Conqueror, with the bell that rang monks into prayer for over 1,200 years. Worse still was the treatment of a chair, owned by the papists, which was believed by many to benefit any who held a piece. Throughout the centuries, many cut away portions to wear around their necks or place under their pillow.

31. Palmer, *Four Years*, 29.
32. Palmer, *Four Years*, 40.
33. Palmer, *Four Years*, 40.
34. Palmer, *Four Years*, 47.

In February of 1860, the Palmers made their way to Glasgow. Her time in Scotland was a difficult one. She was warned ahead of time not to waste her time among the Scots. Too many were connected to the established Church of Scotland, and the prevailing belief was that many could be converted without knowing it. This notion caused Phoebe much angst, as it amounted to a rejection of the Spirit bringing power in the believer's life. She put this up to a national character "The Scotch, as a people, are theologians; and are remarkable for religious technicalities, and the strength of their prejudices. They are, as a nation, greater adepts in hair-splitting, and making a man an offender for a word, than any people I ever saw. For this they are famed."[35] Phoebe loathed hair-splitting and impious lives masquerading as theology. Most people she said only communed quarterly, and were members of churches simply because it was unpopular to not be a church member. People feared eternal repercussions for their children if they were not baptized. The churches would not baptize children if their parents were not members. As such, nearly everyone was a member of a church that they understood very little. The difficulty for Palmer was the real result that they were members of the church without understanding nor experiencing their own conversion. While the success was not as great as Phoebe hoped, there was some measure of accomplishment. One case included the baptism of the Holy Spirit poured out on a local preacher who traveled a great distance to see them.

As time went by, Phoebe's attraction to the Old World grew. She even considered expanding their missionary journey into France, but was hindered because they did not know French. Phoebe appreciated the cultivated land and the numerous beautiful gardens and common hawthorn fences. She also marveled at the differences between the classes. Nowhere was this more obvious than on the Isle of Wight and Windsor. Both of course were residences of Queen Victoria (d. 1901). Phoebe first encountered the Queen in her marine residence on the Isle. The Queen rode in front of the home she was staying in at the time and the atmosphere was full of life when she was about. The Palmers stay was not the typical camp meeting, but they were there by invitation of Wesleyan societies who wanted to give the Palmers a special blessing.

While on the island, Phoebe took advantage of her proximity to the Queen to present her with a copy of her book *Promise of the Father*, her latest publication in which the Queen was mentioned. Palmer was unable to hand a copy to the sovereign personally but was told by a private secretary that she received it. Phoebe received a letter thanking her for the book. A

---

35. Palmer, *Four Years*, 93.

few weeks later Palmer purposed to write the monarch once again; this time it had to do with her own salvation. Phoebe Palmer believed the Queen to be an exemplary leader but feared the accounts of her piety to be overly stated. Palmer wanted to warn her majesty of the sins accompanied by her patronizing of the theater and race courses, not to mention her violation of the Sabbath by cruising on her yacht and having hired musicians to perform for her on the Lord's Day. Queen Victoria sent no reply concerning the lesson in piety. This resulted in Palmer's letters to friends back home, stating "As a Queen, she doubtless merits their admiration. But as an experimental Christian, she cannot be regarded, so long as she patronizes the theatre, and the horse race, etc."[36]

Palmer's concern for the Queen was intensified when she went to Windsor. Here she held a revival where a number of soldiers and musicians belonging to the Queen's band attended. At first Palmer was overjoyed at the outpouring of support she had from the Queen's guards. One of the guards served under four sovereigns of England and professed to pray for the Queen in every room of the palace, including at the foot of the throne. The news was not so joyous from the sanctified musicians. The members of the band who converted to entire sanctification were now faced with a serious dilemma. What were they to do when the Queen ordered them perform on the Sabbath? It was from this point that Palmer understood why some called Windsor, Wicked Windsor. Palmer now realized she was called to a valley of dry bones and not a place that favored revival. How could a Christian serve God and the sovereign? This was likened to Daniel violating the decree and praying to God. The actual consequence of the upcoming performance were not as dour as to be thrown to lions. The Queen was sick on the day of the scheduled performance and it was canceled.

In December of 1860, the Palmers made their way to Oxford. This overjoyed them, as they had an opportunity to see the birthplace of Methodism. Rather quickly their joy turned to despair when they were unable to enter Wesley's former room. The fellow who had until recently resided in the rooms died shortly before their arrival. As such, the room was closed off. Instead they peered through the window to the room exclaiming, "Wesley's room, we thought of the mighty blaze now spreading over the earth through the power of that form of Christianity here first developed, and in derision called Methodism, and exclaimed, 'What hath God wrought!'"[37]

At this same time Oxford was the birthplace of another movement. This one did not follow Wesley but rather Edward Bouverie Pusey

36. Palmer, *Selected Writings*, 268.
37. Palmer, *Selected Writings*, 269.

(1800–1882). Dr. EB Pusey was one of three founding members of what became known as the Oxford Movement. John Henry Newman (d. 1890) credits the movement's birth to John Keble's sermon "National Apostasy," which he heard on July 14, 1833. Together Pusey, Newman, and Keble (d. 1866) tried to move the Church of England back towards the Catholic Church. This took different forms among the three. Early on the view was to support a very High Church Anglicanism. Unlike Germany or France, England had jurisdictional authority on equal grounds to Rome and Greece. As such, Protestantism was not a necessary step taken by Henry VIII, rather England should have appealed to this for its autocephalous status. Rome and Canterbury were one with Episcopal tradition, just different in their history, similar to Rome and Constantinople. Newman broke from the other two and converted to Roman Catholicism in 1843. For decades to come, Newman and Pusey wrote works directed against each other, Newman supporting Catholic teachings while still maintaining limits placed on the Pope's civil authority, and Pusey still uneasy with some issue of doctrine.

Palmer did not understand many of these distinctions and viewed High Church Anglicanism and Puseyism as nearly identical with Papism. She called the Bishop of Oxford the pontiff of the Puseyite party, and saw the Church of England as joining hands with Rome. She was especially antagonistic towards Puseyism, as those churches under the sway warned the poor that if they left the Church of England for the Wesleyan camp, their benefactors could cut off aid. Furthermore, she believed that both Pusey and the Pope possessed the Bible, but did not read it or follow it. Largely this was an exaggerated and inaccurate polemic she used, but it was fairly effective. Palmer, far more than Schleiermacher, echoed the anti-Catholic fervor of Perkins, Spener, and much of America.

In 1861 the Civil War broke out and Palmer was caught in the middle of it. While safely away from the battle lines, in October a Union vessel intercepted a British ship. This was known as the Trent Affair, and caused quite a scandal for a time. The ship had two Confederate diplomats on it, but it was still a British ship. Hostilities erupted and Phoebe Palmer feared British involvement in the war, as she heard the newsboys cry out "War with America! War with America!" Palmer believed that if the British got involved it was as a punishment for the sin of slavery. She told everyone she encountered that she opposed the action that had occurred and could not understand why Lincoln would order such a thing. Lincoln likely did not order it, and eventually the Trent Affair dissipated and the Palmers continued their mission.

Palmer's greatest conflict while in England was not with controversy over the Civil War, Puseyism, Irish Papists, Scottish theologians, or the

Monarch, but with alcohol. English ale, Scotch, and Irish whiskey more than anything else proved to be the greatest barrier to her Holiness message. The greatest conflict came at Poole on the Dorset. That Sunday they began their services, but then heard rumors on Monday that the basement of the church was used to store liquor. The man responsible was the Sunday school superintendent, who just happened to be the owner of the largest liquor establishment in town. Never before had such an affront faced the Palmers. Not only was there someone present who drank, but someone who sold alcohol. Even more appalling, it was stored at the church and they were a respected member of the congregation. That night Phoebe and Walter prayed and decided to end their time in the town if the liquor was not put out. The congregation met and the circuit superintendent met with the Sunday school superintendent and told him to renounce his sin or leave the church. He took his ales, liquors, and spirits and left the church.

On another occasion the Palmers heard rumors that many in the church drank alcohol, and others brewed beer. Their suspicions grew when there was an altar call and no one came forward. Phoebe believed that the only reason why there was not repentance was because there were those who loved drink more than divinity. She confronted the congregation, which had many prominent members who imbibed from time to time and she demanded that they publically renounce all involvement with alcohol. Only a few took the temperance pledge. With such a poor showing, the Palmers left. She told those leaders of the congregation that the blood of those not saved there was on their hands.

At yet another location, Phoebe suspected that the church housed liquors in its cellar but they were not confirmed. Unsure what to do and with no evidence, Palmer attempted to continue her services, but they bore little fruit. Then her fears were confirmed when the church shook with a crash from the basement. They all went outside to see the cause and discovered a man unloading barrels of brew into the basement. Immediately the church repented and the spirits of sin were destroyed. Once this was done salvation poured upon the people.

On October 7, 1863 the Palmers boarded the Steamer City of New York to return to the city by that name. Unsure how long they were to stay, the Palmers now felt called to return home in the middle of the Civil War. Along the return voyage the boat was tossed by the sea and there was fear among some that the steamer would be swallowed up. One passenger fell overboard. As he drifted farther and farther away Palmer prayed that he be saved and if he was saved from the ocean she would labor to save his soul. A lifeboat recovered him, though he remained ill for some time, he lived. Both Walter and Phoebe spoke with him and were encouraged that his soul may be saved. Another passenger died midway from an asthma attack. He was buried at sea with an Anglican service performed by the captain. Palmer found the widow and tried to comfort her. The widow was heartbroken from grief as well as sea-sickness. The Palmers were comforted to hear that the dearly departed was a leader at his Methodist church. When the ship approached America the sun emerged and the waves calmed. The Palmers disembarked and headed home on the nineteenth.

Overall the four year trek to Britain was a worthwhile endeavor. Palmer did not keep a total estimate of the number of those blessed by her trip, but often recorded how many were saved or sanctified at specific locations. Even with the struggle against the intemperate English, the Palmer's time in the United Kingdom approached her efforts in America. Given the conditions in America, she was likely more fruitful in the UK than if she stayed home. Throughout the four years, the Palmers were always moving forward to the next camp meeting and often refused to return to places of their previous victories, finding it more beneficial to advance to the next town. After she left, the Methodists continued the work of revival and her Holiness message undoubtedly contributed to the Keswick movement that sprung up a decade after the Palmers departed the English shores.

BACK AT HOME

"Surely, God takes our treasure to heaven that our hearts may be there also."[38]

No sooner did Phoebe and Walter cross the threshold of their New York home than a delegation from Allen Street arrived to welcome them. In addition to inquiring as to their trip, they requested that the Palmers hold revival services at Allen Street. Less than two hours passed since they were home and the next revival was scheduled. It was obvious to both Phoebe and Walter that they were needed in America and their labors would not cease. To this end Walter retired his medical practice. He gave it up temporarily when he sojourned to England and had planned to resume it if and when he returned. It now appeared that he was a full time missionary and not a man of medicine, regardless of what continent he found himself on. The Palmers also did not require his income. The sales of Phoebe's works supplied them with a constant and substantial living.

In the midst of the Civil War, many common Methodist practices were abandoned. There was no more mourner's bench for the penitent, and class

---

38. Palmer, *Selected Writings*, 239.

meetings for the perfection of the saints ceased. Camp meetings, which just began at the turn of the century and had succeeded in America, Canada, and England, became increasingly rare during the War Between the States. At the outbreak of war the American population who were church members was at 25 percent. The war reduced this and it would not be until 1890 that the numbers rose to that level again.

The Palmer's Tuesday Meeting continued in her absence in Great Britain. Phoebe resumed her leadership role when she returned, even during the war. When the war eventually ended, Palmer and many of her likeminded Methodists were able to turn their attention to other matters. The evil of slavery, which ripped the country and the denomination apart, was settled. Now other evils could be addressed. For Palmer, this focused on women's rights and temperance. Others focused on political reform including women's suffrage, ending polygamy in the Mormon territories, and other pet issues. The number of available causes was seemingly endless.

One matter that gripped Palmer's Tuesday Meetings attention was the assassination of President Lincoln. While he was not a Methodist, many Methodists placed great hope in him personally and in his presidency. After prayers were offered, and Walter read Psalm 91 in honor of the departed president, Phoebe spoke on his death. She proclaimed that he was a noble and good man, but she feared that he was not abiding under the shadow of the Almighty, since he went to the theater that night. Phoebe placed the cause of his death on the theater rather than on John Wilkes Booth and his co-conspirators. God would not protect the president during this time of sin. The Almighty would have if he remained at the Whitehouse that night. The consensus at the meeting was "Would that our dear President had not received his death wound in the theater."[39] The location of his immortal soul was questioned. Shortly after Lincoln's death, his body was brought around the country. When it made its way from Philadelphia to New York, the Palmers, along with tens of thousands of others, went to City Hall to look upon his remains and pay their respects. To avoid the crowds they went at midnight.

A year before Lincoln's assassination, the Palmers decided to purchase *The Guide to Holiness. The Guide* was founded in 1839 by Timothy Merritt. Initially the magazine was known as T*he Guide to Christian Perfection.* Shortly after the Palmers purchased it, they renamed it. Merritt was the editor of the *New York Christian Advocate and Journal* until the Palmers convinced him to start his own magazine. Merritt was also one of the first men to attend the Tuesday Meeting, and his relationship with the Palmers

39. Wheatley, *Life and Letters of Palmer*, 60.

was a long and healthy one. The magazine suffered as most did during the Civil War. Two problems existed. The first was with the country torn in two; the logistics of fulfilling circulations ranged from difficult to impossible. Second, most people simply lacked the ability, funds, or desire to read a subscription. Walter and Phoebe saw beyond the current subscription to its former glory and its future potential when the war concluded. The Palmers paid $13,000 for the magazine. This was one dollar for every name on the subscription list. By most accounts, this was a generous price, since of the 13,000 on the list, less than 7,000 actually paid for their subscriptions and the price of paper was skyrocketing. Paper tripled in price over the next decade.

Phoebe took over as the managing editor. By 1870 it was the largest religious journal in America with 37,000 paying subscribers. This was done through wise business practices as much as a thirst for the publication. Around this same time the Palmers also purchased *Beauty of Holiness* and *Sabbath Miscellany* from Reverend and Mrs. French in Cincinnati. They merged the magazines. By doing so, they essentially purchased the major Holiness magazines, eliminating all competition, and adding subscribers. They also kept the price of the publication down. When the price of paper rose, most magazines had no choice but to raise the price of their publications. The Palmers chose to raise the price of their magazine only a quarter compared to most people doubling it, making their publication cost two dollars a year. *The Guide* was also reduced in size, it went from thirty-two pages to only twenty-four.

The business practices worked rather well. Most magazines in the United States only lasted four years. Under Phoebe's leadership *The Guide* not only survived but more than doubled its circulation and sustained that growth through the rest of her life. Phoebe also redesigned the cover of the magazine and added some ornamentation instead of simple text. The new name also served to prioritize a shift in her own message since the magazines founding in 1839. Christian perfection was now identified simply as Holiness. The new name was also a marketing ploy, Christian perfection was a very Methodist idea. That reduced others who were interested in the interdenominational Holiness movement. By calling it Holiness, it appealed to more Protestants who were inclined toward perfection, rather than simply Methodists. Phoebe argued "Holiness is not sectarian but Christian."[40] Acquiring *The Guide* was a perfect fit for Palmer. The magazine was essentially a short form version of most of her books, camp meetings, and Tuesday Meetings. Throughout all of these enterprises the common

---

40. Hughes, *Fragrant Memories*, 174.

thread was personal testimonies. Palmer's greatest skill was in advancing her notion of Holiness by using other people as the example.

The very year after they returned from England, even during the last years of the Civil War, the Palmers went out on revival tours. Most of the camp meetings were closed, but this did not stop the Palmers from setting up their own throughout New York, Massachusetts, Iowa, and Canada. Two years after the Civil War concluded the Holiness camps resumed in full capacity. In 1867 the National Camp Meeting for the Promotion of Holiness was founded. The National Camp Meeting was opposed to the bourgeois Methodism that dominated Methodist churches over the second half of the century. Eventually the camps fell under the same temptations as Methodism did, and succumbed to a similar gentrified state.

Palmer's involvement with revival and camp meetings was always more dynamic than most. Her focus was always on holding a believing meeting rather than simply an inquiry meeting. Most camp speakers simply probed the visitors with an idea that a sanctified life existed and would be better than not. Phoebe was direct with people and pushed them towards a moment of decision. One example, not surprisingly, centered on an alcoholic. Following one meeting, a man who Palmer identifies as clearly inebriated, was observing her. She confronted the man and asked him if he would trust in God and give up his addiction to strong drink. At first he said nothing. Then Palmer forcibly challenged him, "Will you not resolve, in the strength of the Lord, that you will never taste another drop of liquor?"[41] He still remained silent but staring at her. Undeterred she examined him again, the she told him she wanted to pray for his inebriated soul, that the Lord would strengthen him, but only if he relented. He did and finally spoke, and in a firm voice proclaimed "In the strength of the Lord, I will!" The drunk's wife came from the shadows and they wept together. Palmer's focus on the societal ills resembles Francke's involvement in reforming Glaucha. Both expected that a preacher's persistence could overcome the staunchest sinner, if the Lord called them to the work.

Palmer was far more direct than most speakers. The style most adopted was that of the pilgrim. They borrowed as heavily from John Bunyan's *Pilgrim's Progress*, as they did the Bible. Bunyan's use of the pilgrim crossing into Beulah Land, was a common trope. Hymns were written with this phrase and Beulah was synonymous with Eden, the Promised Land, paradise, and heaven. It worked well with the notion of Holiness, and finally arriving at a place of total sanctification. The main problem with this was that the Beulah pilgrim metaphor was not one the uninitiated was always

41. Palmer, *Full Salvation*, 122.

familiar with. While it played well with the converted, for the uninitiated it meant nothing. Palmer's direct calling was understandable and touched people without relying upon a lost metaphor.

While Palmer continued her revivals and camp meetings, before the National Camp Meeting for the Promotion of Holiness was founded, 1867 was the first year that she traveled much outside of their familiar Northeast territories she was accustomed to. Beginning in 1867 she decided to head down the Mississippi and see if the Southern Methodists would receive her messages as well as those in the North. In all, she attended twenty-two different meetings that year. At the very beginning of the journey she traveled to Leavenworth and Kansas City to see if the West may hold out promises for holiness. She was well received in Kansas. Palmer's presence in Kansas will prove to bear lasting fruit with the birth of Pentecostalism in Topeka in 1900, as will be addressed in chapter five.

Palmer then headed East back to St. Louis and down the Mississippi to New Orleans. The trip South was largely a failure. During the era of Reconstruction, northern émigrés were not looked fondly on, even if they brought with them a message they agreed with. They found that among the Southern Blacks they had greater success than with the Whites. Palmer was surprised at the level of giving that the black congregation offered to build a large sanctuary and a school. The congregation of mostly former slaves were more than willing to offer the little they had to the Lord. A large reason for the willingness to give was the school that was attached to the church. The promise of an education excited them.

With the South mostly closed to her message, Palmer spent the next few years only attending meetings in the Northeast, occasionally going to Illinois or Iowa, and once in 1869 as far West as St Johns, Nebraska, but she never traveled to the South again. In 1870 she decided to go west once more. This year she stopped off at Leavenworth, Kansas again, partly because of the success she had there in 1867. From there she traveled to Sacramento then six other cities in Northern California. Her trip to California was accompanied by a dozen other National Association workers, who planned on settling in California. They brought a four-thousand seat tent with them to Sacramento, and despite some protests they had a peaceful meeting where more than two-hundred professed entire sanctification. Beyond the numbers, Palmer describes her time in Sacramento as lasting two weeks where "All unite in saying that such a meeting was never before known in California. We are now holding afternoon and evening meetings in this city, which are largely attended, and the altar is nightly surrounded with penitents and seekers of the great salvation."[42]

From Sacramento they made a tour of the San Francisco Bay Area. Palmer styled San Francisco as an international city. On the way back from California, Palmer stopped in Utah. No meeting was held, but after gathering with some Mormon women, she roundly condemned Mormonism and the practice of polygamy. From here she went by Oberlin and stayed with Finney. Phoebe continued preaching at camp meetings until her death in 1874. In total she preached at over a hundred and forty different meetings and revivals after her return from England in 1863. Not only was Palmer's preaching style more effective than others, so too was her generosity while traveling. She often did not receive any pay for her appearances and gave the money back when it was offered. The sales from her books and *The Guide* provided Phoebe and Walter a very nice living. She also did not use these meetings as an opportunity to sell her books or sign people up for subscriptions. Others did not always follow her example in these regards.

DEATH

"Only one thing more, and that is the last enemy, Death."[43]

Phoebe Palmer died at the age of 67, but she believed she was going to die much earlier. In 1846 when she fell ill, she was convinced that her life was over. It was partly due to her recovery that she was determined to labor so much until the time of her death. When death eventually came on November 2, 1874, she was well aware that it was finally at an end. That morning she had one last mystical vision while she slept. When she awoke, she told her sister and her husband that she saw a chariot come for her. She proclaimed, "Thanks be to God which giveth us the victory, through our Lord Jesus Christ. O death, where is thy sting; O grave, where is thy victory!" and then repeated the doxology: "Glory be to the Father, glory be to the Son, and glory be to the Holy Ghost. Amen."[44] Following a quick quiver at 2:30 in the afternoon she breathed her last and died in Walter's arms.

After Phoebe's death, Walter continued her work as editor of *The Guide*. The family helped as well. Sarah took much of the responsibility for the magazine. Sarah Lankford then married Walter Palmer sixteen months after Phoebe's death, on March 18, 1776. Thomas Lankford died three years

42. Palmer, *Selected Writings*, 302.

43. Palmer, *Sweet Mary*, 30.

44. Palmer, *Full Salvation*, 22.

earlier. Walter and Sarah were married for seven years before Walter died on July 20, 1883. Sarah Lankford Palmer died on April 24, 1896. *The Guide* continued until 1901.

For those last twenty-seven years *The Guide* was really a family magazine. Dr. Foster, the son-in-law who married Sarah Palmer, was the assistant editor under Walter and Sarah, and took over the magazine until his death in 1898. Phoebe Palmer Knapp, in addition to writing hymns, was rather involved in Holiness camp meetings and after her husband died in 1891 she used some of her $50,000 annuity to keep *The Guide* afloat when its circulation dropped off. Walter Clarke Palmer, Jr. was involved in publishing, and it was his company that published many of his mother's books. He likely would have taken over *The Guide* if he did not die in 1885 just two years after his father.

Phoebe Palmer's life serves as a synthesis of Wesleyan Pietism and America. Palmer took advantage of her wealth and the technological advancements of the time to spread her message across of all America and the United Kingdom. The Promethean spirituality encouraged by Francke is best exemplified with the constant toil of Palmer. While she encountered different perspectives on life, she remained true to her Methodist upbringing and maintained her status as an outsider. While her gender could have limited her ability to spread her Pietist message, she built upon the egalitarian themes in Zinzendorf and Wesley to overcome this obstacle. She also used their theological systems and constructed her own theology which worked to clarify and expand Wesley's notion of Christian perfection. Palmer's interpretation became the center point of her theology and the motivation for her Tuesday meetings, camp meetings, and extensive travels.

IV

Theology of Palmer

"I love my Jesus, yes, I do, O! glory, hallelujah!
I know my Jesus loves me too; O! glory, hallelujah!"[1]

SCHLEIERMACHER WAS A SYSTEMATIC theologian, while Palmer's theology emerged organically. Her theology can best be described as pastoral and devotional. Phoebe Palmer never sat down to create a cohesive overarching theological concept as Schleiermacher did. Nor did she wrestle with her conception of God and how she fit into God's plan of salvation. Following July 26, 1827, Phoebe Palmer never doubted anything concerning matters of faith. At least she never expressed doubt and condemned those who did.

PALMER'S DEVOTIONAL THEOLOGY

"Thus by Thy presence sanctify. This earthly sanctuary, Lord."[2]

Palmer developed a theological system to eliminate doubt and to encourage an active, evangelical, and complete faith. Since her system was narrowly focused and intended to be received by the masses, her theology is nowhere near as complex as Schleiermacher's. Palmer condemns the value of emotions in religion, still religion is experiential for Palmer. Palmer reduced the worth of feelings as they relate to religion, but her theological works were designed to produce an emotional and experiential connection to God. Palmer serves as an interesting juxtaposition against Schleiermacher, who

1. Palmer, *Useful Disciple*, 24.
2. Palmer, *Selected Writings*, 298.

elevated the role of feelings as the basis of theology and then developed a theology around that experience, but did so without inducing that emotional theological experience. Palmer's basic theological message, described as the shorter way or her Altar Theology, runs throughout nearly all of her works. Each work relays her theology of conversion and hope in the lives of different people. Palmer's theology relates the value of a devotional and pastoral approach of the divine, and seeks to express the experience and entice others to share in that experience, more than explaining what the experience is in theological language, as Schleiermacher did.

The Shorter Way—Altar Theology

"Lord, if on Thee I dare believe, The faith shall bring the power."[3]

Palmer's basic theological message concerns Holiness or Christian perfection. The notion of Holiness was present throughout the history of Christianity. What Holiness means varied greatly through the ages. Thomas à Kempis, Johann Tauler, and Johann Arndt all possessed an idea of Holiness that related to a state of perfection. Though for à Kempis this was never a state arrived at before death. For Tauler perfection is abandoning all things that are not of God, and for Arndt it was only a denial of will. Neither à Kempis, Tauler, nor Arndt applied the notion of holiness and perfection to be anything more than a moment where sin did not hinder the Christian's devotion. It was a moment where worship was pure, and it was never complete.

John Wesley challenged this understanding of perfection and developed his own doctrine concerning the matter. Wesley wrote extensively on the subject, but always with enough ambiguity to leave the doctrine incomplete. Wesley's doctrine of Christian perfection grew from his belief that Christians simply could not sin, therefore they needed to be perfect or they were not Christians. The standard and the actuality in no way resembled one another, therefore Wesley wrestled with this idea, often confusing notions of justification and sanctification, equating them, or reversing their order as generally understood. Wesley's notion of perfection did not include angelic, nor Adamic perfection. It also excluded perfection in wisdom and there was no notion of permanence. Perfection was a state of total and complete sinlessness, but one could lose perfection and thus salvation by sinning. The problem with his doctrine was that Wesley tried to elevate perfection beyond the ideas held by à Kempis, Tauler, and

3. Wheatley, *Life and Letters of Palmer*, 543.

Arndt, while still wanting to accept notions of freedom of the will and the limitations of that will. Essentially Wesley's theology of perfection needed to be taken on faith by his followers, as its development was confused and logically inconsistent because he wanted perfection to be complete, yet allow Christians the freedom to reject perfection once attained.

It was Wesley's works on Christian perfection which first captivated a fifteen year old Phoebe Palmer. From this moment she equated her Methodist Episcopal identity with this at best inconsistent and incomplete teaching. Palmer's central theological contribution was to develop and complete Wesley's theology. She did so by removing the ecclesial and theological limitations that Wesley sought to maintain. Those limitations sprung from Wesley's desire to remain within the Anglican Church and appealed to the theological and philosophical trends of the day. Since Palmer was born in America sixteen years after Wesley's death, those limitations did not apply to her, and she had no desire to be united with the Anglican Church, or its teachings. Palmer remained within the Anglican tradition, as interpreted by Wesley, but not as a member of the denomination as it stood in nineteenth-century America.

Palmer also did not develop her interpretation of perfection in a vacuum. Phoebe was influenced by her sister Sarah and her husband Walter. They were influenced through the already emerging Holiness movement with leaders like Timothy Merritt, Charles Finney, and the Oberlin faculty. Merritt published *The Christian's Manual; a Treatise on Christian Perfection, with Directions for Obtaining That State*, in 1825. The book contains little more than a summary of Wesley's view of perfection and a few examples of how to live in perfection. It was later that he came under the influence of Palmer and her Holiness movement.

In a similar fashion, Finney and Palmer influenced one another. Finney is often called the Father of the Holiness movement, and Palmer its Mother. It was really the combined effort of the two that produced the movement as a whole, especially due to the fact that Finney was not a Methodist, but a Presbyterian. This interdenominational emphasis on Wesley's interpretation of perfection is what allowed for the movements success throughout the United States and the United Kingdom. Finney and Asa Mahan (d. 1889), the president of Oberlin College, began examining the doctrine of Holiness a few months before Palmer's second conversion. Mahan was influenced by a student, who asked him what sort of sanctification the Christian should expect, partial or whole. Mahan turned to his theology professor Finney and the two them then came up with their version of Christian perfection. Mahan published *The Scripture Doctrine of Christian Perfection* in 1839. Mahan defined Christian perfection as "the consecration of our whole being to Christ and perpetual employment of all our powers in that service."[4] It is the assimilation of the Christian's character to Christ at all times and under all circumstances. Mahan describes this more as a goal than something easily attained, although he does believe that it is attainable and should be attained by every Christian. The focus of Mahan's perfection was moral in character. He was influenced by Kant, and the concept of moral agency connected to free will.

Finney adapted Mahan's notion of perfection and popularized the Oberlin position. Essentially Finney combined Mahan's simplicity of moral action with a Presbyterian notion of freedom. Finney rejected the notion of indwelling sin as the basic disposition of the heart, therefore the Christian was free to choose not to sin. Part of Wesley's complicated theology on perfection was due to Wesley holding the opposite position than Finney. Finney, believing in a unity of moral action, argued that the mind could only choose one ultimate end. If that ultimate end is Christ and perfection, then it cannot simultaneously hold sin as the ultimate end. All individual acts and proximate ends should line up with the ultimate end. Therefore full obedience is possible, since sin is not a separate consciousness struggling with its own ultimate ends. The existence of sin is only an act that is in conflict with the ultimate end for a Christian, therefore it can be eliminated, resulting in perfection. Finney's notion of perfection is a continued abiding and obedience to God in a very similar way to à Kempis, Tauler, and Arndt. Finney argues that this change can be instantaneous because the ultimate end can be determined in an instant and God's grace permits it within a Calvinist system.

Palmer's concept of Christian perfection was more Wesleyan than Oberlin or Calvinist. Palmer's concept of perfection falls under her concept of the shorter way, which includes full consecration, or her Altar Theology. There are three essential steps to Palmer's shorter way. The first is the altar, the second, faith that the act was done, and finally testimony. The entire shorter way is subsumed under the idea of the Christian altar. For Palmer this is not an altar were the Eucharistic sacrament is performed. There is no separate priest that ministers at the altar either. For Palmer the altar is Christ.

Christ is not laid upon the altar, or transubstantiated over it, but he is the altar. Christ is not the gift upon the altar rather the Christian is the gift. The Christian must figuratively lay themselves upon the altar of Christ. Palmer asserts, "We have an altar. This altar is Christ. His blood is the

---

4. Mahan, *Doctrine of Christian Perfection*, 16.

purifying medium."[5] With Christ as the altar, anything that touches Christ is automatically made holy. God made Christ the altar and commands the Christian to come to it by faith. The Christian is to be a living sacrifice, laying their entire being upon the altar. This is an act of faith and an act of surrendering ones will to Christ. Under the old covenant the animal placed upon the altar is sacrificed. Therefore the Christian presenting themselves on the altar is sacrificing their will. In this act they receive Christ's will and Christ's holiness is swapped for theirs. This is the means of transmuted righteousness, which is essential for justification under the substitutionary atonement theory of the passion of Christ, and it becomes essential for Palmer's view of sanctification.

This act of faith is based upon Christ's declaration in Matthew, where he asks "For which is greater, the gift or the altar that sanctifies the gift?" (Matt 23:19). Palmer interprets this by saying that anything that touches the altar is automatically sanctified. She adds another link to Perkin's *Golden Chain*, between sanctification and glorification lies entire sanctification. Palmer proclaims, "The moment you laid it upon the altar, it became God's property, for it was sanctified by virtue of the altar upon which you laid it. No great venture of faith is called for here. God's word declares it, and it were presumption to doubt. And, now that your offering is on the altar, sanctified and cleansed by the infinite virtue there is in Christ, upon whom you rest, and through whose all-cleansing blood you are presented faultless before the throne, expect the consuming process to begin."[6]

Once the self has been offered on the altar which is Christ, the Christian must now believe that they are sanctified. Faith in the completed act of sanctification is the second step. In the same moment as the offertory act, the Christian must believe that they are sanctified. Borrowing language from John Fletcher (d. 1785) and Hester Ann Rogers (d. 1794), Palmer declares that this is a "naked faith in a naked promise."[7] One does not wait for the witness of the Holy Spirit or for a feeling, rather all is based upon trust in the sanctifying act of the altar sacrifice. It is from faith that this blessing is gained. Palmer's conception of faith is similar to those of other experiential Protestants, with the exception that she connects it within her theological system.

Faith is an act of hope. As her starting point, Palmer quotes Hebrews, "Now faith is the substance of things hoped for, the evidence of things not seen" (Heb 11:1). In *Sanctification Practical* she tells a story of a man who is

5. Palmer, *Incidental Illustrations*, 46.

6. Palmer, *Full Salvation*, 45.

7. Palmer, *Selected Writings*, 120.

hungry and is invited to come to someone's house to eat. The hungry man gets up and walks towards the house of the promised food. "You desire food, and, by virtue of your faith in the promise, you expect food; and hence, as hope is made up of desire and expectation, you now hope to obtain food. Now you comply with the condition. You go with the man; and, as you go, you just as much expect to find and eat the food, as you expect to reach the house."[8] Palmer also likens faith to a banknote. If someone offers a gift of hundred dollars and presents a banknote to that effect, the recipient does not deny its worth. Rather the note has value because of the promise that it contains. The note has value because of the bank, just as salvation has a value because of Christ proclaiming it so.

To this end Palmer argues that faith in complete salvation is reasonable. It is as reasonable as believing a banknote has value or that a generous man is offering food to the hungry. Both can turn out to be false, the man may not have any food and the note may belong to a bank that has no funds, but in the absence of contrary evidence it is not unreasonable to believe the affirmative. Since Palmer believes that God is the one who promises holiness, faith in holiness is reasonable. "Faith is taking God at his word, relying unwaveringly upon his truth. The nature of the truth believed, whether joyous or otherwise, will necessarily produce corresponding feeling. Yet, faith and feeling are two distinct objects, though so nearly allied."[9]

During one of her Tuesday Meetings, Palmer was confronted by a man she calls Brother C. Brother C doubted the reasonableness of the shorter way to entire sanctification while still believing that God desires a holy life. Palmer responds by asking Brother C a series of questions. The first, if he knew he was going to die in two minutes what would he do. Brother C immediately responded that he would place himself on the infinite mercies of God. From here a few more questions led Brother C to admit that he believed doing so would save him from all sin. Palmer concludes "What! Without any more conviction exclaimed his friend. At this point, he manifested much emotion, and, amid tears and smiles, exclaimed, sister, you have cornered me!"[10] Since God would save with only two minutes' worth of faith and repentance why should it require more if he was to live longer? In a similar fashion Palmer, when confronted about the possibility of living a sinless life, once asked if a man can go a minute without sinning. When the answer was in the affirmative, she then asked about two minutes, or a day. If both could happen, then what is to stop from continuing for a

8. Palmer and Boynton, *Sanctification Practical*, 45.

9. Palmer, *Way of Holiness*, 30.

10. Palmer, *Incidental Illustrations*, 94–95.

lifetime? Palmer often extrapolated from a small moment to a larger one to prove her notions of faith.

For Palmer, faith is reasonable, but faith is not a matter of the intellect. She explicitly states "Satan tempts you that your faith is a mere intellectual effort, and not that faith which is through the operation of the Spirit."[11] Faith still contains some mystery and not a sense of omnipotence on behalf of the Christian. It is an act of trust, not reason. Palmer's conception of faith and her Altar Theology slightly resembles Tauler's notion of the new man. A glaring difference lies in in the fact that Tauler and the Pietists, such as Arndt and Spener, who followed after him, advocated that the new man addressed a positional righteousness and the foundation of the relationship with Christ and did not possess any notion of a sinless perfection attached to it.

Palmer applies the same notions of trust to faith as she does feelings. Phoebe Palmer was always troubled by feelings. Unlike Schleiermacher, who saved religion from the Enlightenment by calling it feeling, Palmer saved her notion of faith by declaring that feelings are the likely effects of faith; they should not affect faith. Explicitly and plainly, she declares over and over again, "Remember faith is not feeling. You are not saved by feeling, but by faith."[12] Even her own act of conversion began with her concluding that, "Whatever my feelings may be, I will believe God's immutable Word unwaveringly, irrespective of emotion."[13] Still she maintains that "There is joy in faith."[14] This joy does not save but comes from the knowledge that one is saved. Even if no emotions come, or if emotions are contrary to those expected, faith requires acceptance of one's salvation.

In addition to acceptance, one must understand the relation between faith and action. Another example Palmer gives to explain faith is a father telling a child to jump into his awaiting arms. The child must jump, just as the starving man needed to accept the invitation, and the recipient must go to the bank. Faith always requires an action and but is itself not the action. Palmer often criticized Catholics and other Protestants for what she believed was equating actions with faith. Palmer proclaimed "Fasting, prayers, and tears, are all good, and all helpful; but they will not take the place of saving faith. One act of faith can raise the dead to life, and can do more for us than twenty years of groans and tears without it. Without faith, it is impossible

---

11. Palmer, *Faith and Its Effects*, 67.

12. Palmer, *Full Salvation*, 103.

13. White, *Beauty of Holiness*, 12.

14. Wheatley, *Life and Letters of Palmer*, 41.

to please God."[15] Palmer also did regularly fast and perform similar acts of self-denial to build her faith, but she emphasized that these were not done in order to save, but because she was saved.

The necessity of actions as a result of faith is the third step in Palmers's shorter way. The sanctified Christian must testify publicly about their salvation. If they do not then it can be lost. Proclaiming their own salvation gives honor to Christ. Therefore to not share in the good news of their sanctification withholds this honor. To remain silent is a sin and an act of rebellion from the very God who just saved you, illustrating that the faith was false and they were never truly placed upon the altar, or if so, that some part was withheld. God grants the blessing of sanctification not for the believer's enjoyment alone, but for all who hear and accept this avenue of salvation.

Just like Wesley, Palmer believes that perfection can be lost. The primary way that sanctification is lost for Palmer is the rejection of this third step. Palmer points out that John Fletcher lost his entire sanctification five times, all due to his lack of giving testimony. But one can lose their sanctified status in other ways as well. If one abandons faith, then the blessing of sanctification can be lost. This faith is actively remaining on the altar. One must continually rely upon Christ for their salvation. Palmer calls this walking by faith, rather than sight. Doubt is not acceptable.

Doubt is a temptation that must be wrestled out of the Christians life. In her journals shortly before her death, Palmer proclaims, "It has been many years since I remember to have had a temptation to doubt. Well do I, as a daughter of the Lord Almighty, remember the baptism of fire that fell upon me."[16] Palmer asserts that "Unbelief is the great sin of the world, but who can tell how varied its forms."[17] Unbelief is a temptation that only faith can fight against. One must first trust in Christ and then look to the effects of faith. The effects of faith are primarily love and a pure heart. One must assume that looking towards the effects of faith is still walking by faith rather than sight.

Doubt has another danger. This danger exists for those who have not yet received entire sanctification. Palmer argues that once Christ has offered himself, the response must be immediate, just as it was with the disciples who Jesus called. Peter, James, and John dropped their nets and followed Jesus. Matthew left his tax-collecting table. When Christ calls, it may be only once. Palmer posits one should not assume "that He will ever again

15. Palmer, *Incidental Illustrations*, 92.

16. Wheatley, *Life and Letters of Palmer*, 83. December 10, 1873.

17. Palmer, *Promise of the Father*, 332.

call you."[18] This was also a technique Palmer used in her preaching. She presented the promise of salvation, but pointed out that it may not come again. Palmer's preaching style was personal and always pushed towards action.

Palmer spoke at so many different revivals and camp meetings that she developed quite a routine. Generally she spoke for twenty minutes, but sometimes her messages lasted an hour. Most revivals were multiple day events, so the first day she usually addressed Pentecost and the events that unfolded on that day that birthed the church, and many were baptized with the Holy Spirit. Following this, the subsequent nights expanded on the concepts of full baptism. She argued that once Christians were baptized with the Holy Spirit, the world would be convinced. What was needed was for Christians to take that next step of entire consecration, faith, and testimony.

Essential to these revivals and meetings was that a decision was made, and was made quickly. One reason why the shorter way is shorter is because it is accessible and easy to apply. There were no catechumen classes, but an immediate call to action. She had a few added techniques to encourage decisions. First she used group pressure whenever possible. She also understood some other notions of group psychology. She encouraged everyone to stand up to present themselves as candidates. She knew that once someone was standing they were more likely to come forward than if they remained sitting. Also if they alone were standing, the pressure of those around made them feel obliged to make a decision.

Palmer's preaching was effective. Another reason for her effectiveness was that unlike other revivals, she emphasized lay ministry. This created larger networks to keep the newly sanctified, sanctified. While most nineteenth-century Methodists were abandoning lay ministry and local pastors, Palmer utilized them to the same effectiveness that Wesley and Methodist circuit riders had decades earlier. What is particularly interesting about Palmer's place in American Methodist history was that she witnessed the boom and the decline, the institutionalization of Methodism and its failings. As such, she differentiated herself from the elites whose calcified version was expanding. Palmer maintained Methodism through her Holiness message and the lifeblood of Methodism, the laity, and plain speaking revivals. Finney recognized the same pitfalls and spoke of the value of the laity, but Palmer was really the first American preacher to organize the laity effectively during a revival.

Now that her evangelical revivalist message was delivered, Palmer needed to make sure that doubt had been wrestled away and the Christian

18. Palmer, *Incidental Illustrations*, 14–15.

had laid their entire lives upon Christ, the faith that Christ's work to sanctify them has been accomplished. Following the various testimonies proclaimed, the newly holy were entirely sanctified. Palmer clarifies what holiness is, just as Wesley does. In its simplest form, holiness is heaven on earth. It is full salvation and living in the kingdom of God, where the believer has their heart and lives within Christ and becomes the image of Christ on earth. Holiness implies a duty to others and purity of their own soul. Knowledge of one's own soul is never attainable, nor does the perfect Christian have perfect knowledge. Similarly to Wesley, the Christian is also not in a state of Adamic or angelic perfection. Temptations still exist, but they are not victorious. Perfection is love of God, love of neighbor, and deliverance from sin. Humanities nature is not destroyed in perfection, rather the depravity of man is. Holiness is freedom from sin, but not its infirmities.

It is from this last point that Palmer would disagree with the notions of faith healing which emerged at the conclusion of the nineteenth century. The Holiness movement of which Palmer was a significant part was never a single thing. Portions of the movement advocated 'faith cures' in the same manner that Palmer presented the shorter way to salvation. Those who advocate faith cures rely upon faith to save through consecrating themselves to Christ. They are then to act as if they are healed without external proof to the contrary. Palmer would have opposed this practice, but not denied the possibility that God may choose to save some from their physical injuries. The notion of faith healing never entered Walter's medical practice, and Phoebe Palmer never criticized her husband's practice. Both Phoebe and Walter believed practicing medicine was an excellent way to serve God.

Palmer did not advocate for a healed body but a healed soul. This healed soul also became known as the second blessing. This second blessing was a blessing of the Holy Spirit and is sometimes called the baptism of the Holy Spirit, a second baptism, a baptism of fire, or full baptism. In this full baptism, the Christian receives power in their salvation. This power combats the spiritual struggles and presents a holy life as attainable. The second baptism is not simply a recommitment to Christ, it is a separate act. The imagery of Pentecost is used. The disciples were justified prior to the day of Pentecost due to Christ's atonement. On the day of Pentecost they received the Holy Spirit and were sanctified. They also possessed power to heal and to speak in tongues.

With the second blessing, the Christian is now perfect but this perfection does not signal completion. A tree may be described as perfect in every way; it is the perfect example of what it should be. Still, the following year it will be larger, it will have grown. Similarly Palmer points out that a child may learn how to read perfectly, but having learned how to read does not result in them no longer reading. Rather, once they have perfectly learned how to read, they only then truly begin to read. Perfection is the beginning point, not the conclusion.

This is far more than a subsequent conversion. When Phoebe Palmer experienced her second conversion, it was a leap of naked faith into a different type of Christian life. This was not the same thing as a simple recommitment of her life to Christ. It was also radically different than the second conversion experience of Friedrich Schleiermacher. Schleiermacher's second conversion experience was an act of repentance and dedication. He never expected that it meant his own perfection or was a second spiritual baptism. Schleiermacher openly rejected Wesley's theology which Palmer's understanding grew from. Since the understanding of the act differed, so too were the expected effects. Surprisingly, neither of them believed the Calvinist notion of once saved always saved. Palmer and Schleiermacher both believed that salvation was constant work, but only Palmer believed that it could be complete and affirmed through entire sanctification.

Palmer's second blessing must always be understood as a separate act that takes place after conversion. Palmer points to her own experience to prove it. "My experience continually attests the truth of the assertion, that the life of the believer is a heaven below. The divine tranquility; the deepened communion with the Father, Son, and Holy Spirit; and the accompanying increase of love, faith, light, and humility."[19] Palmer affirms her beliefs through her own experiences. This is also something attainable for everyone.

Palmer's conception of Christian perfection differs from Wesley's primarily in its simplicity. Wesley was conflicted, at times Wesley appeared to suggest that he was perfect, and other times he clearly states the opposite. Wesley also confused the concepts of justification and sanctification, and gave no clear instruction as to how one remains perfect if indeed they attain perfection. Palmer's shorter way and Altar Theology is simple. For Palmer, entire sanctification is a separate request, rather than simple assent to the notions that Jesus is the messiah and the source of salvation. It is faith and a desire to be holy, and wholly given over to Christ. While it can be lost, Palmer posits that one must simply return to the shorter way once again.

19. Palmer, *Faith and Its Effects*, 38.

Feminist Theology

"Not she with traitorous kiss her Savior stung; Not she denied him with unholy tongue: She, while apostles shrank, could danger brave, Last at his cross, and earliest at his grave."[20]

Palmer's second significant theological contribution concerned the role of women and feminist theology. Palmer's feminist theology was simultaneously countercultural and consistent within Pietism, especially among followers of Wesley. For most of nineteenth-century American life, women were relegated to a separate sphere. Gender relations were distinct and possessed a rigid gendered division of labor, especially in the antebellum North. This division of labor gave women primacy over the domestic sphere, while men controlled nearly everything else. Church life was an interesting area, where women were celebrated for superior virtue and piety, while isolated from many of the positions that virtue and piety were naturally inclined to adopt. In the South, the Northern feminine archetype was largely absent, with the notable exception of the power elites. Those women outside of the patriarchal circles of plantation life enjoyed a greater degree of freedom in domestic and other relations.

Palmer's feminism focused on women's participation in the church. As such, her inherited Pietist history was vitally important in her construction of a feminist theology. Pietism, from the time of Spener, privileged women to a greater extent than their scholastic counterparts. Women were included in the various *collegia*. Women's admittance into these small groups, whose purpose was to grow in their Christian lives through pious living and understanding the scriptures, led to widespread fears of educated women in eighteenth-century Prussia. The fears were well founded, as the same women involved in Francke's friend Johann Caspar Schade's *collegia*, eventually were the first women to enter German universities. The Pietist *collegia* directly led to women's involvement in the academic world.

Most important for Palmer was Wesley's view of Christian women. Both John and Charles Wesley were personally very attractive to women converts and followers. John Wesley's connection with some of his acolytes even led his wife and others to conclude he had a series of affairs. While the affairs were never confirmed, Wesley's extra time spent with Sarah Crosby unequivocally led to her prominent position within Wesley's inner circle. In 1761, Crosby led classes in London and was sent to teach other classes as well. This included mixed classes, where she not only instructed men and women in the faith, but gave sermons as well, though Wesley advised her

---

20. Palmer, *Promise of the Father*, 14.

sermons not resemble the traditional sermon in construction. Wesley had long seen the necessity of lay preachers, so non-ordained women preaching was not much of a step. Lay preachers were necessary, and since the majority of Methodists in the UK and US were women, having women teach seemed reasonable, especially in the contexts of Sunday school classes, bandleaders, and those in the medical field, including nurses and visitors of the sick.

Early nineteenth-century America was filled with women preachers who spread Methodism and other forms of Protestantism. There were over one hundred itinerant female preachers active during the first half of the century, and roughly a quarter of them were Methodists. Following Crosby's example, women's preaching styles differed from men. The feminine style was often more successful in generating converts. Women generally had a calm demeanor that carried over in their preaching. This demeanor presented an air of refinement and intellectualism, even if their message was the same as a man's. The success of women preachers in the early nineteenth century is similar to IM Lewis's treatment of women in East Africa and the *sar* possession. Lewis points out that women found a culturally acceptable medium to voice their grievances, arguing that "Women may thus resort to spirit possession as a means both of airing their grievances obliquely, and of gaining some satisfaction."[21] While no Methodist women were ordained to speak at this point, their commission to speak was accepted and their concerns were heard, both those concerning salvation as well as temperance and increasingly suffrage. Palmer's lay preaching, as well as her mystical dreams, follow a very similar pattern.

After a decade of preaching, Palmer wrote *The Promise of the Father: A Neglected Specialty of the Last Days*, in 1859. This work spells out her concerns for women in the nineteenth century. Palmer concerns herself with three distinct areas in this, her largest work. First Palmer seeks to elevate the position of women, which she believes was demeaned during the first half of the century. Second, she wants to address the prohibition against women preaching. This is the bulk of the work and she points to examples of prominent women in the Bible and Christian tradition. Special attention is paid to the role women played during Pentecost. Finally she tries to understand Paul's command for women to keep silent in the church (1 Cor 14:34).

The work opens with Palmer pointing out that she does not intend on addressing "'Women's Rights' or of 'Women's Preaching,' technically so called."[22] Rather she confirms that women have a legitimate sphere of

21. Lewis, *Ecstatic Religion*, 77.
22. Palmer, *Promise of the Father*, 1.

action which differs from that of a man, a sphere she maintains that leads women to be both happy and useful. Palmer's initial concession to different spheres and her desire to not directly address ordination are intended to halt immediate objections to her work. She goes on in the next four hundred or so pages to illustrate how the separate spheres, as well as the blanket ban on women's ordination from all ecclesial positions, do not stand up against reason, history, or Biblical criticism. It is interesting that in this work Palmer utilizes these techniques which are absent from all of her other works. She continues to say that the facts show that women are occasionally charged by God to break their ordinary sphere and occupy a vital role in the church or state.

Palmer conceived that the work was necessary for a few reasons. First, in the opening decades of the nineteenth century, as Methodism grew, it became more institutionalized. With greater institutionalization, a greater antipathy towards women emerged, especially in the middleclass and upper-class neighborhoods. The stronghold women had within Methodist leadership was eroding, including informal leadership roles. Palmer was also concerned that women's roles outside of Methodism were increasingly base and unequal. New York itself witnessed several restorationist and eschatological churches whose views on women and sexuality were concerning. Palmer, likely thinking of the Oneida community, Kingdom of Matthias, and Mormons, said "The idea that woman, with all her noble gifts and qualities, was formed mainly to minister to the sensuous nature of man, is wholly unworthy a place in the heart of a Christian."[23] Christian wives are intended by God to be more than sex objects, used by their husbands to fulfill the lusts of the flesh. Palmer believed that women contributed intellectually and spiritually within a Christian marriage. Palmer alleged that God judges the sins of countries. The US had a long list of sins that Palmer expected God to hold the nation accountable for, including slavery, the treatment of women, and the sins against the family. These and others serve only to bring condemnation.

Palmer next turns her attention to Paul's prohibition against women speaking in church, arguing "The Christian churches of the present day, with but few exceptions, have imposed silence on Christian woman, so that her voice may but seldom be heard in Christian assemblies." The reason for this silence is Paul, who decreed "Let your women keep silence in the churches."[24] The way Palmer treats this passage from Corinthians is noticeably different than others, including Soren Kierkegaard who also challenged this verse.

---

23. White, *Beauty of Holiness*, 196.

24. Palmer, *Promise of the Father*, 5.

Kierkegaard's appeal was a mix of possible misogyny and an object to show the value of silence. Palmer's treatment of this verse is to illustrate how it is misapplied and misunderstood. Palmer's convictions do not allow her the luxury of simply dismissing the verse or ignoring it. Therefore, she must dissect it and contextualize it in a way that supports her convictions. The notion of "plain gospel truths" that dominated Protestant theology in and out of both Great Awakenings, is made less plain. Palmer seeks to use reason and traditional Protestant practices to aid in interpretation.

The first avenue she takes is to demonstrate that it is inconsistent. If women were to remain silent, as the verse commands, women would not be able to participate in any public worship whatsoever, no church accepts this. She points out that even the Episcopalians fail to live up to this standard and they trespass against this prohibition every service "in calling out the responses of women in company with the men in their beautiful Church Liturgy, and when they repeat our Lord's Prayer in concert with their brethren. And thus also do they trespass against this prohibition every time they break silence and unite in holy song in the church of God of any or every denomination."[25] Either the prohibition is universally ignored, or else it was not a universal decree but a local solution to a local and particular problem. Palmer argues that Paul told the Corinthians to keep silent, not all women. The church of Corinth had a number of unseemly practices that needed to be eradicated. In an interesting reversal of exegesis, Palmer shifts her view of the Bible as a work that is intended for all Christians in every age to a work that is bound and limited by historical development and historical circumstances.

To support this conclusion, Palmer looks to other places in the Bible to confirm her conclusion that there was no biblical warrant for denying women a vocal place in the church. Beginning in the Old Testament, Palmer points to the Judge Deborah, the Prophetess Huldah, and Moses' sister Miriam. Deborah was called not because there were no men, rather Palmer argues "because God, in his wisdom, had so ordained; and it was also by the direction of Providence she was compelled to take the lead in the orderings of the battle."[26] Furthermore when Josiah found the Torah in the temple, they turned to the prophetess Huldah rather than Jeremiah and Miriam responded to Moses before Aaron or others.

In the New Testament, there are many more examples that Palmer uses. Surprisingly Palmer does not use the Virgin Mary as an example, in fact, she is never independently mentioned. Twice the phrase mother of

25. Palmer, *Promise of the Father*, 5–6.
26. Palmer, *Promise of the Father*, 2.

Jesus is used, but both cases were scriptural quotations, and the attention was never on the Virgin Mother. Palmer also never uses the phrase Virgin Mary. Palmer's anti-Catholic bias extended to demoting Mary the Mother of God to a footnote, and for some even an object of scorn, especially when connected to devotional practices of Catholics. Palmer hints towards these sympathies when she tells the stories of Catholics who convert, proclaiming "no Virgin Mary for me."[27]

Palmer does speak of a Mary with greater detail, but the Mary she references is Magdalene, who is listed as a disciple. Mary Magdalene is exalted because she spoke to the disciples and revealed the resurrected Christ to them. The Samaritan woman is also mentioned and called the first apostle for Christ in Samaria. This title obviously serves to validate women's leadership and shows that women are often called while men are not. In the New Testament, Phoebe Palmer mentions her namesake as well, the deaconess Phoebe. Palmer reminds her readers that "Deaconesses were ordained to the office by the imposition of the hands of the bishop."[28]

In addition to scriptural references, Palmer argues that early Christian tradition also utilized women in speaking and leadership roles. In no other work does Palmer reference patristic writings, but here she uses the writings of St. John Chrysostom and Justin Martyr as sources. Palmer evokes Justin Martyr when addressing Pentecost. In Justin's dialogue with Trypho, Justin argues that "both women and men were seen among them, who had the gifts of the Spirit of God."[29] Chrysostom is invoked a few times, first to show that women among the early Christians were free to worship. Palmer references Chrysostom's mother first. Libanius proclaims that Chrysostom's mother possessed a noble appearance, and was moved to declare, "What women these Christians have!"[30] Later Chrysostom and Theophylact are used to illustrate that Junia, mentioned in Romans laboring for God, was in fact a woman rather than a man. "But Chrysostom and Theophylact were both Greeks; consequently, they knew their mother tongue better than our translators, and they say it was a woman."[31]

Palmer also tries her hand at hermeneutics, or a further attempt at biblical criticism, by dismissing Paul's decree as a cultural command rather than a universal one. She argues, "It was also customary amongst the Greeks and Romans, but amongst the Jews it was an express law, that no

27. Palmer, *Four Years*, 40.

28. Palmer, *Selected Writings*, 36.

29. Palmer, *Selected Writings*, 35.

30. Palmer, *Selected Writings*, 36.

31. Palmer, *Promise of the Father*, 26.

woman should be seen abroad without a veil. This was and is a common custom through all the East."[32] These ventures into patristics and biblical criticism are rather short lived, but it illustrates Palmer's attempt to engage the rationalists and scholastics on their level, rather than simply dismissing their critiques.

Palmer dismisses Paul's command in light of further revelation. Palmer argues she is now living through the second Pentecost. It may be the third Pentecost if we want to include Zinzendorf's or any others. Since Palmer believed that she was living through a second Pentecost, the dispensation to which she was not obliged was not the same as history nor the same as the early church. Therefore, the gift of power that was given on the first day of Pentecost needs to be re-appropriated and accepted in these later days. Palmer queries, "has not a gift of power, delegated to the church on the day of Pentecost, been neglected? Or, in other words, has not a marked specialty of the Christian dispensation been comparatively unrecognized and kept out of use?"[33] Both men and women were present at the day of Pentecost, and both received power. In the interim women have either neglected their power or it has been denied them by others. Palmer interprets Acts Two by saying, "The Lord our God is one Lord. The same indwelling spirit of might which fell upon Mary and the other women on the glorious day that ushered in the present dispensation still falls upon God's daughters. . . . The same impelling power which constrained Mary and the other women to speak as the Spirit gave utterance impels them to testify of Christ."[34] Acts 2:17 states "And it shall come to pass in the last days, saith God, I will pour out My Spirit upon all flesh; and your sons and your daughters shall prophesy." Therefore Palmer wants to recapture women's gifts of prophecy. This call for women to preach echoes Spener's 1677 *The Spiritual Priesthood*. Both Spener and Palmer argue that the priesthood of all believers comes from the anointing of the Holy Spirit and purchase by Christ.

Since her aim is to allow women a space to prophesy, she must define prophesying. Palmer's treatment of prophesy follows Perkins in *The Art of Prophesying and the Calling of the Ministry*. Perkins separated preaching from public prayer, and Palmer attempts to reunite them. While Palmer opened the work saying she was not trying to justify women preachers, she has now concluded that since she is living in the end times, the promise of the Father is being fulfilled. Women will prophesy. Furthermore, Palmer contends "the scriptural idea of the terms preach and prophesy stands so inseparably

---

32. Palmer, *Promise of the Father*, 44.

33. Palmer, *Promise of the Father*, 14.

34. Palmer, *Promise of the Father*, 30.

connected as one and the same thing, that we should find it difficult to get aside from the fact that women did preach, or, in other words, prophesy, in the early ages of Christianity, and have continued to do so down to the present time, to just the degree that the spirit of the Christian dispensation has been recognized."[35] Both preaching and prophesying is little more than edification, exhortation, and giving comfort. Men and women are called to do these things as prompted by the Holy Spirit.

Palmer then addresses another biblical prohibition against women speaking. This one is found in 1 Timothy 2:12. "But I suffer not a woman to teach, nor to usurp authority over the man, but to be in silence." For Palmer the question is about usurpation rather than teaching. The issue of silence she has already dispensed of. The solution is simple for Palmer; women do not speak on their own authority, rather the authority of the Holy Spirit. "Women who speak in assemblies for worship under the influence of the Holy Spirit assume thereby no personal authority over others. They are instruments through which divine instruction is communicated to the people."[36] Sometimes women preach in front of a congregation, other times a class room, and still others publish works. In all of these, the idea is that the Christian woman is simply speaking what God has given her and with God's authority rather than her own. If indeed someone is called by the Holy Spirit to minister and oversee a congregation, Palmer cannot foresee the manner in which they would lord it over their flock. Echoing Zinzendorf, she maintains that male or female should make no difference.

To apply the issue of teaching authority consistently Palmer contends, leads to an unobtainable standard nowhere practiced. If women were not allowed to teach, Palmer maintains "No woman is to keep a school. No woman is to teach her children to sew, or cook, or read, or write, &c. No woman is to write books; for this is one excellent method of teaching. No woman is to pray in public; for praying is one method of conveying instruction upon doctrinal, experimental, and practical religion."[37] Just like the prohibition against women speaking, conclusions are not consistently drawn out. While Catholics or Orthodox may choose to respond that these verses are interpreted through ecclesial tradition, Protestants have no such authority, therefore her objections must be addressed on that level.

In *The Promise of the Father*, Palmer also launches her attack against Puseyism and High Church practices. Shortly after this work was published, Palmer comes directly into contact with these practices in England while on

---

35. Palmer, *Promise of the Father*, 34.

36. Palmer, *Promise of the Father*, 9.

37. Palmer, *Promise of the Father*, 48.

her four year voyage to the Old World. It is in this work that she addresses civil issues as well. The issue of women's authority of men is circumvented not only in the church, but also in civil governments. Against the Puseyites Palmer raises up an example of "Her Most Gracious Majesty Queen Victoria, the reigning sovereign of the most mighty, intelligent people of this or any other age. Who questions her ability for her station, and talks of her as having transcended the bounds set by public opinion of the sphere of woman?"[38]

The result of Palmer's work was to open the floodgates ever so slightly. Palmer did not seek ordination, nor ecclesial office herself; neither would have changed her mission. Other Methodist women who came later benefited from Palmer's work. In 1866, Helenor Davison was the first woman ordained within Methodism to the diaconate. Shortly thereafter Methodism employed deaconesses to carry out social ministries. In 1880, six years after Palmer's death, Anna Howard Shaw was ordained to the diaconate. A few years later Ella Niswonger was the first woman to graduate from the denominations seminary and be ordained. In 1869, Isabella Thoburn and Dr. Clara Swain were the first single female missionaries. Women's involvement as missionaries grew to the point that by 1910 more than half of Protestant missionaries were women.

Palmer's feminist message reached many contemporary women as well who were crucial for the development of early feminism. Many nineteenth-century feminists were deeply rooted in evangelical revivalism as their primary focus, while other concerns were expressions of their piety. Martha Wheat, Harriet Beecher Stowe, Frances Willard, Hannah Whitall Smith all serve as examples of women who were impacted by Palmer's life and works.

Martha Wheat (d. 1874) was a southern evangelical who desired to be a missionary and was encouraged by *The Promise of the Father*, shortly after its publication. Martha sought numerous occasions to preach, believing that public prayer and oratory was consistent with true womanhood. Palmer's book aided Wheat with her mission in the face of widespread criticism. "When I read of the Christian women, who obeyed God rather than man, and thereby saved souls," Wheat wrote, "I am afresh encouraged to renew my efforts, with redoubled diligence."[39]

Harriet Beecher Stowe (d. 1896) was reared on Calvinism and revivalism. The Beecher family were well acquainted with the Palmers, and Phoebe publically criticized Harriet's brother, the Reverend Henry Ward Beecher (d. 1887), for his inclusion of bowling alleys in the Brooklyn

---

38. Palmer, *Promise of the Father*, 3.
39. Kierner, "Woman's Piety within Patriarchy," 93.

YMCA. Harriet sought to spread her religious message, especially concerning slavery. To this end she wrote one of the most influential books of the nineteenth century, *Uncle Tom's Cabin*, but she did so by adopting an impersonal, third-person voice in the work. This denied her agency and made the work a devotional inspired by the Holy Spirit and belonging to the Christian community. At the time Palmer admired the work but condemned it because it was too easy to adapt into a play, which enticed people to sin. She even provides an example of a pious woman who attended the theater for the first time because of Stowe's work.

Frances Willard (d. 1898), the leader of the Woman's Christian Temperance Union (WTL) was also influenced by Palmer. The WTL was the largest American woman's organization formed, having 176,000 members at the close of the century.[40] Two years earlier, before the WTL was formed in 1879, Willard preached in Boston. She was encouraged by D.L. Moody, but was given the justification to do so from Palmer. Willard professed sanctification at one of Palmer's meetings, and the similarity in speaking styles produced at least one study on the effects Palmer's preaching had on the rhetoric of Willard.

Palmer's Holiness message also extended to Hannah Whitall Smith (1911), a significant leader in Holiness revivals in the United States and United Kingdom. Her conversion took place during the Businessman revival, but continued to grow in holiness through the works of Palmer. Palmer's works advanced women's causes among the Quakers and Salvation Army as well. Her sales alone demonstrated the thirst for holiness and the acceptability of women in print.

GOD, SIN, AND REDEMPTION

"God is thine, disdain to fear the enemy within; God shall in thy flesh appear and make an end of sin"[41]

Palmer's view of God, sin, and redemption differs greatly from Schleiermacher, but remains consistent with Wesley's position. Since it is essentially Wesleyan, there are many similarities concerning God and sin akin to Perkins and the Anglo-Calvinist understanding of God's sovereignty, with an emphasis on the substitutionary atonement. Yet unlike Perkins and his *Golden Chain*, Wesley and Palmer reject the notion of a predestined election. Wesley supported the Armenian position that was defeated at the Synod

40. Brown "Publicizing Domestic Piety," 43.

41. Palmer, *Sweet Mary*, 22–23.

of Dort. Dort prioritized Perkins teachings on Calvin, sin, and redemption over those of Jacobus Arminius.

Phoebe Palmer's conception of God would not have been controversial during her life time as she affirmed the traditional doctrines of the Methodist church. God is eternal, "Jesus Christ, the same yesterday, today, and forever."[42] Palmer professed the trinity and that God is holy. God's holiness is understood to be grounded in love. Palmer maintains "God is infinitely holy, and whatever flows out from him on man tells enduringly in lessons of love and power."[43] This power and holiness are connected with God's justice. This form of divine justice rewards those who are with God and condemns those who are not. God cannot be united with evil. While God is love, Palmer, along with Wesley, Perkins, and Calvin, declare that God hates sin. "Daughter, God hates sin now just as much as He hated it in the days of Adam. God is unchangeable in His nature. With Him 'there is neither variableness nor shadow of turning,' 'the same yesterday, today, and forever.' Think of the effect of one sin in the days of Adam—how it has been felt along down through time, even till the present hour! We are feeling it today, and its effect will be felt down to the end of time!"[44]

God's sovereignty has its limits for Palmer, primarily in the allowance of free will, even a will that could tend toward sin, the very thing God hates. This is a typical Methodist view, as Catherine Kelsey argues that for Wesleyan-Armenian Methodists, individual human responsibility is the chief concern. "While the sovereignty of God is also adamantly affirmed, no description of divine sovereignty is acceptable if it can suggest to individuals that salvation will work itself out regardless of the level of their active participation."[45] Humanity has used this free will to sin. For Palmer there are only two logical and theological conclusions. First, that humanity and those who have sinned are rightly condemned to hell. She proclaimed "The sinner is condemned already."[46] The second is the necessity of the doctrine of the substitutionary atonement.

What is striking is not these beliefs from a nineteenth-century Methodist, but rather the divergence of views from Schleiermacher, the other nineteenth-century Pietist addressed. Schleiermacher and others, including Kierkegaard, denied or demoted the concept of hell and the need for a substitutionary atonement. Schleiermacher was revolutionary by treating

42. Palmer, *Faith and Its Effects*, 118.

43. Palmer, *Recollections and Gathered Fragments*, 49.

44. Palmer, *Present to My Christian Friend*, 90.

45. Kelsey, "Methodism in America," 24.

46. Palmer, *Recollections and Gathered Fragments*, 14.

the incarnation as the redeeming act of God rather than a penal substitution. Schleiermacher understood the incarnation as a world altering event where the earth was sanctified by God entering into it. Christ's death was not a vicarious suffering; this was the very notion which got Schleiermacher kicked out of his Moravian schools and made his father question his very salvation. Rather for Schleiermacher the death was a consequence of the incarnation and God humbling himself in Christ to approach the lowliest of men and women. Schleiermacher's decree that he was a Moravian of a higher order centered on the prioritization of the incarnation over the death of Christ. He went so far as to believe that Christ's incarnation signaled the election of humanity as a whole, and as such provided the means of salvation. Palmer does not even consider this a viable Christian position. Palmer's rejection of the Schleiermacherian position illustrates her consistency within Methodism as well as the potential divergence within Pietist theology.

Palmer maintained the notion of hell as a justified punishment for all who are not believers. She argued "Thou art this moment prepared either for the abode of the believer or for the home of the unbeliever. No alternative presents. There is no middle state."[47] Sin grieves God, and as such God turns away from a fallen humanity. While Schleiermacher viewed the incarnation as a larger redemptive act, Palmer only views this as efficacious for those who accept the universal offer of redemption. For those who don't, they are judged and rightly condemned to eternal damnation. Palmer addresses universalism specifically at one of her Tuesday Meetings. When a Universalist was fearing his own death, Palmer asked him why he was afraid to die, since he believed in universal salvation. They both concluded "when death stared me in the face, I found the doctrine of Universalism would not stand the test."[48]

For Palmer, like Perkins, the only means of salvation is the substitutionary atonement. Christ must offer himself as a substitution for the sins of every individual. As such, the individual must accept the gift of the substitution. Palmer's Christology is also contained within this doctrine. Christ must be understood as "Immaculate purity, ineffable beauty of holiness, who was once personified, and walked and talked with men."[49] This life ransomed humanity, not just the elect. Palmer's Christianity is based upon this sacrifice. She argues "The foundation of the Christian religion is laid in sacrifice. The Father gave his Son, who, from all eternity, dwelt in his

---

47. Palmer, *Recollections and Gathered Fragments*, 14.

48. Palmer, *Incidental Illustrations*, 176.

49. Palmer, *Present to My Christian Friend*, iv.

bosom. The Son left the throne of his glory, and came to earth in the form of a servant. As our Exemplar, he lived a life of toil and sacrifice, enduring the contradiction of sinners, despising the shame, and suffering the agonies, of the cross. In his vicarious death, we may not follow him."[50]

Throughout her works Palmer points to the redeeming blood of Christ. While she does not emphasize the wounds themselves as the source of redemption like Zinzendorf, Palmer seizes upon the idea of sacrifice. Christ sacrificed himself on the cross, and now the Christian must sacrifice themselves upon the altar that is Christ. Palmer pronounces, "We are not unmindful of the fact, that Christ set Himself apart as a vicarious sacrifice and that there can be nothing vicarious in the sufferings of the Christian but there is a sense in which the Christian is left to fill up that which is behind of the afflictions of Christ."[51] Christ's sacrifice was only the beginning. The Christian must then advance in His vicarious sacrifice.

Christians are redeemed in order to be sacrificed and ultimately sanctified. As Palmer argued with her shorter way, "Sanctification implies the whole heart and life devoted to God."[52] Christ's vicarious death was the Christian's justification, and sanctification moves from this. Sanctification also implies holiness and perfection. Palmer uses Abraham as the prime example of the perfect Christian. She elevates Abraham as the example for contemporaries to live by. The anguish of Abraham is inconsequential, rather he serves as the model because he obeyed. He did what God commanded. Palmer asserts "It was enough that God had made the demand, But it won the design of God, that Abraham should stand out before all succeeding generations, as the father of the faithful—the friend of God. 'Ye are my friends, if ye do whatsoever I command you.'"[53]

Abraham is rewarded for his obedience. He was strong in faith and gave God glory. The Christian is to follow Abraham's example by laying what is most prized upon the altar. For Abraham, that was his son, for the Christian it is themselves. Palmer understood that the act of laying one's self upon the altar varies depending on the individual and not everyone can have such a definitive moment of faith as did Abraham. She concedes, as did Wesley, that for some this is an instantaneous work, and for others salvation is gradual. In light of the work of Christ there is no anguish connected with Abraham, rather Palmer insists that sanctification takes away fear. Death and its consequences of damnation or eternal reward should only cause the

50. Palmer, *Four Years*, 84.

51. Palmer, *Present to My Christian Friend*, 86.

52. Palmer and Boynton, *Sanctification Practical*, 77–78.

53. Palmer, *Faith and Its Effects*, 136.

unredeemed trepidation. For those living in Christian perfection, there is no anguish, no fear, and no concerns that are matched to eternal blessedness.

The hope in eternal blessedness requires the Christian abandon this life and its concerns for Christ. Still, Palmer expresses that future blessedness does not require a renunciation of life itself. Christians must continue to live and not desire death. To continue to live demonstrates that the Christian has a purpose in this world. They can always spread the gospel a little further, and with every breath. There are also still earthly affections which the Christian maintains. These are not in themselves bad or to be avoided. Palmer holds that as long as the Christian is willing to follow Christ with these affections they are acceptable, and reason enough to desire to stay living.

The Christian must understand that their reward is not these earthly attachments, but is waiting for them in heaven. Schleiermacher addressed the concept of heaven and redemption as communion with Christ and as a mystery. While Palmer views heaven as communion with God, she also connects the idea of a reward waiting for her in heaven. Heaven is a personal reward that varies depending on the Christian's level of obedience. Some Christians will receive eternity in heaven but the rewards given to them will be minor, while others will have an abundance. Palmer maintains a consistent imagery concerning her heavenly reward. All those who are redeemed and in heaven will receive a crown. Palmer extols her readers to, "Hold that fast which thou hast, that no man take thy crown. Yes! thy crown is now awaiting thee! It is thy crown; for at an infinite expenditure it was purchased for thee. If earthly crowns are valuable in proportion to the expenditure of wealth, toil, and blood which they have cost, who will attempt to estimate the value of thy crown?"[54]

Palmer also believes that not all crowns are equal. Upon the crown there are various numbers of jewels or stars which adorn them. The crown imagery is so important to Palmer that the ninth chapter of *Entire Devotion*, is simply titled "Thy Crown." The jewels or stars upon the crown each represent a soul won for God. They represent the fruit that the Christian produced. This is rather similar to Angela da Foligno, calling those Franciscans who attached themselves to her, "her crown and joy in the Lord."[55] Beyond Foligno's love for the monastics surrounding her, Palmer viewed the redemption of souls as an eternal reward. Palmer queries "Who should be satisfied with a starless crown, when, after a little lingering on

---

54. Palmer, *Present to My Christian Friend*, 70.
55. Foligno, *Classics of Western Spirituality*, 109.

earth, it may be set with many brilliant stars?"[56] Palmer posits that this is the reason why the Apostles themselves labored so mightily. "The ambition for a starry crown—an abundant entrance, is of the inspiration of the Holy Spirit, and should be cherished. With such inspirations were the apostles and the holy martyrs fired."[57]

Palmer viewed God as very transactional. Debts need to be paid and rewards granted to those who earn them. This transactional relationship with God applies with Christ as well. Christ's sacrifice was not merely a selfless act of love, but also a payment to redeem. Upon redemption those snatched from the flames belong to Christ. Every soul won is a soul delivered to Christ, to be placed in his crown. Palmer declares "If I die, I shall be a gem in my Savior's crown."[58] Christ, as well as the Christian, all have the same desire. Palmer relays a vision she had where Jesus showed her a gleaming crown and then instructed her to be faithful, saying "thou shalt have a crown glittering with as many stars as the one thou hast just beheld."[59]

The starless crowns likely belong to those whose Christian life was fruitless or to those who converted but never reached the place of entire sanctification. In *Sanctification Practical*, Palmer is asked what happens to someone who is converted never reaches the place of sanctification. The question concerns if they will go to heaven at all. This is a practical concern, since justification and sanctification are separate events and one may grow into the sanctified life. Palmer concluded that "dying under these circumstances, we should be saved."[60] This does not open the door to universal salvation though as it does for Schleiermacher. Palmer does not accept the idea that one may accept the atonement after death.

THE CHURCH AND ITS PEOPLE

> "Head of the Church! Oh wilt Thou still, Thy Church in this our house behold, With greater grace Thy people fill, Give power beyond the days of old."[61]

Palmer's conception of the church first begins with the laity. She herself was never ordained. Palmer believed that most of the church's functions could

---

56. White, *Beauty of Holiness*, 170.

57. Palmer, *Incidental Illustrations*, 221.

58. Palmer, *Sweet Mary*, 32.

59. Palmer, *Present to My Christian Friend*, 69–70.

60. Palmer and Boynton, *Sanctification Practical*, 96–97.

61. Wheatley, *Life and Letters of Palmer*, 151.

be performed by the laity, including preaching. Lay preaching was long a hallmark of American Methodism and a good reason for its success in the early half of the nineteenth century. Beyond just the lay preacher, Palmer insisted that the task of converting the unbelievers belonged to every Christian, not just the itinerant preacher or ordained clergy. Palmer's promotion of the laity redrew the lines of ecclesiology. Palmer simultaneously criticizes the church and redefines what it is through her understanding of the laity, promoting a new doxa of exclusion that removes the standing benefits and responsibilities of the church hierarchy and officials.

In her Pietist *collegia*, the Tuesday Meetings, Palmer models her vision of the church. Believers led other believers without regard to rank, position, or denominational affiliation. In these meetings Palmer seizes on the Protestant refrain of the priesthood of all believers, arguing that when a Christian is entirely sanctified they are a living sacrifice and are holy to God. At this point they are "made priests unto God."[62] The laity, who now serve in most functions as the clergy, also serve as confessors. The booth is replaced with public confession and though it has lost its sacramental character, it becomes a regular part of her meetings. Palmer put it this way, "in order to be continually washed, cleansed, and renewed after the image of God, the sacrifice must be ceaselessly presented. I believe it does us good not only to confess our faults before God, but before one another."[63] It is from this confession of faith that entire sanctification occurs and the Christian remains upon the altar, which is Christ.

Palmer specifically elevates the laity in her works as well as her Tuesday Meetings. In both *The Guide to Holiness* and her earlier published works, Palmer constantly lends her voice to the pious conversions and stories of the laity. This is why her theology is pastoral and devotional rather that systematic. Palmer seeks to demonstrate the intrinsic value in individual experiences of God and sanctification. Her greatest skill was in advancing her notion of Holiness by using other people as the example. Three of her published works are entirely devotional stories, recounting the lives of pious women. In *Recollections and Gathered Fragments of Mrs. Lydia N. Cox of Williamsburg, Sweet Mary*, and, *The Useful Disciple: Or, A Narrative of Mrs. Mary Gardner*, Palmer elevates Mrs. Lydia Noyes Cox, Mary S. (called sweet Mary), and Mrs. Mary Gardner.

Mrs. Lydia Noyes Cox was a Presbyterian who embraced Holiness. Palmer argues that "Holiness to the Lord was her continual watchword. Nothing less than the advancement of holiness in the membership would

---

62. Palmer, *Present to My Christian Friend*, 7.

63. Palmer, *Incidental Illustrations*, 75.

answer her ardent wishes."[64] Palmer presents Cox modeling Holiness as an all pervading principle rather than a theological afterthought. Mary Gardner was also a Presbyterian who was initially unaware of Palmer's doctrine of Holiness. Palmer's use of Gardner was to assert that her Holiness doctrine was not her own, but was found in the Bible. Mary proclaims "I knew it was a Bible doctrine, that we should present our bodies a living sacrifice but I did not know it by the name of sanctification, perfect love, or Christian perfection."[65] Palmer strategically confirms her theology through the mouth of another to eliminate doubt or suspicion in the minds of her readers.

The same could be said of Palmer's treatment of Mary S. Sweet Mary is eulogized by Palmer, who proclaims "Mary had her trials, But with her, every new trial was made the occasion of a new triumph."[66] Sweet Mary faced many temptations and Palmer uses her struggles and her victories to encourage others to follow her example. From Mary's spiritual battles Palmer asserts "there is no sin in being tempted. The sin lies in yielding to the tempter. "The people that do know their God shall be strong and do exploits."[67] Mary is also used to address the notion of sanctification as both a gradual and singular act. Mary was pardoned before backsliding into a state of lukewarm Christianity. Each time she returned to the altar and surrendered herself more fully to Christ.

In these three cases Palmer gives voice to women who otherwise would not have one, while using them to advance her doctrinal understandings. Still, Palmer insists that her authority does not come from the laity or from ordination, rather from the Bible. As is the case with earlier Pietists, the Bible becomes the head of the church for Palmer. The Bible is not the book of the church; the church is the people of the Bible. Palmer plainly decrees, "The Bible is the voice of God speaking to man. If holy men spake as they were moved by the Holy Ghost, the words thus uttered are in verity the words of God."[68] Beyond simply being the book of the people, Palmer equates the Holy Scripture to Christ himself. Calling the Bible the word of God, Palmer then shows that Christ is called likewise. "His name is called The WORD OF GOD." Here the word is personified as Christ himself.[69]

Since the scriptures are one with Christ, and Christ is one in the trinity, Palmer proposes that "the voice of the Scriptures is the voice of the

64. Palmer, *Recollections and Gathered Fragments*, 71.

65. Palmer, *Useful Disciple*, 41.

66. Palmer, *Sweet Mary*, 4.

67. Palmer, *Sweet Mary*, 6.

68. Palmer, *Faith and Its Effects*, 60.

69. Palmer, *Faith and Its Effects*, 85.

Holy Ghost."[70] For Palmer the Bible is divine, not only in origin, but also in its presence. Since the Bible is available to all, and it is the supreme authority over all, all are made equal under it. "The Bible being the only infallible standard, and no human authority being comparable with it, the latter being only right as far as it is found one in sentiment with it, let this book, above all others, be the Book of books with us."[71]

The Bible gives the laity its power, while depriving power from the episcopacy. The Holy Spirit itself interpreted the Bible, since it, as the word of God, is personified in the second person of the trinity. The simplest believer who truly wishes to understand the Bible will learn unhindered from the text itself. While Schleiermacher attempted to understand the Bible through historical analysis, Palmer asserts that the Holy Spirit is sufficient. Furthermore Palmer does not believe that under the tutelage of the Holy Spirit one can come to error. "The Holy Spirit never takes us beyond the written Word, neither does it take us aside from it."[72] Palmer believes the text is plain and simple to understand, especially when read by an obedient sanctified Christian. Complicated verses only require devotion and prayer.

Following this, Palmer accepts as true that no evidence is necessary. The Bible is interpreted by God and was given to humanity by God, as a manifestation of God. Therefore Palmer proclaims, "God's word is its own evidence."[73] Schleiermacher's hermeneutical approach to scriptures demonstrates an inherent lack of faith from Palmer's perspective. The task for all Christians is not to question the Bible, nor try to understand it from a position of human reasoning but to become Bible Christians.

The concept of a Bible Christian is central to Palmer's ecclesiology and theology. Again the church is the people of Bible, not the other way around. The concept of a Bible Christian, as Palmer calls it, is understood to be a Christian who trusts wholly in the Bible as the singular source of authority. As such, Palmer equates being a Bible Christian with being a perfect Christian, declaring, "If you are not a holy Christian, you are not a Bible Christian."[74] She also says "Holiness is the great leading doctrine in the Bible, rather than as a doctrine peculiar to any sect."[75] Palmer believes that Christian perfection is not only a Methodist or Presbyterian phenomenon, but one intrinsic to the scriptures.

---

70. Palmer, *Full Salvation*, 188.

71. Palmer, *Full Salvation*, 155.

72. Wheatley, *Life and Letters of Palmer*, 518.

73. Wheatley, *Life and Letters of Palmer*, 539.

74. Palmer, *Present to My Christian Friend*, vi.

75. Palmer, *Present to My Christian Friend*, iii.

To this end Palmer, while a Methodist, is also a leader of the ecumenical movement. She views denominations as secondary to entire sanctification. Palmer's treatment of ecumenicalism is similar to Zinzendorf's *tropus*. Zinzendorf tried to unite the magisterial Protestant denominations together under the umbrella of Herrnhut. Zinzendorf ultimately failed. Schleiermacher, as addressed in chapters one and two, tried to do the same thing in Berlin and had moderate success. The advantage that both Zinzendorf and Schleiermacher had was that their attempts at uniting the Protestant Churches were fairly limited. Both focused their attentions on uniting Reform with Lutherans, believing that the other smaller denominations in Germany would follow suit. By the middle of the nineteenth century the sheer number of denominations, especially in America, made the top down approach of Schleiermacher and Zinzendorf impossible. Instead, Palmer chose to promote a single doctrine, Holiness, and have that unite American Protestants. Those Protestants that objected to this doctrine Palmer counts as lost. They are outside of the truth as she understands it. As she maintains, "The truly pious of all denominations, and of all classes, both of the ministry and laity, are seeking for the truth. There is a literal uprising of the people."[76]

After encountering Mormons, Palmer deduced that they were not of the same spirit as the Holiness denominations. Since Joseph Smith's early years were spent around Methodists, there is a level of similarity in their preaching styles and messages. Mormons often joined in with the Holiness meetings, poaching members. Mormonism's early success came directly from Methodists. Douglas Strong puts the number at least at 28 percent, at a time when Methodists were nowhere near that in the general population. Palmer's antipathy towards Mormons only grew when she was in Utah and witnessed polygamy first hand. Palmer was especially attuned to the emotional torture one wife had, having to share her husband with fourteen other women.

According to Palmer the Catholics and Orthodox are equally lost to the truth. Palmer's aggression towards Catholics was not well hidden. She called the Pope and members of the Catholic Church the "Man of Sin." She also viewed the Catholic Church as a "kingdom of darkness," while Protestants were the "kingdom of light," in *Full Salvation*. This was the cause of joy for the Catholic girl's conversion, rather than her acceptance of a doctrine, as was the case with her Protestant converts. She believed that the Pope was in need of repentance just as everyone else, and there was no holiness in either Pope Pious IX, or the office. Palmer declared, "The Pope may enter paradise, like any other sinner. Yes, Pius IX, if he repent, No more his claim need

76. Palmer and Boynton, *Sanctification Practical*, 6.

borrow; For Christ would to his claim consent if he'd show godly sorrow."[77] Worse still was Palmer's treatment of Orthodox, whom she did not even consider Christians, but heathens in her vague mention of those in the East.[78]

While Palmer did not value the Roman Church nor the Eastern Churches, she did place some value on "the Church." Properly understood, Palmer's conception of "the Church" was Wesley's church and those who subscribe to Holiness, her reinterpretation of Pietism. Those who belonged to her denominations who accepted Holiness were close enough to count as Christians. She believed that her duty was to save souls. This was also the mission of the church, "But if sinners are to be saved, it is to be through the agency of the Church. The Church must be clothed with the garments of salvation."[79] Many individual churches failed to live up to this standard, primarily when they became too costly. Once a church becomes too opulent, worship fails to live up to the standard that Christ desires. Palmer calls this "proxy worship." This occurred within the Methodist churches as well. Palmer describes proxy worship as worship where "Only the minister kneels to pray. He is paid to do so by the church members, who sit comfortably and listen."[80] The same applies to singing in these churches. The choir is paid and the congregation sits. These churches become performances rather than devotions.

Noticeably minimized in Palmer's ecclesiology is the clergy. Palmer's emphasis on the laity reduces the ordained clergy to only a few roles, including weddings and funerals. The other duties of worship and prayer are performed by the laity. Palmer still valued those who were ordained, calling them "ambassadors of the King of Kings."[81] She would not have supported anyone criticizing the ministers in general, but they needed sanctification as must as anyone else. In fact, Palmer generally only speaks of ministers as those present in her meetings, those who are lost, and those who are experiencing sanctification. "Occasionally a clergyman is awakened and converted the same as any other poor sinner"[82] is a common refrain.

Also missing from Palmer's ecclesiology are the sacraments. Since preaching and conversion is the task of the laity, the sacraments are the remaining vestiges of the minister. Palmer's Methodist inheritance of the sacraments minimizes their salvific efficacy, to the point that they are rarely

---

77. White, *Beauty of Holiness*, 146.

78. Palmer, *Promise of the Father*, 45.

79. Wheatley, *Life and Letters*, 137.

80. White, *Beauty of Holiness*, 151.

81. White, *Beauty of Holiness*, 172.

82. Palmer, *Four Years*, 215.

if ever mentioned. Palmer does not see water baptism as all that necessary or beneficial, except as a dedication. At one point Palmer echoes the lament of one convert who was disappointed in her baptism. "She found that being immersed in the water had not the efficacy to wash away her sins. Her distress of mind increased after her baptism; and fearing that she had sealed her damnation by taking upon herself the profession of religion when she was yet in an unregenerated state."[83] For this poor lady, her baptism was not a symbol of joy, nor a sacrament, but a testimony of condemnation. Palmer argues that she experienced the baptism of the Holy Spirit later.

This second baptism is the only sacrament that Palmer truly identifies. This sacrament is also not performed by a priest but by the individual, who by laying themselves on the altar, saves themselves. Palmer's ecclesiology promotes a church of one. Everyone eagerly works for their own salvation and saving others. Salvation is an individual act rather than a corporate one. The church exists only as a collection of individuals, not as the single body of Christ present on earth and in eternity.

Similarly, the Eucharist is absent from Palmer's theology. She makes mention of taking it a few times in her life, but little value is given. Rather the absence of the rite serves as a lack of piety on behalf of a congregation for Palmer. Communion exists within a healthy Christian church but it does not possess any power for those who take it. Unlike Wesley who prioritized the Eucharist, to the point that those early members of the Holiness Club began with taking communion weekly, Palmer's general silence on the issue only illustrates the lack of value the sacrament, and indeed all sacraments had for her.

83. Palmer, *Selected Writings*, 148–49.

PALMER AS A MODEL OF NINETEENTH-CENTURY PIETISM

"When from this altar shall arise, Joint supplication to Thy name,

Accept, O, Lord, our sacrifice, Thyself our answering God proclaim.

When here Thy ministers shall stand, O, give them hearts and tongues of flame,

Hold them as stars in Thy right hand, And seal the truth in Thine own name."[84]

Phoebe Palmer was the first woman widely known as a religious leader in America. A few other women may have predated her, but not amongst mainstream Protestantism. Palmer's life was constant toil by her own choosing. She spanned the continental United States, preaching in New York, Louisiana, Kansas, and California. She spread her message to Canada and Great Britain as well. Charles White estimates that over 1.5 million people converted to Holiness while she was in England and more than that in the United States.[85] Palmer's eighteen books sold more copies than Schleiermacher did in his lifetime. She was widely accepted as the mother of the Holiness movement at the time of her death in 1874. Yet within a generation of her passing, she was all but lost to history and scholars. Her Holiness theology continued and her experiential Protestantism survived in the twentieth century, becoming the basis for both fundamentalism and Pentecostalism.

Palmer's example of experiential Protestantism best fits my definition of Pietism. She was a mystic who pushed for experiential revivalism. Her entire life was dedicated to advancing revivals, believing that she was witnessing the second Pentecost. During the second Pentecost, Palmer alleged that the rules which governed the previous Christian dispensation no longer applied. Rather at this point, the new Christian receives power from a second blessing, a baptism of the Holy Spirit that was poured out equally to men and women. Her world was remade through her experiencing the divine.

It is also this new perspective of baptism of the Holy Ghost that made relationships valuable. Palmer gained rewards in heaven for her sacrifices on earth and condemned the frivolity of this world. It did not matter if it came from a Christian source or a secular one, every action that was not based in her understanding of being a Bible Christian was anathema. Institutionalized forms of Christianity did not matter, only sanctification did.

---

84. Palmer, *Selected Writings*, 299.
85. White, *Beauty of Holiness*, 232.

It is amazing that Palmer vanished from the public record so quickly. Just like Angela da Foligno, Palmer's life and work vanished within a generation after her passing. George Hughes, Richard Wheatley, and a few others wrote about her shortly after her death, but then she was lost until Timothy L. Smith rediscovered her in 1957. After this, another few decades passed before Charles White and Harold Raser both wrote new biographies about her in 1986 and 1987 respectively. Elaine Heath was the next to seriously look at Palmer, but this was not until 2009, over thirty years since the last serious work on Palmer. It appears that every thirty years Palmer is mentioned briefly, often times in connection to understanding the Holiness movement or the effects of it. Palmer's place within Protestant history for most is only a footnote, yet without this footnote, twentieth-century Protestantism is unmoored.

Palmer's life appears destined to be lost to history, but not her legacy. She cobbled together an ecumenical movement consisting of Baptists, Presbyterians, and Episcopalians, in addition to Methodists, and produced the Holiness movement. In doing so, she expanded the reach of experiential Protestantism beyond the institutional and denominational forms that existed at the beginning of the nineteenth century. Her contribution to the Pietist edifice was not simply to remove portions like Schleiermacher, rather Palmer built upon the Wesleyan protrusion and cobbled together a concrete patch with its own individual nuances at the dawn of the twentieth century.

The Holiness movement, which will be addressed in greater detail in chapter five, touched nearly every aspect of American and English life in the nineteenth and early twentieth century, from camp meetings that became permanent vacation destinations like Martha's Vineyard and Ocean Grove, to the founding of schools, and the involvement of women in American politics through temperance and the suffrage movements. The nineteenth century was the Methodist century in America, but Methodism dwindled in the latter half, fragmenting and morphing into two different types of churches. One remained institutionalized, resembling Wesley's Anglicanism, with the other becoming the Nazarenes and the charismatic Assemblies of God. The division centered on the Holiness controversy. Palmer's advocacy of Holiness and the antipathy it possesses towards religious formalism presents itself as a modern expression of experiential Protestantism, which has its origins at the dawn of the Reformation, but whose journey to fundamentalism and Pentecostalism could only have occurred through Zinzendorf, Wesley, and Palmer.

V

Holiness, Pentecostals, and Liberalism
The Direct Heirs of Schleiermacher and Palmer

> *"I began to realize that the Reformation had implicit emotional dimensions."*[1]
>
> —*Susan Karant-Nunn*

SCHLEIERMACHER AND PALMER EACH reconstructed their Pietist inheritances. Pietism moved from an innovative and dynamic chord of Protestant Christianity into an ossified lifeless series of institutions which spanned Europe and America by the nineteenth century. The challenges of institutionalization and the growing ascendency of modernity over the daily lives of Protestants in Prussia and America forced Schleiermacher and Palmer to abandon the establishments conceived of by Perkins, Arndt, and Spener and return to the experiential roots of Christianity. In doing so, Schleiermacher and Palmer remained within their denominations and fashioned their own version of Pietism, a new version that each believed was better equipped to address the challenges of modernity.

Modernity remained connected to the experiential medieval Christian mysticism of Angela di Foligno, Thomas à Kempis, and Johannes Tauler. By reconstructing their spiritual inheritance Palmer and Schleiermacher founded new theological systems and forever changed the mindset of Protestantism. The impact of Schleiermacher and Palmer was not entirely uniform, and movements such as Holiness, Pentecostalism, and Liberalism have a direct line to their ideological parents. Other movements

---

1. Karant-Nunn, *Reformation of Feeling*, 5.

such as Protestant fundamentalism and neo-orthodoxy come about in part in opposition to the earlier movements. This chapter will focus the expansion of Holiness in the nineteenth century and the resultant birth of Pentacostalism at the dawn of the twentieth, as well as the pervasive effect of Schleiermacher's liberalism throughout the nineteenth century and the post war metamorphosis this had with the emergence of neo-liberalism. Fundamentalism and neo-orthodoxy will be addressed in the next chapter.

HOLINESS AND PENTECOSTALS

"Therefore are they next the throne, Serve their Maker day and night: God resides among his own, God doth in his saints delight."[2]
—Phoebe Palmer

In America, nationalism took on a new dimension in the nineteenth century, namely populism. Beginning with Andrew Jackson's rise to the Presidency, the movement continued to grow throughout the nineteenth century as dissatisfaction with industrialization and modern capitalism took root. American populism was far more than the failures of William Jennings Bryan and the Populist Party. American populism sought to redeem the masses of Americans from a country that passed them by. Lawrence Goodwyn argues that "At bottom Populism was, quite simply, an expression of self-respect. It was not an individual trait, but a collective one, surfacing as the shared hope of millions organized by the Alliance into its cooperative crusade."[3] It should come as little surprise that the very territories of the West and South that saw the largest attraction to Populism were also the same regions where revivals continued to burn past the Civil War. The emergent Holiness movement grew from the same dissatisfaction with modernity that fueled populism, but added a religious dimension to the earthly struggles. Holiness assured not only the promise of a better future, but also gave meaning to current sorrows and provided a mechanism to combat those struggles as well.

Just as populism was not one thing, Holiness was not one thing either. While Phoebe Palmer's contribution to the Holiness movement cannot be and should not be diminished, she was not the only voice advocating Holiness. Phoebe was converted to Holiness from her sister Sarah, and many Methodists believed Christian perfection was the essential theology of Wesley. In addition to these Methodist voices, perfectionism was in the

2. Palmer, *Promise of the Father*, 125.
3. Goodwyn, *Populist Moment*, 35.

air in the 1830s. Charles Finney, the Oberlin School under Asa Mahan, and William E. Boardman (d. 1886) all advocated for entire sanctification from a non-Methodist perspective. The Holiness movement continued to grow throughout the century in the United States and England with the Keswick movement. As the century came to a close, Holiness was purged from Episcopal Methodism. The result was the formation of Holiness denominations that themselves split into two camps. The radical camp became the Pentecostals at the beginning of the twentieth century, while the reactionary Holiness camp became evangelicals and fundamentalists. These two Protestant phenomena were a byproduct of the Holiness movement, its contributing members, and a wider Protestant world. Unlike Schleiermacher, who introduced a new perspective within Pietism and the Protestant world, Palmer's voice was one in a chorus. Hers was likely the loudest voice, contributing the most to the Holiness movement and its future growth. To understand the resultant denominations and ideologies, Palmer's inheritors of Holiness should be briefly addressed. These inheritors include Asa Mahan, William E. Boardman, Hannah Whithall Smith, Charles Fox Parham, William J. Seymour, and William Cooke. Only then will the explosion of Pentecostals and fundamentalists at the dawn of the twentieth century make sense, and only then will Palmer's legacy be understood.

Oberlin

"May the presence of thy love Rest upon us from above; May thy glory and thy grace Shadow o'er this holy place; Shield us by thy power divine O thou God of Oberlin."[4]

In 1832 when Phoebe and Walter Palmer were engrossed in the Allen Street Revival, another essential step occurred in the history of the Holiness movement. Oberlin College was founded by Asa Mahan, the Tappan Brothers, and anti-slave rebels expelled from Lane Theological Seminary. Initially the school dedicated to teach manual labor skills, but before too long it was a hotbed of Holiness. This was in part due to the selection of Charles G. Finney, who never graduated from college, to head the theology department. The school sought to unite the head, hand, and heart in instruction, as well as all people regardless of race or gender. It was revolutionary in its acceptance of blacks and women. Admittance to the school was based upon merit, regardless of color or sex.

4. Hambrick-Stowe, *Charles G. Finney,* 213.

The school really came into its own in 1835 when they erected a large tent in the front of a few buildings. The tent could hold three thousand people and had a large ten foot blue flag from the center pole which read "Holiness to the Lord." The school resembled a tent meeting, both in its construction and content. This was the same year that Finney and others flirted with the concept of retrenchment. The idea was to reject the materialism of the Jacksonian era and to live a minimalist lifestyle. This retrenchment away from things of this world eliminated fancy dress, furniture, and diet. The dietary restrictions eliminated all stimulants, including tea, coffee, spices, and tobacco, as well as most meats and grains. The Oberlin retrenchment diet was largely the work of Sylvester Graham (d. 1851), who inspired the Graham cracker, and nearly entirely consisted of fruits and vegetables. For the next two years fasting and the Graham diet dominated Oberlin, until rumors of mass starvation circulated. Finney and Graham were called "starvation monarchs" and styled champions of "evangelical anorexia."

Amidst the experimental retrenchment and evangelical anorexia, Finney's awakening to Christian perfection occurred. This was prompted by Asa Mahan in 1836, whose understanding of Holiness grew in Palmer's parlor and Tuesday meetings, as mentioned in chapter three. Through Mahan and Finney's numerous discussions of theology, a distinct version of Holiness emerged. Central to both was the notion of free will. They both equated the will with the heart, and maintained both must be free and voluntarily consecrated to God. Mahan further contributed the concept that it was the baptism of the Holy Ghost that produced Christian perfection. This understanding of Wesley's doctrine was rooted both in his familiarity with Palmer, as well as his background in philosophy and theology.

While Mahan is central to the further development of Holiness, it is Finney who is often called the father of Holiness. This is the case despite his conversion to the doctrine late in his career, and well after his popularity as a preacher began to wane. Still, his name lent credence to the doctrine of perfection and supported Palmer's notion of Holiness as they both matured at the same time. Finney added to his notion of Holiness a belief that it was the privilege of Christians to live without known sin, but sinlessness was not an impossibility along antinomian lines, rather it was an ongoing voluntary act which the Christian chooses. Finney believed that God was obliged to provide the ability for entire sanctification since God desires holiness. Holiness is nothing but obedience to the law, unwavering and perfect. His early lectures on the subject state "Sanctification is obedience, and, as a progressive thing, consists in obeying God more and more perfectly."[5]

5. Hambrick-Stowe, *Charles G. Finney*, 185.

Finney, like Palmer, separated perfection from feelings, but Finney's perfection involved emotionalism to a degree not found with Palmer. Finney records a few instances of conversions to Holiness that include some people dropping down and others groaning so loudly that they could be heard throughout the house after the Holy Spirit fell upon them.

As Oberlin was fixed with retrenchment, both Mahan and Finney further equated perfection and simplicity. As such, notions of what constituted a sin or immoral action were also reduced to more basic volitional acts, rather than a Calvinist notion that all acts which do not directly glorify God constitute sin. Much like Wesley, eliminating the distractions of the world served as a means to achieve perfection. Morality was also equated with simplicity and moral actions were by their definition simple and therefore perfect.

Finney further contributed to the Holiness movement by lending his voice to the movement overseas. By the 1840s, Finney's popularity in America dwindled further. Finney's works, published in England as well as the United States, remained a popular attraction overseas. Finney's first wife, Lydia Andrews, died in 1848 and his second wife, Elizabeth Atkinson, urged him to travel to England. Following the advice of his wife, he traveled twice to England, once in 1849 and again in 1858. Just like Palmer, his trips included Scotland, Wales, and Ireland as well. His journeys were equally successful there. Upon his return from his 1849 trip he assumed the role of president of Oberlin. It was at this time that his mature theology can be seen as a synthesis of his earlier message, which resonated during the Second Great Awakening, and Palmer's Altar Theology. The subsequent liberal trends towards Pentecostalism and even the more conservative tendency of fundamentalism run through Finney and his application of Palmer, especially as this message developed and dominated Oberlin.

In America it was Presbyterian William E. Boardman who best serves as an example of Holiness growing from both Palmer and Oberlin. Boardman attended Palmer's Tuesday Meetings and read Finney and Mahan. Like Finney, Boardman defined Holiness in non-Wesleyan terms, while still focusing on a second conversion which was central to Palmer's Altar Theology. Boardman's interpretation of the doctrine of justification as an instantaneous pardon is best expressed in his popular work *The Christian Higher Life*, published in 1858. Here justification is understood as a pardon of past sins, while providing the basis for a future where sin no longer dominates the Christian's life. Sanctification therefore was the ongoing process of shedding sins while the Christian apprehends Christ and his ongoing work in the lives of Christians. All together Boardman's notion of sanctification is not radically different than a traditional Christian understanding of the doctrine, except that he was willing to declare along with Palmer, Finney, and Mahan that the Christian is perfect, even though sanctification is not truly complete. Boardman differs largely in his language that the second conversion is when the Christian puts on Christ and therefore begins the process of gradually conforming their heart to Christ's. Boardman calls sanctification complete in order to align himself with Palmer and other perfectionists, even though he really argues that it is ongoing and as such is not complete.

Keswick

"The Divine Order is Fact, Faith, Feeling."[6]

Boardman was followed by a whole host of others who were wrestling with the notions of Holiness and perfection. This message was taken by Palmer, Finney, and others throughout America and to the United Kingdom. It was England, a decade after the Palmers returned to New York, which saw one of the largest Holiness revivals of the nineteenth century. Beginning in 1873 the seeds of Palmer's Holiness began to bear fruit. The seeds were watered and cultivated by R. Pearsall Smith and his wife, Hannah Whithall Smith. As was the case for the Palmers, Hannah's fame was greater than her husbands and she was the more convincing preacher. As mentioned in chapter four, Smith was greatly influenced by the writings of Palmer. Both women had unemotional conversion experiences and sought after the facts of salvation before anticipating feelings. Both were also urged towards conversion after the tragic death of their children. Smith's occurred during the Businessman Revival of the 1850s. Following Smith's conversion, she began a series of campaigns to reform society. This societal reform mirrored personal reform preached by Palmer and her notions of entire sanctification.

The Smith's message of entire sanctification came at a crucial moment for the three thousand or so souls in the small village of Keswick on the south bank of the Greta in the North of England. Small meetings were also held in London that connected the Holiness message and victory over sin. Conventions were held in and around Keswick for nearly the next thirty years. The next thirty years also saw a dramatic change for Hanna Whithall Smith, who grew tired of the Holiness message. By the mid-80s she considered her old Holiness friends "dreadfully religious,"[7] and was embarrassed by constant requests that she preach with them. Smith

---

6. Pierson, *Keswick Movement*, 32.
7. Campbell, "Hannah Whitall Smith," 96.

developed a new feminist theology that she called "The Unselfishness of God." In her feminist theology, she argued that women could hold God responsible to meet the same standard of selflessness that good mothers require of themselves. Divine love is linked to selfless motherhood more than entire sanctification. Still, even without Smith's continual support, Keswick grew. Ironically, as Smith grew less radical, so too did Keswick.

Smith illustrates the next step in Palmer's feminist theology. In Palmer's *Promise of the Father*, she repeatedly argued that she was not advocating for female ordination, yet by appealing to notions of prophesy like Perkins she blurred the lines between deaconess and presbyter, lay and ordained. The cause for female ordination was also championed by Palmer's very message and leadership role in the nineteenth century, an example that Smith and others built upon.

It was the perfectionist message which dominated early Keswick theology. Keswick took the Oberlin message of simplicity and reinterpreted it along more traditional Calvinist lines. Keswick's notion of simplicity argued that all things that were not simply of God were sinful. Alcohol, tobacco, and luxuries were all evil indulgences and not matters of faith. This new hypersensitivity to sin resulted in a new power to discern motives as either good or sinful, largely based upon the agent and effect. If the agent was a justified and sanctified Christian and the effect was one which brought glory to God, the actions were acceptable. If the result only brought vain pleasure, it was a sin. Actions deemed acceptable in Oberlin were condemned as sinful at Keswick, yet both based the decree upon notions of simplicity.

The Keswick movement began in 1873, but the following year it matured as the details of the Oxford convention were settled, and the call for the Oxford Union Meetings for the Promotion of Scriptural Holiness began on August 8. Oxford provided a key development within the Keswick movement since the city possessed respected and ordained ministers, as well as theologically knowledgeable laymen. The atmosphere of the Oxford Union was harmonious. Scores of pastors from different denominations prayed together and studied scriptures along the Keswick model.

The Keswick convention continued to grow, now reinforced by Oxford. Like many of the revivals that Palmer and Finney heralded in the United States and United Kingdom, Keswick put up large tents to house the thousands assembled. At the beginning of the twentieth century it was estimated that nearly ten thousand people took part in the annual meetings, with forty to fifty different speakers. The message of these speakers was perfection, along with Palmer's, Finney's, and Smith's insistence that "Faith, is not to be confused with feeling."[8] As with the other Holiness leaders, feeling is the final step rather than the initial cause. Keswick deemed the divine order to begin with the fact of John 3:16 that God loves them, and following this faith proceeds. This faith, like Palmer's notion of faith, is grounded in the belief that God loves and accepts them. The feeling comes last and is directed towards God, who loved them first.

The Keswick notion of fact, faith, and feeling all connected with divine love produces seven features of a perfect Christian life. The first is sinlessness. The Christian must first be sanctified not simply justified. Once the Christian is sanctified they now possess authority, to which obedience, communion, and consecration follow. From these, blessedness and eternal glory rightly follow. As with Palmer, the glory of the individual is stressed, along with the glory of God. Sanctification leads to faith and continual surrender and reliance upon Christ. It was this message from the Keswick movement that returned back to the United States and eventually produced Pentecostalism at the beginning of the twentieth century, partly from Dwight Lyman Moody in the 1890s, and in conjunction with other Holiness transplants.

Holiness Controversy

"We believe also that the baptism of the Holy Ghost is obtainable by a definite act of appropriating faith on the part of the fully cleansed believer."[9]

—Benjamin Harden Irwin

A decade after the Keswick revival began, the Holiness movement as a whole began to face large scale resistance from the very denominations where the doctrine had flourished earlier in the century. While there was an anti-revival stance advocated by many Presbyterian Calvinists in the first half of the century, resulting in the Presbyterian synod of 1837 splitting between the Congregationalists and more evangelical elements within the denomination, the 1880s saw a large scale division between Methodists. Following Wesley, Methodism was the initial home of Christian perfection which served as the basis for Holiness theology. Now many took this doctrine and grew it to ever more radical extremes, pushing the limits of sinlessness and evidence of the outpouring of the Holy Spirit, including snake-handling, speaking in tongues, and fainting spells, later identified as being "slain in the

8. Pierson, *Keswick Movement*, 32.
9. Dayton, *Theological Roots of Pentecostalism*, 97.

spirit." The majority of these extreme measures took place in the South and West, largely among rural Methodists, the same areas where Populists and Palmer found the greatest success in the later years of her life. Since a good portion of the Holiness movement took place within Methodism itself, a rift grew between the New England Methodists and the rest of the Methodist Episcopal Church. George W. Wilson highlighted the tension that only continued to grow in the thirty years after Palmer's death with his work *Methodist Theology vs. Methodist Theologians*, which came out in 1904. Wilson argued that much of New England Methodism was dying. His analysis mirrors the critiques of others, as addressed in chapter three and four.

One example of the slow death of Methodism and the gradual disappearance of the Holiness movement in New England was the evolution of the Holiness camps. During the 1880s and 90s the more radical Holiness camp associations of the South and West spun off of the National Camp Meeting Association. The National Camp Meeting Association became the camp association of New England rather than the country. It also became the canary in the coalmine for the Methodist Episcopal Church, which was doing the same thing with the Holiness movement in general. Just like the dynamic growth of Methodism during the first half of the century, the camp meetings were always energetic and capable of great change. By the middle of the century, the change began to exclude mobility and certain sites that had regularly hosted revivals became permanent.

Instead of moving to where the revival was, the Camp Meeting Association dictated the location of a revival and even scheduled them. By 1856 the camps lost their tents and permanent cottages rose up in their stead. When the Civil War ended, these cottages resembled middle-class resort communities, including streets that radiated from the outdoor auditorium. A decade after the Civil War concluded, camp sites such as Martha's Vineyard and Ocean Grove began to lose their religious identity to tourism. The revival sites became vacation destinations for those who were in no way inclined to Holiness but wanted to vacation at a seaside resort. The evangelical push towards physical vigor and exercise only added to the sites appeal as vacation hotspots. Throughout the 1870s and 80s the Holiness camp sites remained committed to Holiness and forbade alcohol and transport on the Sabbath. Hundreds still came down to the altar in the auditorium to receive the second blessing, convert, or reclaim grace. The slide away from Holiness was drastic, as the 1894 Ocean Grove reports read, "Several persons were at the altar and some were converted,"[10] a far cry from the hundreds who experienced entire sanctification a decade earlier. The

10. Stark and Finke, *Churching of America*, 168.

Holiness camps founded to secure revivals were born again, but not into Holiness, rather their new birth was as a camp site and vacation destination of the wealthy.

With the slow death of traditional Methodism, the more extreme Holiness Methodists only continued to grow in power and in numbers. The two factions of Methodism shared a common ancestry back to Wesley, but most American Methodists were relatively new members of the church. Within a few generations, Methodists grew from obscurity to the largest denomination in the country, but loyalty to the denomination did not run deep. By the 1890s, the educated and established Methodists undertook a series of maneuvers to expel their Holiness counterparts. These maneuvers included denouncing prominent Methodist clergy who participated in the Holiness movement. The Holiness movement was always suspect to some degree. Since the movement and the corresponding National Holiness Association were independent of the Methodist Episcopal Church, and many of its members did not even identify as Methodists, the conclusion was to break ties with pastors and churches connected to Holiness.

The result was the gradual development of new Holiness denominations, the largest of which were The Church of God [Anderson, Indiana], The Church of the Nazarene, The Evangelical Church of North America, and the Salvation Army. Not all of these Holiness churches became Pentecostal. Another division took Holiness, also known as evangelicalism or fundamentalism. By 1887, the Holiness Association had two hundred six evangelists who preached full time. Four years later, that number grew to over three hundred. A common trait of Holiness churches was a weekday meeting for the promotion of Holiness, modeled after Palmer's Tuesday Meetings. The meetings outnumbered full time Holiness pastors by at least fifty.

In the later decades of the nineteenth century, the future divisions between the Holiness movements were already taking place. Largely the division was regional rather than ideological. The southern Holiness churches remained far more conservative than did their western counterparts. Even those deemed too radical to remain within the Methodist Episcopal Church did not always embrace the second blessing as much as they advocated for Holiness. Georgia was the key Holiness state in the South. Methodist Bishop and president of Emory University, Warren Akin Candler (d. 1941), the brother of Asa Griggs Candler (d. 1929), the founder of Coca-Cola, was the central figure in Atlanta Holiness. In 1884 Warren Candler hosted the annual convention of the North Georgia Holiness Association. Throughout the meeting, Candler denounced sin through fiery sermons. He railed against the temptations of this world and the need for sanctification, still he never fully embraced the notion of the second blessing of the Holy Spirit.

In the West the more radical forms of Holiness grew. Following the examples of Palmer and Finney, the Holy Spirit took a preeminent position in the burgeoning ecclesiology. Like Palmer, the idea that a second or subsequent Pentecost was upon the people only transformed the older theological expectations held by Methodists and other evangelical Protestants into a more evangelical and charismatic association. The notions of dispensationalism that grew from the Plymouth Brethren echoed and reinforced these Holiness preachers. John Nelson Darby (d. 1882) founded the British Plymouth Brethren earlier in the nineteenth century, and as dispensationalism spread, it influenced American revivalism. Following Darby, many Holiness preachers spoke of different dispensations or covenants God had with humanity. The first covenant was with Adam, then Abraham, Moses, and the Old Testament Prophets. Following these Old Testament dispensations where God operated under a covenant of works, a covenant of grace emerged with the Christian dispensation. Much of the languages of differing covenants existed before Darby's dispensations, and similar claims can be found with Wesley and even the Puritans. Darby's innovation was the extent to which he took these claims of dispensations. Darby echoed the second century heresies of Montanism and Marcionism, where new prophesies coming from Montanus or Marcion superseded earlier claims. Both also pointed to themselves as the third age and the new covenant of the Holy Spirit.

Under the spreading view of dispensationalism, the new dispensation was upon the Holiness preachers of the nineteenth century, and the era of the Holy Spirit was upon them. With the advent of the Holy Spirit, the previous era of Christ was over, along with its rules and expectations. The promise of the Father sending the Holy Spirit reworked the rules concerning prophesy for Palmer, but it also brought new blessings. The new blessings quickly became known as the threefold, or for some fourfold, blessing. The three blessings consisted of justification, sanctification, and now the baptism of the Holy Ghost. Neither Palmer nor Finney fully advocated for this third blessing to the extent that was expected at the dawn of the twentieth century. For both Palmer and Finney, the baptism of the Holy Ghost largely consisted of entire sanctification, an expansion of traditional Christian notions of sanctification. For them perfection was the blessing. For those who came later, the baptism of the Holy Ghost included tangible signs, most noticeably glossolalia, or "speaking in tongues." Other blessings followed as well, including being slain in the spirit, and holy laughter.

Those who advocated for a fourfold blessing rather than a threefold blessing abandoned the theme of sanctification and instead identified salvation, healing, baptism of the Spirit, and the second coming of Christ as the four blessings. Another name for fourfold blessing was the "full Gospel," or "fourfold Gospel." With the continual outpouring of the Holy Spirit, the belief that Christians were living in this final eschaton grew to supreme status for some. From here the miracle of speaking in tongues was not only possible, but expected as evidence of a Pentecostal baptism. Other blessings, such as divine healing of the body and regeneration were added to the more common themes of repentance, justification, and sanctification.

This early Pentecostalism was attractive for those who were already inclined towards Holiness and Pietism. The individualism and subjective encounters of the divine inherent in these ideologies found a new life completing the Christian message in the lives of individuals themselves. The drama of creation, fall, and redemption became personal with their own accounts of creation and sin before turning to Christ. Christ's birth was now a birth within, his death was echoed in conversion, and the coming of the Holy Spirit was also present with the triumphant glory of the third blessing of the Holy Spirit, glossolalia.

Speaking in tongues grew from an anticipated or rare practice to one that in the 1948 Pentecostal Fellowship of North America was codified. In article five of their statement of faith, the Pentecostals affirm, "We believe that the full gospel includes holiness of heart and life, healing for the body and baptism in the Holy Spirit with the initial evidence of speaking in other tongues as the Spirit gives utterance."[11] Other practices, like being slain in the spirit, and holy laughter, increasingly became common, especially in the latter half of the twentieth century. Both involve a form of Holy Spirit possession where the believer is rendered incapable of autonomous movement, either through involuntary jerks, including falling over, or uncontrollable laugher. Examples of holy laughter are found within Wesley's Baldwin Street meetings as well as modern Pentecostalism.

Holiness is not and cannot be one thing, rather as a movement each leader has a different interpretation of what Christian perfection should entail. Palmer's view of Holiness differed from Wesley's, just as Wesley's view differed from those of Tauler, Arndt, and Spener. Finney and the Oberlin faculty's main contribution to the debate over Holiness was bringing Wesley and Palmer's conception of Holiness to a non-Methodist audience. Once here other theological conceptions, especially those connected with Calvinism, reinterpreted the doctrines of Holiness as espoused by Wesley

11. Dayton, *Theological Roots of Pentecostalism,* 18.

and Palmer. In England Hannah Whithall Smith laid the groundwork for the Keswick conventions and their interpretation of Holiness that was mixed with charismatic exuberance and refined theology. In America the experiential enthusiasm of Holiness melded with populism and American individualism, which only served to fuel the birth of Pentecostalism in the same areas that denominational affiliation was at its lowest and Palmer's revivals had the greatest success.

The Birth of Pentecostalism

"He had a special work for me to do."[12]

—*Charles F. Parham*

The official birth of Pentecostalism was January 1, 1901 in Topeka, Kansas at Charles Fox Parham's small Bethel Bible School. Parham (d. 1929) began a healing service on New Year's Eve, and during the early hours of the New Year, Miss Agnes Ozman was heard speaking in other tongues. Parham expected the outpouring of the Holy Spirit. He received training from Methodist Holiness teachers and the Baptist Benjamin Harden Irwin. Irwin was the most controversial Holiness preacher of the late nineteenth century. Irwin expected his disciples to receive a baptism in fire. This figurative fire was the influence of the Holy Spirit beyond sanctification. In 1895 Irwin's Fire-Baptized Holiness Church was born in Iowa.

Irwin spent the majority of his life moving from one place to the next. Born in Lincoln, Nebraska, and raised in Northern Missouri, he eventually made his way to Iowa. Like Finney, Irwin was a lawyer. Unfortunately for Irwin he was a rather poor lawyer. His failing law practice forced him into a church to plead with God. He entered a Baptist church, converted, and soon was on his way to becoming a Baptist minister. From the Baptists, Irwin learned Holiness and how to preach. His sermons and doctrine of fire baptism soon spread through the entire Holiness movement. Irwin echoed and advanced Palmer's notion that the Holy Spirit brings power. While Palmer believed this was power to overcome sin and lead a life of entire sanctification, Irwin understood this power to have other manifestations as well. This power or fire was the third experience of the Holy Spirit.

Irwin's theology of fire was very much like fire itself. It was attractive and dangerous. There were very few Holiness publications or preachers who did not have an opinion on Irwin and his fire baptism, and most were negative. Even the Iowa Holiness Association was split over Irwin's teachings.

12. Parham, *Voice Crying in the Wilderness*, 14.

Still, people not even connected to Irwin himself fell under the power and experienced the fire. Irwin took his message into the South and held a series of revivals from 1896 to 1898. During these revivals, personal holiness and moralism grew as it did in Keswick and with Palmer. Assemblies condemned chewing gum, Coca Cola, rings, bracelets, earrings, and neckties as luxuries, unnecessary, and sinful. Most Holiness associations condemned Irwin and many even lampooned him and his followers. Still the fire grew beyond Irwin himself. The inferno engulfed Charles Parham in 1900.

Parham learned from Irwin that the Holy Ghost brings a separate baptism to Christians following sanctification. Parham was the first to clearly identify this blessing as speaking in tongues, and that this activity of the Holy Ghost should be a normal part of Christian life and worship, and not simply a religious exuberance. Several years before Parham encountered Irwin he was already familiar with Holiness teaching. His ministerial career began as a supply pastor for the Linwood Kansas Methodist Episcopal Church. Palmer's teachings on entire sanctification were central to his understanding of the Christian life. Likely the two never met, since Parham was born in 1873, a little more than a year before Palmer's death, but there were many surrounding him who had adequate opportunity to do so.

As the Methodist Episcopal Church pushed Holiness preachers out of their denomination, Parham left in 1895, the same year Irwin's Fire Baptism began. Like Finney, Parham adopted an anti-denominational view to the church. Within a few years, Parham met Irwin and brought a portion of his fire to Topeka. In 1898 Parham was convinced that divine healing could be expected and he began a "divine healing home" in Topeka. The thought was that faithful Christians would gather and use the power of the Holy Spirit to heal the sick and infirmed through prayer. This began the Bethel Healing Home, and a paper called *Apostolic Faith*. As the healing home grew, it became the Bethel Bible School in 1900.

It was in 1900 that Parham also first really encountered people speaking in tongues. Unsure as to the nature of tongues, he urged his students to seek the scriptures concerning the practice. Like Irwin, Parham believed there was something more than entire sanctification, and that God was about to deliver a special blessing for the new century, in addition to Christian perfection and faith healing. His students returned and unanimously affirmed that the Holy Spirit manifested itself through the speaking of tongues. This report launched the all night prayer service on New Year's Eve 1900. Agnes N. Ozman was the first of many to receive the gift of tongues under Parham. They all believed she was speaking Chinese as a "halo seemed to surround her head and face."[13] Ozman was so taken by her experience that she could not speak English for three days, and even wrote in Chinese characters rather than English. Years later the writings of Ozman were evaluated and it was concluded that they were not Chinese, but the movement began with her not quite Chinese tongues.

Parham experienced a similar divine encounter a little while later. Following Ozman, speaking in tongues became a central tenet of Parham's Holiness theology, in addition to sanctification and faith healing. The Topeka press heard of the experience at Bethel and soon the message spread to Kansas City where the Holiness message was primed by Palmer and more recently D.L. Moody. Parham took his message on the road with him to Kansas City, and from there to Lawrence and south along the Missouri Kansas state line. He eventually settled in Houston, Texas in 1905. In Houston Parham began another Bible school.

Along the southern journey, Parham took his family and his household staff, which largely consisted of one African American woman named Lucy Farrow. Farrow was the children's governess. She received the gift of tongues and also served as an altar worker who helped those who sought the blessing of the Holy Spirit. It was through Farrow that William J. Seymour (d. 1922) encountered Parham. Seymour was born in 1870, the Baptist son of former slaves in Louisiana. When he was fifteen years old he traveled to Indianapolis where he became a Methodist, joining the African Methodist Episcopal Church (AME). Shortly thereafter, he encountered the Holiness movement and was taken with the doctrines of entire sanctification, after which he moved to Houston.

In Houston, Seymour could not legally attend Parham's tiny school. The twenty five white students were legally enrolled, but Parham desired that all could attend his classes. The law was circumvented as Seymour was allowed to sit in the hallway and listen to the lectures through the open door. This went on for months and was the theological education that Seymour needed before he could become a pastor. Parham even allowed Seymour to pastor his Houston church when he was away on revival tours to add vocational training.

Theologically Seymour learned that the Holiness movement was incomplete when it equated baptism of the Holy Spirit with sanctification, that there was indeed another experience, another blessing that God wished to bestow upon faithful Christians. Sanctification only cleansed the believer and prepared the way for the baptism of the Holy Spirit, where God would

13. Synan, *Holiness-Pentecostal Tradition*, 91.

come in power. Seymour defined this power as "just more of God's love. If it does not bring more love, it is simply a counterfeit."[14]

Seymour took this message and the blessing of Parham and accepted an invitation to become the pastor of an African American Holiness Church in Los Angeles. The previous pastor, Julia Hutchins, decided to become a foreign missionary. When Seymour came to his new church he found that his message was not welcomed. The church was not going to accept this brand of Holiness. Seymour's and Parham's message was too close to Irwin's, and speaking in tongues was too foreign a concept. Seymour found himself barred from the pulpit of the church he traveled two thousand miles to lead. Undeterred, Seymour resolved to meet with those members of the congregation who would have him in their homes instead. It was in April 1906 in one these homes that the baptism of the Holy Spirit was first evidenced in tongues in LA. Seymour records "One sister was baptized with the Holy Ghost on the front porch. She lay under the power of God for something like two hours, praising God and speaking in an unknown language."[15] This caused great attention and shortly thereafter Seymour moved these crowds into an abandoned and dilapidated old AME church on 312 Azusa Street. The Azusa Street Revival was born, and Pentecostalism came into its own during the three year revival.

312 Azusa Street once housed the first black Methodist church in LA, but in 1906 it was a tenement house and livery stable and not suited well to either. The city would have gladly condemned the building and threatened to do so several times before and after the revival. Housed in the business district, everyone in LA made their way over to the church to see what was taking place. Interracial crowds gathered around. Blacks, Whites, Chinese, and even Jews came to the revival to hear Seymour preach. He delivered his sermons on a makeshift pulpit on the porch of the building. As the crowds grew, they made their way onto the porch as well. The church began to fall down as the porch collapsed from the weight of the swelling congregation. No one was hurt, and many prophesied and spoke in tongues. The interracial congregation showed the power of the spirit to all in attendance. Race did not matter; the black pastor spoke to all races equally and for a brief time the majority of the congregation were white. One man exclaimed, "The color line was washed away in the blood."[16]

In addition to speaking in tongues, the Spirit was manifest in other ways including weeping, shouting, dancing, falling into trances, laughing,

14. Knight, *Anticipating Heaven Below*, 112–13.
15. Seymour, *Azusa Street Papers*, 20.
16. Synan, *Holiness-Pentecostal Tradition*, 99.

and singing, which Seymour called the heavenly choir. These additional spiritual exuberances attracted many, but they also scared off many who were interested in Holiness. One person that rejected the Azusa Street Revival was Parham. In October of 1906, Parham was finally able to make his way to LA. Both Parham and Seymour expected to greet one another with admiration concerning the outpouring of the Spirit. Instead Parham quickly surmised that this was not the work of the Holy Spirit and what was taking place was "beyond the bounds of common sense and reason."[17] Parham sought to counter the revival by holding his own down the street. Parham's revival failed to dissuade any from following his disciple. Parham was banned from Azusa and the two leaders of Pentecostalism never fully repaired their relationship. Parham always maintained that Azusa was nothing more than prostituted spiritual power, full of awful fits and spasms of "holy rollers and hypnotists."[18] The revival ended in 1909. Seymour traveled the country spreading his message, leaving his church in Azusa to his wife to pastor until she died in 1931. Shortly thereafter the church was torn down as a fire hazard and the city confiscated the land for non-payment of taxes.

Growth of Pentecostalism

"God was in His holy temple-The Shekinah glory rested there."[19]

—*Frank Bartleman at Azusa*

Pentecostalism grew beyond Azusa, in part to reliance upon the success of the Holiness movement. Parham and Seymour's messages resembled the teachings of Palmer and Finney. Palmer's Holiness theology was further adapted by British Methodist William Cooke, who argued that God's holiness was a specific type of glory. Cooke identified this as Shekinah. Shekinah is a loose transliteration of the Hebrew term שכינה, and the concept is applied to God's spirit resting upon the mercy seat in the holy of holies of the temple. The term is used to address God settling in a place and sanctifying it. Cooke applied this idea to Palmer's Altar Theology. From here it was used to describe nearly any powerful manifestation of God among the Holiness movement during the latter half of the nineteenth century. The Shekinah of the altar was the same as the Shekinah of Pentecost. John Inskip, during one of Palmer's and his Holiness meetings in Sacramento,

---

17. Synan, *Holiness-Pentecostal Tradition*, 102.

18. Synan, *Holiness-Pentecostal Tradition*, 102–3.

19. Knight, *Anticipating Heaven Below*, 131.

described the tangible power of the Holy Spirit in those meetings along the same lines as God's spirit descending upon the tabernacle altar, "a haze of golden glory encircled the heads of the bowed worshippers—a symbol of the Holy Spirit."[20] Similar claims are later used by Pentecostals about their meetings, including the Azusa Street Revival.

Pentecostalism also grew among the disenfranchised Americans. That God's Shekinah glory would descend upon all regardless of race, gender, and economic status only served to accelerate the movement. The American frontier afforded many preachers the opportunity to move away from the established urban centers and into communities that needed ministers. The Holiness movement, and later Pentecostalism, gave the otherwise voiceless a voice, along with esteem they could only get from a supportive congregation. Since Protestantism does not require apostolic succession or theological training to claim authority to preach, one's own abilities of persuasion, combined with a degree of charisma, prove effective in converting those who desire a spiritual answer to the problems of the material world. Pentecostals are often called charismatics because of the excitement that their services produce. The egalitarian message opposed in word or practice by many established Protestant churches also served to provide an opportunity for Pentecostals. The derisive connotations of Pentecostalism as illiterates, snake handlers, and holy rollers only served to disengage the weakening mainstream Protestants from understanding the surging inheritors of Palmer's Holiness and Wesley's Pietism.

Throughout the twentieth century, Pentecostalism grew from a few revivals in Topeka and Los Angeles into a worldwide movement. By 1908, Pentecostal revivals were found on six continents. Six years later the Assemblies of God was formed. The Assemblies of God is the largest Pentecostal denomination in the United States and is the engine of growth for many of the Pentecostal revivals throughout the world. In 1995, less than a century after its inception, there were over 200 million Pentecostals around the world attached to a Pentecostal denomination, and another 250 million who are associated with charismatic or Holiness movements.[21] The same dissatisfaction with modernism and racial, gender, and economic segregation found in America was present throughout the world. As industrialization grew, so too did dissatisfaction with modernity. Radical Holiness, as advocated for by Palmer, as well as a missionary zeal from Pentecostals, provided both the opportunity and remedy for modernism. Success also begets success. As American and European Pentecostals were

20. Knight, *Anticipating Heaven Below*, 131.
21. Synan, *Holiness-Pentecostal Tradition*, ix–x.

marginalized by their respective societies, news of missionary success fueled enthusiasm, which then produced more missionaries. The general antipathy towards Christian culture and secular culture inherent to Pietism is also found within Pentecostals. The mystical encounter with the divine becomes the answer.

Essential to the Pentecostal message is the notion of a second blessing and subsequent conversion experiences. Without Palmer's Altar Theology which served as a valid interpretation of Wesley's notion of Christian perfectionism the Pentecostal message could not have existed. Holiness, especially as understood by Palmer, provided the theological justification for glossolalia, faith healing, and fire baptism, even though Palmer would have rejected these ideas. Without ecclesial control over doctrine and practice further revelations and marginal experiences become centralized and new religious groups emerge.

LIBERALISM

"If I had written my book with the intention of founding a sect or school, then I could have opponents. But I know that I had no such thing in mind."[22]

—*Friedrich Schleiermacehr*

Schleiermacher is the father of modern liberal Protestantism, though he did not intend on founding any movement, nor creating a new ideology. In many ways Schleiermacher did not found a new movement, rather it was an approach to theology and an ecclesiastical ideology. After all, it is said that he had no children, only grandchildren. Liberalism was adopted and to a great degree decimated by a series of backlashes from fundamentalists and neo-orthodox theologians by the middle of the twentieth century. The remaining tenets of liberal Protestantism survive within some mainline traditions, but not as a movement, rather only as a pervasive trend in theology, or the prevailing position divorced from its theological foundations. Liberalism as advocated by Schleiermacher is therefore simultaneously absent and ubiquitous from mainline Protestantism by the end of the twentieth century. The greatest strand of liberalism that survives in the twentieth century is a new liberalism or neo-liberalism that emerges after World War One. This liberalism shares many traits in common with Schleiermacher, but less with the theologians that occupied the interim period. Neo-liberalism occupies an alternative to the weakened or the ubiquitous trend within mainline

---

22. Schleiermacher, *On the Glaubenslehre*, 34.

Protestantism, therefore two distinct discussions of liberalism need to proceed. The first concerns Schleiermacher and nineteenth-century liberalism, the second follows Tillich and twentieth-century neo-liberalism. In part, both liberal movements guided mainline Protestantism and provoked criticism from fundamentalists and neo-orthodoxy, to which our attention will turn to a greater degree in the next chapter.

Schleiermacher intended on preserving what he believed to be essential to Christianity, by stripping away what was unnecessary. The superfluous doctrines, dogmas, and practices were not merely supererogatory, but were dangerous appendages that weakened the Christian faith. Schleiermacher's liberalism was not haphazard, rather it was a surgery performed to remove the gangrenous growth, which left untreated could kill the host. His diagnosis was likely overstated and much of what Schleiermacher removed, comforted rather than condemned. Schleiermacher saw the barrage of attacks coming from modernity and the cultured despisers of religion and reacted. The result was a systematic theology based in Pietisms call, that experience trumps scholastic theology and rationalism. Modern liberal Protestantism saved Protestant churches by challenging the origins of Christianity and redefining essential doctrine accordingly.

At the dawn of the nineteenth century, Schleiermacher produced a new Christian apology with his work *On Religion, Speeches to Its Cultured Despisers*. Just like early Christian apologists such as Justin Martyr, the purpose of the polemic was to defend Christianity over and against the wider profane culture which despised Christianity. Both early Christians and Christians in the Early Modern period were faced with a similar threat to the gospel message. As Schleiermacher saw it, the very survival of Christianity was at stake in both eras. Christianity grew by affirming what it believed was necessary to overcome its challenges. These obstacles were both legal and philosophical, and a theology was developed to answer these objections. In doing so, the early church developed an ecclesiology and theology that preserved it against a Greco-Roman and Jewish context. As the church triumphed against those challenges, new challenges emerged, but much of the older apologetics survived. Those tools were contextually valid and effective, but outside of that historical context the same polemics could harm. Schleiermacher's construction of a new apology mirrors his own conception of earlier discourses at the dawn of Christianity but framed within a new cultural context.

This is why in both *On Religion* and *The Christian Faith*, Schleiermacher attempted to separate religion and dogma. In his earlier work he argued, "If you have only given attention to these dogmas and opinions, therefore, you do not yet know religion itself, and what you despise is not it."[23] The problem with dogmas is twofold. First they are held up as the expression of faith and second, they equate piety with knowledge of doctrine. For Schleiermacher and liberalism following him, as well as Pietism preceding him, religion is not knowledge. One can be knowledgeable about religion without in any way being devout. Rudolf Otto, a twentieth-century disciple of Schleiermacher, argues that in the first centuries of Christianity the numinous idea of the holy was connected both to the notion of God as father and the disciples calling each other holy. Holy was not morally perfect, nor did it carry notions of entire sanctification, rather it referenced a positional difference. The holy disciples were holy because they focused not on this profane world but on the sacred world which was to come, and indeed in the act of becoming.

It was from this context that Schleiermacher and liberal Protestantism sought to redefine the origins of the Christian faith, not simply as something delivered from on high, but people who engaged with the incarnate God and a profane and hostile world. The dogmas and doctrines of the church and the scripture of the church comes from this era and from these conflicts, and only after this context is understood can Christianity be preserved. Theology derives from the apology, and when the apologetic concerns erode, the theology needs to adapt to the current conflict.

Christian theology must therefore line up with both reason and experience. The experience of God remained central to Schleiermacher's theology. This God-consciousness is a given, but the language used to describe it was not. This is why theology must always be defined and redefined in light of contemporary experience. Heresies are those experiences that are outside of the community's religious orbit and understanding. The affirmed doctrines are those experiences that resonate with others and are validated by a shared experience of the infinite, experiences that the community believes increase the God-consciousness rather than diminishing it. As Schleiermacher says in *The Christian Faith*, "The piety which forms the basis of all ecclesiastical communions is, considered in itself, neither a knowing or a doing, but a modification of feeling, or of immediate self-consciousness."[24]

Since theology is experiential, the church must constantly return to theology and ensure it lines up with the lived experiences of its members. This allows for doctrines to change, in addition to being abandoned when they are contextually no longer necessary. Schleiermacher's liberalism answers the challenges of empiricism but runs a risk of too much subjectivity. This is

23. Schleiermacher, *On Religion*, 15.
24. Schleiermacher, *Christian Faith*, 5.

also why for Schleiermacher ecclesiology and Christology is essential. These experiences of God, which liberalism elevates over other doctrine, must remain centered on Christ as the incarnation and first of the new creation, and second within the fellowship of the Church. The church, both visible and invisible, mediates these experiences and the church is the one who needs to reflect upon the value of doctrines rather than this belonging to the domain of the individual. For Schleiermacher the churches experiences remain of higher value than those of the individual.

The church must evaluate doctrines based upon historical and scientific challenges. Schleiermacher's contribution of hermeneutics is key to the first evaluation. Some challenges remain similar, and even though context changes, doctrines may only need to evolve slightly. Equally important is the relationship that must exist between the church and science. Schleiermacher argued that the church must endeavor "to establish an eternal covenant between the living Christian faith and completely free, independent scientific inquiry, so that faith does not hinder science and science does not exclude faith."[25] This relationship allows for scientific discovery to inform faith rather than becoming a rival.

Schleiermacher's conception of science and reason shifted his views of biblical authority as well as the miraculous. Early in his life he abandoned biblical literalism from both his understanding of historical criticism as well as a scientific one. Both views contributed to a shift in his theology. The scriptures themselves were only expressions of the incarnation and where they were not consistent with science, reason, or experience, Schleiermacher abandoned them or was silent. Schleiermacher maintained that religion was a combination between the supernatural God and the natural world. As the natural world works within its laws, science is necessary and miracles less so. Miracles are largely operations of nature, the greatest of these miracles is the incarnation. Therefore Schleiermacher surmises that there must be something within humanity that allows for the possibility of the divine.

Since humanity possesses the capacity for the incarnation of God, it follows that humanity also possesses the capacity to relate to that God. The first half of *The Christian Faith* concerns itself with notions of natural religion and this universal capacity. Neither liberalism nor Schleiermacher argue that all people share the same basic beliefs. What is shared is the natural capacity for belief. Some people have a greater capacity than others and are more pious, but this condition is present in all.

Schleiermacher's liberal legacy shook the Protestant world, but how this eruption is understood and approached is not uniform. The different

25. Schleiermacher, *On the Glaubenslehre*, 64.

critics grow from the varied ways Schleiermacher and liberalism were absorbed. To both to his benefit and detriment, Schleiermacher did not found any theological school and he appointed no theological heirs. His works were taken up by Albert Ritschl (d. 1889) and Ritschl's protégé Wilhelm Herrmann (d. 1922), who largely shaped his legacy and the trajectory of liberalism.

Ritschl was also the one whose caricature and criticism of Pietism reduced its history to a footnote until recent years. Ritschl's treatment of Schleiermacher did much the same, this one from a point of admiration. Ritschl embraced the Enlightenment to an extent unfitting for the dominant voice concerning Schleiermacher over the next century. Ritschl understood Schleiermacher from a Kantian perspective instead of vice versa. Kant's appeal to reason became the ground from which Ritchl sprung. More than Hegel and any others, Ritschl believed that modern man desires to live a life according to reason. Ritschl's notion of reason included his own interpretation of Christian perfection. Reason dictates that since man is justified, this justification must contain within its capacity the means of attaining the desired object. In addition to morality, Ritschl's perfection takes place in faith in divine providence, humility, patience and in prayer. Perfection is a life work and perpetually includes insights concerning imperfection and is culminated in love of neighbor. To this end he opposed justification as interpreted as the forgiveness of sins, rather he argued justification is interpreted as placing the Christian in relation to one another and with God. From this perspective, Ritschl radically reinterpreted Schleiermacher and condemned Pietism, mysticism, and Roman Catholicism as traditions that view justification as something different than the impartation of the God-consciousness.

Herrmann took a slightly different tact than his teacher, but he still valued Schleiermacher as the harbinger of the new theology. Herrmann believed that *On Religion* was the most important Christian writing after the New Testament. Like Ritschl's interpretation of Schleiermacher, the emphasis is on experience as the heart of theology. For Herrmann this is the only appropriate way faith can be understood. Herrmann equated faith and historicity of culture, and argued that Schleiermacher's conception of *Anschauung* (intuition) was the answer to how justification and election become fact for individual Christians. The feeling of absolute dependence is the presence of the God-consciousness and therefore the evidence of justification and the means of securing election. Herrmann was convinced that the Christ outside was the same as the Christ inside, that through the feeling, the God-consciousness was not only a consciousness of God, but actually God, that Christ incarnated himself in the believer throughout this relationship. Theoretical knowledge played only a very small role in confirming this belief.

Neither Herrmann nor Ritschl accepted Schleiermacher's liberalism on its own grounds. Not surprisingly, the inevitable critiques of their theology were laid upon Schleiermacher, as the notion of absolute dependence and the God-consciousness superseded the rest of Schleiermacher's theological contributions. Liberalism, following Ritschl, embraced the Enlightenment, though Schleiermacher believed it was incomplete without a Pietistic heart. Such an accommodation only contributed to the widespread perception that Schleiermacher was a nominal cultural Christian who only measured Christian truth by its ability to adapt to modern culture. This perception was especially true in English speaking areas where Schleiermacher's works were not as prevalent. Equally absent from the English depiction of Schleiermacher was his life and his conflicts with Napoleon and the Prussian aristocracy.

While Ritschl and Herrmann's distortion of Schleiermacher's legacy perverted his legacy, Schleiermacher's liberalism engendered its own critiques during his lifetime. To answer these critiques, Schleiermacher wrote his own defense. Fittingly he declares "Very many of their objections are based solely on the fact that statements have been imputed to me which I have never expressed and could never acknowledge as mine."[26] In his defense Schleiermacher reasserts his orthodox theology by pointing towards his Christology and ecclesiology. While Schleiermacher may be called a Universalist, his universalism is one within the church. Never does he argue that regeneration can take place outside of the Christian church. Universal salvation occurs through the church and for many this occurs after death.

The term feeling is also a common source of confusion and attention. Hegel equated the feeling of dependence with his dog, while Schleiermacher believed that this feeling was a deep seated and all-encompassing inclination of humanity that went beyond mental formulations and simple assent to doctrinal matters. Schleiermacher insists that the feeling of absolute dependence and piety is grounded in God and not arbitrary or accidental. He also defends his works as Christian works and concedes that the organization of *The Christian Faith* leads to misunderstanding. Beginning with universal and moving towards the particular tenets of Christianity, many opponents regard his claims about humanity to supersede all others. Schleiermacher asserts, "No one could have failed to recognize that the description of the consciousness distinctive to Christianity is in truth and

26. Schleiermacher, *On the Glaubenslehre*, 36.

in actuality the real aim of the book."[27] Regardless of how his theology is interpreted, Schleiermacher's modern liberal Protestantism has the same aim.

Neo-Liberalism and Paul Tillich

"Many of those who reject the Word of God reject it because the way we say it is utterly meaningless to them."[28] – *Paul Tillich*

With the success of neo-orthodoxy, which we will address in the next chapter, the attack against liberalism and Schleiermacher was near complete. Some forms remained, but theological liberalism needed to adapt in order to answer the challenges of the neo-orthodox and the fundamentalists. In many ways the new liberalism or neo-liberalism is simply liberalism after World War One. The name is used only to differentiate the concerns of liberals following the war from those of liberals in the nineteenth century. In large measure neo-liberalism is not nearly the ideological break from the past that existed akin to Pentecostalism, fundamentalism, or neo-orthodoxy and the vestiges of Protestant scholasticism. Practically speaking neo-liberalism is a renewal of Schleiermacher's liberal legacy in the twentieth century. The chief architect of the new liberalism or neo-liberalism is Paul Tillich (d. 1965).

In many ways Paul Tillich was the Schleiermacher for a new generation. Like Schleiermacher Tillich was uneasy with the direction of Protestant theology. While liberalism, as the product of Pietism, sought to approach people where they were, rationalism and scholasticism were not. Rather than addressing practical concerns with their theology, Protestantism was possessed by a "demonic absolutism which throws the truth like stones at the heads of people, not caring whether they can accept it or not." Tillich continues arguing, "It is what may be called the demonic offense the churches often give while claiming that they give the necessary divine offense. Without adaptation to the categories of understanding in those toward whom the expanding functions of the church are directed, the church not only does not expand but even loses what it has, because its members also live within the given civilization and can receive the verity of the message of the New Being only within the categories of that civilization."[29] Tillich was afraid that as Christianity expanded into new civilizations and civilization expanded

---

27. Schleiermacher, *On the Glaubenslehre*, 58.

28. Tillich, *New Being*, 121.

29. Tillich, *Systematic Theology*, 3:186.

within Christian domains, the truth of Christianity would be lost and only a struggle would remain. For this reason, his decision in theology was, as he said "thoroughly on the side of Schleiermacher."[30] Schleiermacher's acceptance of culture allowed Christians to really experience God and understand God through that experience, rather than existing only as an impersonal and often adversarial abstraction.

Tillich accepted Schleiermacher's premise that theology is based upon the person of Christ and the churches historical encounter with the God who became man. In his first volume of *Systematic Theology* Tillich argues, "Christian Theology is based on the unique event Jesus the Christ, and in spite of the infinite meaning of this event it remains *this* event and, as such, the criterion of every religious experience. This event is given to experience and not derived from it. Therefore, experience receives and does not produce."[31] Tillich clarifies Herrmann's interpretation of Schleiermacher by once again separating Christ from residing solely in the God-consciousness. While Christ manifests himself in experience, the experience of Christ is a receptive one rather than a creative one. Humanities understanding of God can still reside in experience as the Pietists argue, but Tillich rescues experience by removing God from the isolated sphere of the domain of individual subjectivity.

As Schleiermacher argues the church then produces dogmas and doctrines based upon these experiences which are bound by history and culture. Tillich echoes Schleiermacher by arguing that theology is "a product of the collective experience of the church."[32] Theology therefore is not only the churches view of God as an object of knowledge, but understanding that the churches existence is contained in God. With this understanding, Tillich melds Schleiermacher's experiential theology with Kierkegaard and Martin Heidegger's existential one. Tillich posits, "Dealing with the meaning of being as far as it concerns us ultimately dealing with man and the world, with nature and history, as far as our ultimate concern appears in them, we must know the meaning of being, we must know the structures and powers controlling the different realms of existence."[33]

Of course this existential understanding of humanity and ones relation to God must be taken on faith, and it is through faith that the self is constructed and remade. "Faith means being grasped by a power that is greater than we are, a power that shakes up and turns us, and transforms

---

30. Tillich, *Perspectives*, 91.

31. Tillich, *Systematic Theology*, 1:46.

32. Tillich, *Systematic Theology*, 1:52.

33. Tillich, *Protestant Era*, 88.

us and heals us. Surrender to this power is faith."[34] Since surrender is faith, the individual remains responsible for some involvement with their relationship with the divine, but the divine power remains the object and subject of faith. In *Dynamics of Faith*, Tillich gives his famous definition of faith and God as ultimate concern. "Faith as ultimate concern is an act of the total personality. It happens in the center of the personal life and includes all its elements. Faith is the most centered act of the human mind."[35] This notion of faith is remarkable similar to Schleiermacher's feeling of absolute dependence. Both ultimate concern and absolute dependence consume the totality of the individual and mark the object as greater than the individual. Tillich continues that "Where there is faith there is an awareness of holiness," therefore "What concerns one ultimately becomes holy."[36]

Even when God is the ultimate concern, the potential for idolatry exists. After all, one can easily elevate any object of love to a status that consumes their entire being. In these cases the ultimate concern is only ultimate to a single individual and not truly ultimate but finite. When the ultimate is finite, the faith is genuine but the object of that faith is not. Tillich argues that "Even God can be made a finite concern, an object among other objects; in whose existence some people believe and some do not. Such a God, of course, cannot be our ultimate concern."[37] God as a concept, or a doctrine, cannot be the ultimate concern, but following Schleiermacher, God as the incarnation can. Not only the incarnate God, but what this God then does for and to humanity really becomes the ultimate concern.

In *The New Being*, Tillich defines what ultimate concern really is and what he believes the essential message of Christianity is. The answer to this question comes from Paul's letter to the Galatians.[38] "It is the message of a 'New Creation.'" Tillich advances this point by saying "The New Creation—this is our ultimate concern; this should be our infinite passion—the infinite passion of every human being. This matters; this alone matters ultimately."[39] Every other point concerning Christian theology follows from this central message. A careful reading of Schleiermacher's *Christian Faith* points out that the doctrine of the New Creation propels the Christian message. While Schleiermacher does not commit a section to the doctrine individually,

34. Tillich, *New Being*, 38.

35. Tillich, *Dynamics of Faith*, 4.

36. Tillich, *Dynamics of Faith*, 12.

37. Tillich, *New Being*, 159.

38. "For in Christ Jesus neither circumcision nor uncircumcision avails anything, but a *new creation*" (Gal 6:15).

39. Tillich, *New Being*, 15, 19.

he argues that Christ was the first New Creation, and from this Christians join with Him and become New Creations as well. When Tillich places the doctrine of the New Creation as ultimate concern, he goes beyond Schleiermacher and incorporates Kierkegaard. While Schleiermacher's theology of the New Creation is contained in his Christology, Tillich's is based in subjectivity, but a divine subjectivity. This is the prevailing theme of Tillich and his often overlooked doctrine. It is only by engaging in this doctrine that neo-liberalism advances something new and engaging for the twentieth-century audience while remaining grounded in the nineteenth-century Pietism of Schleiermacher.

VI

Fundamentalism and Neo-Orthodoxy
The Qualified Heirs of Schleiermacher and Palmer

"When men look into themselves they discover not self-love but the moral law, and that this moral law is a fact of reason and condition of freedom."[1]

—*Helmut Walser Smith*

THE PREVIOUS CHAPTER ADDRESSED the direct theological and ecclesial heirs of Palmer and Schleiermacher. In many ways these movements demonstrated the liberal trends associated with Palmer's Holiness and Schleiermacher's modern liberal Protestantism. Those trends have a lasting effect in producing religious and civil structures, which dominated the history of not only the nineteenth century but the twentieth century as well. In addition to these liberal trends in Protestant theology, Schleiermacher and Palmer also produced a conservative legacy. In many ways the more conservative heirs of Schleiermacher and Palmer are qualified beneficiaries of their theology. This term has obvious double meaning. Many of the leaders within fundamentalism and neo-orthodoxy hold more theological heft than do some of their more liberal counterparts, though this is not always the case. They are also the heirs only as qualified or contextually understood. Fundamentalism and neo-orthodoxy come about in part as oppositionary movements to Pentecostalism and liberalism. Noticeably they speak the same language and similarly understand the nature of Christian theology,

1. Smith, *Continuities of German History*, 61.

174

though from the opposing position. It is no accident that both emerge during the twentieth century rather than the nineteenth. This chapter will address the qualified conservative response found in fundamentalism and neo-orthodoxy to the theological world created by Schleiermacher and Palmer. These conservative alternatives interacted with and counterbalanced the liberal tendencies addressed in the previous chapter.

HOLINESS AND FUNDAMENTALISM

"Let us expect that God is going to use us. Let us have courage, and go forward, looking to God to do great things."[2] *– D. L. Moody*

In a fairly surprising turn of events, the fundamentalists who emerged in the twentieth century did not come about through a resurgence of Protestant scholasticism or rationalism. The ancestry of fundamentalism was the Holiness movement, a movement whose origins were significantly based in Wesley's expression of Pietism and Palmer's understanding of Holiness as prioritizing an experience of God over reason or orthodoxy. Before the rise of Protestant fundamentalism in America, the Holiness churches in America split. Some tended toward Pentecostal, while others were more conservative. They appealed to morality and the Bible as the source of a holy life, rather than a third or fourth blessing from the Holy Spirit. Both strains shared the Holiness associations of the nineteenth century.

Palmer and Finney, the mother and father of Holiness, lent their voices and contributions to the spiritual and ideological ancestry of both movements. As the Methodists pushed the Holiness camps out of their denomination in the 1880s, the differences between the two became more and more apparent. The Pentecostals were swept up in revivalism and the gifts of the spirit, as articulated by Irwin, Parham, and Seymour. Eventually the Assemblies of God was created as the largest home for Pentecostals. The conservative Holiness movement soon dominated the Southern Baptist Convention, the largest Protestant denomination in the United States, as well created a number of new denominations that split off of the Holiness associations of the nineteenth century.

The largest of these is the Pentecostal Church of the Nazarene. In 1919 they dropped the term Pentecostal from their name to disassociate themselves with the Pentecostal movement growing at the same time. The Church of the Nazarene became the largest denomination formed out of the Holiness movement and was a bastion of anti-Pentecostal thought.

2. Belmonte, *D.L. Moody*, 159.

Phineas Bresee (d. 1915) founded the church in 1895 after he conducted mass Holiness meetings in LA. The Church of the Nazarene's articles of faith proclaim they will seek "the simplicity and the Pentecostal power of the primitive New Testament Church" through "the conversion of sinners, the sanctification of believers."[3] Most of the early Holiness language is still clearly present.

Those members of the Holiness churches within the Nazarenes and Southern Baptists produced the evangelicals and fundamentalists. It is the split within Holiness that gives both Pentecostalism and fundamentalism their life in the twentieth century. Both still advocate for a Pietistic prioritization of experience, though one is more tempered and restrained in their expectations about religious feelings. The fundamentalists' restraint was largely due to the third leader of nineteenth-century Holiness, Dwight L. Moody (d. 1899) and his disciple Reuben A. Torrey (d. 1928). Moody was the chief conservative Holiness preacher of the nineteenth century.

Fundamentalism

"Because there is a Devil. He is cunning, he is mighty, he never rests, he is ever plotting the downfall of the child of God; and if the child of God relaxes in prayer, the devil will succeed in ensnaring him."[4] – R. A. Torrey

Dwight Lyman Moody was born in Northfield, Massachusetts on February 5, 1837 and remarkably grew into one of the foremost Holiness preachers and theologians in America, laying the groundwork for fundamentalism at the dawn of the twentieth century. It is remarkable because Moody received no formal education; even his elementary education was suspended after the fifth grade. His lack of education was clear to most who encountered him. Years later when Moody was in England, C. H. Spurgeon (d. 1892) remarked that Moody was the only man he knew that could pronounce "Mesopotamia" in two syllables. Moody's preaching and writing lacks all pretension found in others, largely because he lacked the skill to do other-wise. He was never ordained, but founded the Chicago Bible Institute, later known as the Moody Bible Institute, which was open to men and women of all denominations. While lacking the skill of others he still recognized the need for low-cost evangelical print and established the Bible Institute Colportage Association (BICA). He held titles such as the vice-president

---

3. Jones, *Perfectionist Persuasion*, 108.

4. Torrey, *How to Pray*, 5.

of the Chicago Sunday School Union and president of the Chicago YMCA. Moody even preached in front of Abraham Lincoln. His accomplishments outweigh his limitations and he was an innovator as much as he was an heir of the Holiness message of Palmer and others.

Too often, Moody is credited as the inheritor of Finney, but this claim has little support other than identifying them both as profound Holiness preachers. Moody learned from Finney but took far more from Palmer. Both in the United States and United Kingdom, Moody launched a series of lay run crusades modeled after those of Phoebe Palmer. Palmer's emphasis on the laity prepared them to play a vital role in a variety of revivals. Unlike Finney, whose revivals remained largely controlled by his fellow ordained ministers, Palmer and Moody were never ordained and used that to advance their ministerial aims. Moody decried many of the professional preachers as sophists of the pulpit and "silver-tongued orators."[5] Moody used his poor speech to his advantage at his crusades, since it had a tendency to disarm many who were weary of smooth talking stories that held the audiences captive but did little the second they stopped. Eloquence was nice, but without conviction it amounted to little. It was estimated by Theodore Cuyler at Moody's funeral that he spoke to 40,000–50,000 people a week after the great Chicago fire of 1871, and A. T. Pierson estimated Moody converted at least 100 million people.[6]

Not only did Moody utilize the laity like Palmer, he also avoided most of Finney's new techniques. The emotionalism found within Finney was muted by Moody. Finney had the anxious bench and Moody had the inquiry room. Both may initially appear similar as they moved potential converts around the revival tent, but as Finney moved them closer to the front to make them feel anxious and proclaim a decision for Christ, Moody often moved them farther away from the front to more quiet areas to speak with counselors or pray in silence. Finney used his revivals to rack up converts. Moody borrowed from Palmer the idea that converts themselves are not what the minister should ask for, but disciples. Both Moody and Palmer pushed for decisions, but they also wanted a level of follow through after the revival ended, Moody to a far greater extent than Palmer.

Like Finney and Palmer, Moody's basic theology was interdenominational. All three valued the ecumenical spirit of the age, and the Holiness movement was anything but a single denominational movement. Moody's preaching was based around what he called the three R's of the Bible: ruined by the fall, redeemed by the blood, and regenerated

5. Moody, *Moody's Stories, Incidents, and Illustrations*.

6. Gundry, "Demythologizing Moody," 13.

by the Spirit. After sin entering the world with the fall, Moody argues "unbelief is, the mother of all sin."[7] Humanity is then redeemed by Christ. Like Palmer and Finney, Moody maintained the substitutionary atonement model of justification against the views of Schleiermacher. Moody identified Christ's redemption as a divine act of love; "Nothing speaks to us of the love of God like the cross of Christ."[8]

Moody believed that Christ's death redeemed humanity, not just the elect. Rejecting the doctrine of the limited atonement, Moody declares, "God has put the offer of salvation in such a way that the whole world can lay hold of it. All men can believe."[9] Like Palmer, the next act is simply belief. Moody does not hold to universal salvation but rather universal offer to salvation. Faith is necessary and faith is trusting in God. In his work *Sovereign Grace Its Source, Its Nature and Its Effects*, Moody presents a conversation where Mr. R answers the question about what it is to believe God, "To take Him at His word." "When they take God at His word, and cast themselves upon Him, whether they feel it or not—when they confess Jesus Christ as their Lord—the Holy Ghost will come as a power to make them realize it."[10] This message of faith and redemption is identical to Palmer's.

The third R, regeneration, differs from Palmer though. This was Palmer's notion of entire sanctification, but Moody was never comfortable with the notion of perfection. Moody attested that Christians sin, but Christ calls them back to repentance. Moody argues "the Shepherd will not turn His poor wandering sheep away; He will go after it, and bring it back. He has promised that He will save His people from their sins."[11] This constant act of God leads some at Keswick and later America to believe that Moody altered his views and supported the second blessing. If Moody did support entire sanctification it was not to the extent of Palmer or Finney and no definitive work articulates this position.

While Moody never stresses entire sanctification, he articulates in *The Way to God* that faith is composed of three essential steps, knowledge, assent, and appropriation. The Christian must first be knowledgeable about Christ and Christ's offer of redemption. Upon hearing this, the message must be received and the individual must give assent to God to dictate the Christian's future. Following this, they must appropriate the gospel and repent of their sins. Moody, like Palmer, emphasizes that repentance is

7. Moody, *Secret Power*, 33.

8. Moody, *Way to God*, 18.

9. Moody, *Moody's Stories, Incidents, and Illustrations*.

10. Moody, *Sovereign Grace*, 109–10.

11. Moody, *Sovereign Grace*, 109.

not fear, and repentance is not feeling. Sanctification is the life's work of repentance and this third step of faith. A life of repentant faith is the new birth. For Moody it is also the only way to heaven. Moody proclaims, "This doctrine of the new birth is therefore the foundation of all our hopes for the world to come. It is really the A B C of the Christian religion."[12]

Moody's contribution to experiential Protestantism serves as a prime example of the mixture of Palmer's Holiness message with Calvinist theology. While Finney, the faculty of Oberlin, and Parham all took the perfectionist message and explained it through a radical dispensational shift towards the Holy Spirit, eventually giving birth to modern Pentecostalism, Moody's theology served to cool the growing emotional theology. While credited as fathering fundamentalism, it is more appropriate to place Moody in the line of Palmer, who advocated for increased lay involvement in the lives of Protestants. Like Palmer, Moody cared little for denominational affiliation and called for an increase in Bible reading and personal piety. For this reason it is fair to call Moody the founder of contemporary American interdenominational evangelicalism. It is not quite accurate to call him the father of fundamentalism though. The stern doctrinaire conception of fundamentalism grew from Moody's conservative Holiness rather than a rationalist or scholastic source. Still, it took Moody's successors to develop fundamentalism beyond the Biblicism of Palmer and Moody.

Moody died before the split between conservative and radical Holiness really occurred. His death allowed for another voice to dictate the conservative response to Pentecostalism. That voice was Reuben Archer Torrey. Torrey was Moody's hand appointed successor, so while he was quite the opposite of Moody in many respects, it would be far more difficult to argue that Torrey did not reflect what Moody believed to a large extent. Torrey was likely selected because he was everything Moody wished were true of himself.

Torrey was born in 1856, the same year as Moody's conversion. Moody's early life was spent trying to eke out a living and never taking religion too seriously. Torrey's wealthy father instructed Reuben to read his Bible and pray daily from a very young age. Though he had the image of a Christian, Torrey, like Finney, was afraid of being one. When as a lad he encountered a book that posed a simple question "Will you be a Christian now?" Torrey refused, believing that if he said yes he had no choice but to become a preacher. Both Moody and Torrey entered late adolescence seemingly irreligious, Moody ignorant, and Torrey fearful. Still Torrey entered Yale at fifteen, imbibing and reveling in the life of sin, all along attending church

12. Moody, *Way to God*, 29.

and prayer meetings. His junior year at Yale he saw the vanity inherent in his conflicted life and conceded to become a Christian and to be a minister if God would have him. Torrey met Moody his senior year at Yale. Eager to hear him, Torrey recounted "When Mr. Moody first came to New Haven we thought we would go out and hear this strange, uneducated man." Later he concluded that Moody "may be uneducated, but he knows some things we don't."[13] Torrey received his BA in 1875 and his divinity degree three years later. Around this time, Torrey fell away from Moody's influence and became skeptical of biblical inerrancy.

Even before completing his degree, Torrey was invited to become the pastor at a Congregational church at Garrettsville. After receiving ordination, Torrey moved to Ohio and was discouraged with the rampant quarrelling and infidelity that occurred in this country town. While Torrey encountered the conservative Moody at a young age, his theology was liberal along Schleiermacher's lines. Torrey did not believe in an everlasting hell, and accepted the tenets of the higher biblical criticism. While in Garrettsville, he read the biography of Finney and therefore expected a revival. The revival did not come. While he prepared for its coming, he was discouraged by others in the town. Torrey heard a constant voice telling him to take his message to Horton & Thompson's saloon. Torrey never imagined that being a minister included interacting with people, he always saw the office consisting of preaching good sermons and little more. Still he listened to that voice and entered the saloon, asking those there to put down their cards because he had a prayer for them. Startled, those present complied. A few weeks later the rival saloon owner asked why Torrey did not enter his, so Torrey entered the saloon and preached there. Having imbibed a few times, Torrey was less strict concerning the prohibition of alcohol than Palmer and others. Remarkably, the real leader of fundamentalism was willing to enter a bar when others in the Holiness movement were appalled by the very notion of their existence.

After four years as pastor in Garrettsville the revival never materialized. Torrey resigned his post and travelled to Leipzig and Erlangen to learn biblical criticism. Already believing many of Schleiermacher's liberal views, he sat under Delitzsch, Luthardt, Kahnis, and Frank. Under these German scholars, Torrey rejected their liberalism and moved gradually back towards a conservative camp. He also chose at this time to follow Palmer, Finney, and Moody and become a teetotaler. When he returned to America, Torrey accepted a position at a poor Minneapolis parish instead of a wealthier Boston one. As a result of this decision, Torrey grew ever closer to Moody

13. Davis, "Dr. R. A. Torrey," 3.

and eventually became his successor. A revival occurred in Minneapolis and Torrey's small congregation grew. He also took on additional philanthropic duties, but like Moody, he grew tired of his administrative tasks. He was called to be a preacher, not a paper-pusher.

Surprisingly it was this conviction that led Torrey to become the superintendent at Moody's new Bible school in 1889. Four years later, Moody's Chicago Avenue Church was vacant and Torrey became its pastor, succeeding Moody both in his school and congregation. During Moody's 1893 World's Fair campaign Torrey served as Moody's right hand man. When Moody reluctantly turned down preaching the rest of his proposed nights in Kansas City before his death, Torrey was telegraphed to continue in his stead. Later that same year when Moody died, Torrey took over as the president of the Moody Bible Institute. In 1912 Torrey left Chicago and founded the Bible Institute of Los Angeles (BIOLA). Just as Pentecostalism took root at Azusa Street, it was from LA that fundamentalism officially began, though fundamentalism did not begin with a revival but with the four volume publication of *The Fundamentals*, in 1917. Torrey died in Asheville, North Carolina on October 26, 1928.

Moody was fairly vague with his opinion concerning the "Baptism with the Holy Spirit" that was extremely popular in the Pentecostal West. Torrey was not. He declared that what was taking place in Topeka and Azusa Street was "emphatically not of God." Not to be outdone, H.A. Ironside, an evangelical preacher, decried Pentecostalism as "disgusting . . . delusions and insanities"[14] in 1912. The polarization occurring within the Holiness movement was never more pronounced than when BIOLA was founded about twenty-five miles away from the Azusa street revival. Moody may not have needed to voice his opinion about Irwin, Parham, and Seymour, but Torrey had little choice. Fundamentalists following Torrey were compelled to condemn not only Pentecostal leaders but its central practice of glossolalia. Speaking in tongues, if genuine, gives evidence to a miraculous change occurring in the church. These remarkable claims, left unchecked, characterize Holiness as chaos. Glossolalia may be approved only in remarkable circumstances, but cannot be expected for every believer or as an essential part of any church service. Conservative attacks against this blessing of the Holy Spirit identify the language as gibberish rather than a real gift of tongues, illegible when written and incomprehensible when spoken to all present. This critique maintains that the tongues used as evidence of a spiritual baptism do not conform to their biblical counterparts,

14. Synan, *Holiness-Pentecostal Tradition*, 146.

since they are not orderly, nor are they properly interpreted, as dictated by 1 Corinthians 14:27.[15]

Torrey's rejection of biblical criticism resonated with the Holiness movement. Both the radical and conservative wings of the Holiness movement looked to the Bible as the source of revelation and the authority for life. As the Pentecostals emerged, they began placing greater emphasis on the role of the Holy Spirit in the lives of Christians, but the conservative Holiness rejected any authority beyond the scriptures themselves. As the Bible was the last remnant of authority, any measures to contextualize or challenge scripture necessarily were rejected. Unlike Schleiermacher and those who followed his liberalization program of reading the Bible, the fundamentalists believed the Bible to be in its current construction since the first century. Basic questions concerning authorship of texts and even the formation of the canon were quickly dismissed as either irrelevant or delivered by the Holy Spirit to the early Church, despite the councils and Church Fathers, not because of them. The entire first volume of *The Fundamentals*, and half of the second volume, are dedicated to combating biblical criticism. It is only at the beginning of the second half of volume two, as well as volumes three and four, which actually address doctrines that the fundamentalists believed were crucial to the Christian life. It should be noted that the Protestant construction of the Bible without the Deuterocanonical texts was maintained. The fundamentalists, following Perkins, applied a whole set of techniques to dismiss any books found in the Catholic or Orthodox canons.

An early fundamentalist leader J. Gresham Machen (d. 1937) spelled out the difficulty of any type of liberalism in 1923. Machen argued that the battle between fundamentalism, which he equated with Christianity, and the modern world, was a conflict for the very souls of everyone. Machen believed that modernism was itself a competitive religion, a religion that used traditional Christian terminology and promised redemption in this world. This new religion of liberal modernism used Christian language but applied this to naturalism "that is, in the denial of any entrance of the creative power of God."[16] Machen characterizes modernism as a false gospel that speaks like a Christian but has the heart of a deist, a Unitarian, or an atheist. According to Machen, the chief rival of Christianity for the soul of the modern world is liberalism. He argues that "An examination of the teachings of liberalism in comparison with those of Christianity will

---

15. "If anyone speaks in a tongue, let there be two or at the most three, each in turn, and let one interpret" (1 Cor 14:27).

16. Machen, *Christianity and Liberalism*, 2.

show that at every point the two movements are in direct opposition. That examination will now be undertaken, though merely in a summary and cursory way."[17]

In addition to the already acknowledged conflict concerning biblical criticism, there are primarily three areas that liberalism and fundamentalism collided in, science, economics, and the formation of doctrine. By the early twentieth century, liberalism grew beyond the confines of Schleiermacher, as his liberalism only briefly addressed science and did not touch upon economics. Machen maintains that liberalism is the anti-scientific movement. Rather than combating science, Machen and the fundamentalists combat the application of science and the conclusions that are against the Bible or the world view of the fundamentalist. When faith and science collide, this only points to the inherent flaws in a system of reason based in liberalism and an attempt to rationalize a sinful existence that does not take in mind the grandeur of God or God's creation. Twentieth-century fundamentalists attempt to strike a middle ground with science, along the lines of Spener. The natural phenomena of the universe are not inherently signs of prosperity or doom, but they are created to glorify God. When the signs fail to do so science is incomplete.

The discussion of economics and materialism is used as an example of the willful ignorance present within the liberal ideology. The great economic evil in the 1920s, according to Machen, is socialism. In an odd twist, the Holiness movement that grew as a religious form of Populism now combats the prevailing economic concerns of Populism. Fundamentalism rejected any economic form that restricts choice. Freedom of choice and individual liberty are essential traits to the fundamentalist world view. The apparent contradiction addressing freedom concerning moral issues is glaring.

The fundamentalist has conflicting motivations when it comes to overall freedom. Freedom is necessary to allow people the ability to sin or reject sin and embrace Christ. This concern for freedom is found within Palmer and Wesley as well. Both argued for Christian perfection, but wanted to maintain room for free will. In trying to square that circle their declarations did not always coincide with the definitions of their doctrines. While individuals must be free to make the decision on their own, obvious temptations should be removed in order to ease the sinner's choice towards redemption in Christ. This, along with the shift towards moralism in the nineteenth century, provide the justification in legally prohibiting things like alcohol. In the sphere of economics, the sinful actions perpetuated by greedy corporations or business owners must be condemned, as Moody

17. Machen, *Christianity and Liberalism*, 53.

did, but not made illegal. In volume four of *The Fundamentals*, socialism is warned against, and Charles Erdman who wrote the section, was deeply concerned about the identification of socialism with Christianity. His main concern was the reduction of Christianity to an economic system rather than a spiritual one. Erdman does allow freedom on the issue, urging churches to allow for its members to choose which economic systems they believe are most beneficial. "The church leaves its members free to adopt or reject socialism as they may deem wise."[18]

While Erdman allows churches freedom on economic theory, Machen does not. Socialism is a cure worse than the disease. Machen argues that limiting economic choice through "materialist paternalism. . . will rapidly make of America one huge 'Main Street,' where spiritual adventure will be discouraged and democracy, will be regarded as consisting in the reduction of all mankind to the proportions of the narrowest and least gifted of the citizens."[19] Machen believes that limited economic freedom will actually increase materialism in addition to reducing liberty. In many ways Machen agrees with Marx, that it is a great sin to reduce someone to a commodity, the difference is that Machen believes that socialism does this rather than capitalism.

Liberalism also conflicts with fundamentalism over the issues concerning the formation of doctrine. Here Machen directly addresses the proposals of Schleiermacher's liberalism. Machen roundly rejects that Christian doctrine is an expression of Christian experience. Rather, following Perkin's interpretation of scripture, Machen maintains that Christian doctrine is simply a reflection on the unchanging word of God, the Bible. Doctrines concerning sin, the incarnation, atonement, grace, faith, regeneration, and others are all simply present in scripture for any to accept. *The Fundamentals* address each of these issues in detail, roundly rejecting any other view proposed as preposterous. While the authors of *The Fundamentals* and fundamentalists all believe doctrine is clear from the Bible without need of any interpreting body except the Holy Spirit, arguments over doctrine are apparent and inevitable.

With the construction of *The Fundamentals*, conservative Holiness launches a theological attack against Pentecostals, other Protestants, and Catholics in a way that was noticeably absent from the Holiness luminaries which preceded them in the nineteenth century. It is worth noting that both Finney and Moody were not reflexively anti-Catholic like Palmer was. Both men recount different events when they encountered Catholics and

18. Erdman, "Church and Socialism," 100.
19. Machen, *Christianity and Liberalism*, 14–15.

even learned issues of the faith from them. Palmer was a radical exception and possessed the anti-Catholic vehemence that was so widely popular, but Moody and Finney were more open to the possibility that a Catholic could be numbered among the redeemed. In volume three of *The Fundamentals*, T.W. Medhurst answers the question "is Romanism Christianity?" The answer given by Medhurst is a resounding no. Medhurst takes the polemics of Perkins and Spener, and advances past their anti-Catholic rhetoric. Medhurst defined Christianity as consisting in "The Bible, the whole Bible, nothing but the Bible," and "Romanism denies all this; and therefore Romanism is not Christianity." Medhurst continues his polemic by asserting that Catholics acceptance of councils and creeds is a de facto rejection of the Bible, that "Romanism teaches men to hate,"[20] and furthermore that the Mass puts Christ to death every time it is offered, contrary to Scripture, which attests Christ died once and for all. Medhurst continues his condemnation of Catholics, contending that the Catholic Church is in error on issues of justification, and the institution of the papacy and bishops is the work of Satan. Machen is a little more kind to Catholics than Medhurst, arguing "The Church of Rome may represent a perversion of the Christian religion; but naturalistic liberalism is not Christianity at all."[21]

The causes and definitions of fundamentalism remain a hot topic. Very few scholars are able to agree upon the best way to describe the movement. One common theme within the views of Richard Antoun, Martin Riesebrodt, and Malise Ruthven is that fundamentalism is a movement that emerged out of the crisis of modernity. Modernity is in such a crisis because the shift away from traditional social relations outpaced the conventional understanding about what should be expected in life. The dawn of the twentieth century is usually depicted as an era of radical transformation, and fundamentalism provides an answer to those dissatisfied with this metamorphosis. While many of these statements are true, the shifts in nineteenth-century American religious life, especially with the growth of the Holiness movement are overlooked or minimized. Furthermore, many of the challenges in defining the origins of fundamentalism as a distinct movement are hampered when historical analysis is applied to earlier periods of Christian life. Seventeenth and eighteenth-century Pietism easily fit many of the definitions of fundamentalism. This includes Antoun's assertions that fundamentalists "see themselves as the true believers and the proponents of official religion as hypocrites who advance a superfluous

20. Medhurst, "Is Romanism Christianity?," 291–92.
21. Machen, *Christianity and Liberalism*, 52.

brand of religion and use it for their own purposes."[22] Pietism also resembles fundamentalism with Riesebrodt's conception that "society is in severe crisis, for which there is but one solution: a return to the principles of the divine order once practiced in the original community, whose laws have been handed down in writing."[23] Furthermore, a similarity can be found with Ruthven's belief that fundamentalism is essentially "a religious way of being that manifests itself in a strategy by which beleaguered believers attempt to preserve their distinctive identity as people or group in the face of modernity and secularization."[24]

The difficulty with defining fundamentalism as a distinct movement, rather than understanding that Protestant fundamentalism emerged out of a long and complicated history, is the challenging relationship between the desires of a traditionalist and the fundamentalist. While there is certainly a large degree of overlap, a traditionalist is not the same thing as a fundamentalist. Many traditionalists in America and Europe were opposed to the drastic changes occurring in their countries, but would not have lent their support to fundamentalists. Other traditionalists opposed the radical nature of the Holiness movement and may have supported elements of Schleiermacher's liberalism as lining up with a more traditional understanding of doctrine formation than Machen and other fundamentalists would. In fact, it is often the fundamentalists that opposed the traditionalists, who were seen as becoming too liberal in the beginning of the twentieth century.

A further complication arises when not all conservative Holiness members subscribe to *The Fundamentals*. Just as there were different types of Pentecostals, there are also different types of conservative Holiness churches, and not all are fundamentalists. Many of the conservatives preferred the term evangelical, since they opposed both the extreme theological positions of fundamentalists and the charismatic elements of Pentecostals. In 1978 this division was made all the more clear when the fundamentalists affirmed the "Chicago Statement on Biblical Inerrancy" against the evangelicals. In a series of twenty-five articles, the fundamentalists affirmed and denied specific doctrines concerning the Bible. This included Article one, which affirmed that "the Holy Scriptures are to be received as the authoritative Word of God," and denied "that the Scriptures receive their authority from the Church, tradition, or any other human source."[25] The further articles

22. Antoun, *Understanding Fundamentalism*, 92.

23. Riesebrodt, *Pious Passion*, 47.

24. Ruthven, *Fundamentalism*, 8.

25. Hankins, *Evangelicalism and Fundamentalism*, 21.

articulated that the entire Bible is literally true, including Genesis creation accounts, and that creeds and councils have authority on a similar level to the Bible.

Evangelicals and fundamentalists often share churches and literature though. One common tract issued by evangelicals is Bill Bright's *Four Spiritual Laws*. Bright posits that just as there are laws of nature, there are spiritual laws as well. These laws begin with "God loves you and offers a wonderful plan for your life,"[26] then move to sin causing separation, Christ's death as the only provision for man's sin, and everyone individually receiving Christ to experience God's love and plan for their lives. Both the evangelicals and fundamentalists still focus within these laws on experiencing God rather than scholasticism and reason. Evangelicals even published a popular book with corresponding devotionals, under the title *Experiencing God*, illustrating the priority that experience still holds.[27] While Fundamentalists often oppose their Pentecostal counterparts, both have their origins in Palmer's conception of Holiness. It was only the fragmentary growth of Protestantism that produced the disparate movements.

NEO-ORTHODOXY

"Within the Bible there is a strange new world, the world of God."[28]
—Karl Barth

Fundamentalism was not the only resistance to Schleiermacher or modern liberalism. Neo-orthodoxy joined the chorus voicing their dissent. As the twentieth century began, the Protestant position was unclear. In America, the Holiness movement had grown to the point that most Protestants were connected to or reacting against some strain of the movement. The churches that refused to accept Holiness were wrapped up in liberalism or trying to find a way to survive in an untenable climate. In Europe things fared slightly better, but liberalism dominated most mainline denominations and any appeal to traditionalism seemed lacking. The answer for many Protestants was to return to the basic themes of the Reformation. This was the attempt of neo-orthodoxy.

Schleiermacher had succeeded in redefining Christianity. This work preserved Protestantism through the nineteenth century by focusing the attention onto humanity and the human response to God. This allowed

26. Bright, *Four Spiritual Laws*.
27. Blackaby, *Experiencing God*.
28. Barth, *Word of God*, 33.

Christians to find God by looking within. When the First World War began, the optimism of looking within faded. Neo-orthodoxy answered by shifting the focus back onto God. God's transcendence was now far more important that God's imminence. As God is beyond human understanding, cultures become largely irrelevant, not to the person, but to Christianity. Human aspirations and constructions are only valuable to themselves. God, and therefore Christianity, remains above culture and above the individual. Schleiermacher's answer that God is found in feeling was combated by once again looking at the fall and the pervasive power of sin in the world. Individuals and their feelings are corrupted, therefore relying upon a feeling, any feeling, including those of absolute dependence is suspect. Furthermore, since God is transcendent and utterly different from humanity, human feelings cannot be the fount for this encounter, it must be God.

Neo-orthodoxy also has an interesting response to religion in general. Karl Barth posits that "Religion is never and nowhere true as such and in itself." True religion contains both knowledge and worship of God and everywhere this is rejected. Due to the fall, humanity is incapable of fully approaching God, therefore any effort at approaching God is incomplete, only partially true, or false. God is the only truth, and besides this, "No religion *is* true. A Religion can only *become* true." This is the divine hope. God can justify sinful humanity and cleanse religion, but only from without. The essence of a religion can be remade, and made into a religion that worships God. The same applies to individuals as to religions; it is only from outside that they can be cleansed and made into a right relationship with God. This is through God's grace. Still it is maintained that "We must not hesitate to state that *the Christian religion is the true religion*."[29]

The answer proposed by the neo-orthodox mirrors the fundamental response, to look at the Christian scriptures to find God and God's grace. It is only here that religion can be found true. Like the Reformation teachers proclaimed, it is the scriptures that give the answers to dilemmas of this world. The Bible itself does not automatically give the answers like the fundamentalists assume. The neo-orthodox accept a degree of liberalism while struggling against it. The Bible left alone is simply a text like other texts. It becomes something wholly different when read by a Christian. When the Bible is encountered in faith it becomes the Word of God. The person reading it does not make the change, rather God does. God chooses to speak in scripture to God's creation. Barth argues that "The Bible tells us now how we should talk with God but what he says to us; not how we find the way to him, but how he has sought and found the way to us; not the right

29. Barth, *On Religion*, 85.

relation in which we must place ourselves to him, but the covenant which he has made with all who are Abraham's spiritual children and which he has sealed once and for all in Jesus Christ."[30] Reading scripture is always from God to the Christian.

This view is not terribly different than what Perkins said in *The Art of Prophesy*, or what Francke said in *Guide to the Reading and Study of the Holy Scripture*. Both maintained that different hearts would receive the words of scripture differently. For Perkins scripture only truly spoke if the one reading it was one of the elect. For Francke it was largely dependent upon the preparation of the heart. If the man or woman was impious then God would not speak. If they approached the word with an open heart God would hear their prayers and answer them accordingly.

It was primarily this view of the Bible that brought fundamentalist condemnation upon neo-orthodoxy. Charles Calwell Ryie argues, "It has been hailed as the new or neoorthodoxy; in reality it is nothing but a false or pseudoorthodoxy."[31] Ryie's criticism sounds very familiar to Machen's criticism of liberalism, namely that neo-orthodoxy takes on the form and language of Christianity but lacks the substance behind it. Since the Bible only becomes the word of God when approached in faith, it remains fallible and without inherent authority. For the fundamentalists this is not the Bible.

There are several voices that stand above all others in the neo-orthodox world. Without contradiction, the first and loudest voice is from Karl Barth, who deserves the title the father of neo-orthodoxy. Others contributed as well in America, the Niebuhrs, Reinhold and Richard were the loudest voices and in Europe, Emil Brunner and to a lesser extent Rudolf Bultmann. Barth's contribution to neo-orthodoxy was not only shaped by his understanding of the Bible but also his understanding of Schleiermacher.

The admiration Barth had for Schleiermacher cannot be understated, and several stories circulate about his admiration of the nineteenth-century theologian. The first is told by Barth himself. Barth often told stories that when he reached the kingdom of heaven, the first person, after Mozart, than he wished to converse with was Schleiermacher. One should assume that since this is a heavenly encounter, he was not planning on chastising him. The second narrative is told by Richard Niebuhr, who described an encounter he had when he visited Barth after writing his book on Schleiermacher. Barth's home contained a staircase that rose to the living quarters. Along the staircase there were pictures hung of great theologians, with Kant and Schleiermacher on one side and others following. Niebuhr dared to ask

---

30. Barth, *Word of God,* 43.
31. Ryie, *Neo-Orthodoxy,* 6.

Barth if the pictures were in ascending or descending order. Barth's response was in descending order, because after Kant and Schleiermacher things got steadily worse.

These two stories paint a picture of Barth as an admirer of Schleiermacher that is not always evidenced in his writings. Schleiermacher remained the starting point for Barth's theology, often as the whipping boy and foil, but he always began with Schleiermacher. Barth is as much an inheritor of Schleiermacher as Tillich is, though he rejected this inheritance. This is understood through a third story concerning Barth and Schleiermacher. The story goes that Barth kept a bust of Schleiermacher on his desk to remind him what a true theologian was and what he had to overcome with creating his own theology. While this story is likely apocryphal, it demonstrates Barth's connection to Schleiermacher and how deeply indebted he and neo-orthodoxy are to Schleiermacher's liberalism. Neo-orthodoxy is as much a product of liberalism as neo-liberalism is. It is an ironic twist of fate that Barth became the last word on Schleiermacher for decades and it is only after Barth's voice began to fade that Schleiermacher was approached again.

Barth's critique of Schleiermacher begins with Schleiermacher's stated aims. Schleiermacher wanted to be both a Christian and a modern man. These two ideas were antithetical to Barth, who lived in the modern world but was never at home in it. Barth maintains that the world must be freely and wholly rejected. If the world is valued, it changes the fundamental relationship between God and the world. The world must begin as fallen or at the very least other than God. Barth launches two very pointed critiques at Schleiermacher. The first, published in 1922, was entitled *The Word of God and the Word of Man*. The second is a more restrained criticism, in his work *The Theology of Schleiermacher*, specifically the postscript.

In *The Word of God and the Word of Man*, Barth lists the teachers in his spiritual ancestral line. It contains Kierkegaard, Luther, Calvin, Paul, and Jeremiah. Barth considers adding Melanchthon to this list, but he pronounces, "I might explicitly point out that this ancestral line—which I commend to you—does *not include Schleiermacher.*" Not only does Barth leave Schleiermacher off his list to the surprise of his readers, but he then points out why he is leaving Schleiermacher off. Schleiermacher is not considered a good teacher in theology because "he is disastrously dim-sighted in regard to the fact that man as man is not only in *need* but beyond all hope of saving himself; that the whole of so-called religion, and not least the Christian religion, *shares* in this need; and that one can *not* speak of God simply by speaking of man in a loud voice."[32] The fundamental difference between Barth and Schleiermacher is the condition of man. Barth believes that Schleiermacher never fully possessed a clear and direct apprehension of the truth. This truth is that man is made to serve *God* and not God to serve man. Largely the difference is perspective but the perspective for Barth is everything. It is also worth noting that Barth's view of Schleiermacher came from his theology teacher Wilhelm Herrmann, who as we already addressed, put his own spin on Schleiermacher. It was from this perspective on Schleiermacher that Barth records that "I absorbed Herrmann through every pore."[33] Herrmann and his view of Schleiermacher created the liberalism that neo-orthodoxy initially rejected. A closer reading of Barth's work points out that he rejected Herrmann far more than Schleiermacher.

Later in *The Word of God and the Word of Man,* Barth reasons that Schleiermacher diminishes Jesus by failing to give adequate attention to the absolute miracle of the Bible, namely the resurrection. As stated earlier, Schleiermacher's focus was on the incarnation. For him, once God became human nothing else mattered. If he lived an hour or a thousand years, rose from the dead or not, it did not matter to Schleiermacher. That God would condescend was a radical change in the relationship between the creator of the universe and the creation. Christ's death and resurrection only illustrates that Christ was God rather than changing the new relationship that began at the Nativity or possibly the Annunciation.

In *The Theology of Schleiermacher,* Barth references Schleiermacher as "my old friend and enemy, Schleiermacher!"[34] Barth's later work is more reflexive on the adversarial relationship he had with Schleiermacher. He laments his abrasive tone in his first edition of *the Epistle to the Romans.* He also admits that "in my holy zeal at that time I did not really do justice to pietism."[35] Both Pietism and Schleiermacher are condemned based on their worst traits in Barth's eyes. Barth also reexamines the benefits of Schleiermacher's approach. While still rejecting humanity as the starting point, he realizes that taking human nature in its totality has merit. Apparently he was not able to fully overcome Schleiermacher and remained a true admirer. For Barth, and as such for neo-orthodoxy, Schleiermacher was always at the forefront of his mind. His name loomed like a specter throughout his works, sprinkled in as either the hero or the villain and more often the latter.

32. Barth, *Word of God,* 195–96.
33. Webster, *Cambridge Companion to Karl Barth,* 2.
34. Barth, *Theology of Schleiermacher,* 269.
35. Barth, *Theology of Schleiermacher,* 262.

VII

Conclusion

"I propose, therefore, to take a new look at Protestant theology in the nineteenth century."[1]

—*Claude Welch*

OUR STUDY BEGAN WITH Friedrich Schleiermacher, and overcame the myopic common to nineteenth century Protestant Christianity by including Phoebe Palmer. When treated together, the father of modern liberal Protestantism and the mother of the Holiness movement provided not only a new look as Welch advocated in the 1970s, but a comprehensive picture of the religious landscape which gripped the long nineteenth century. Now we must conclude by briefly revisiting the lives of two theologians in addition to the diverse movements which they launched.

Schleiermacher and Palmer not only share a common Pietistic heritage, but similar family lives. Both grew up fairly wealthy, and inherited their faith from their fathers. Their fathers each had their own distinct conversion experience and moments of shame that scarred their relationship with God and spurred them to instill a sincere piety in their children. Schleiermacher's and Palmer's fathers both fell into Enlightenment traps. Both lived at especially trying times in their countries' histories and were followed by a gilded if not golden age. Personally both Palmer and Schleiermacher lacked faith during adolescence. Schleiermacher temporarily turned his back on the faith of his father and Palmer's fear of her own salvation isolated her from her God. Each experienced a second conversion, though Palmer never had a first, and each of them viewed the idea of a second conversion as something

1. Welch, *Protestant Thought*, 2.

fundamentally different. The basic construction of their lives were rather similar and not terribly atypical from religious leaders of any age. What bound them together was not the events of their lives or the lives of the fathers as much as the expectation that they could and would understand God first and foremost through experience. What this experience was and what the catalyst would be was unique, as every life is, but the expectation was key. Through this expectation they understood their place in the cosmos and planned on fulfilling God's mission for them.

Palmer and Schleiermacher share a Pietist background, but not a similar confessional identity. Palmer's commitment to Wesley and Wesley's Episcopal Methodism is unmatched in nineteenth-century America. Schleiermacher came from a long line of Reform preachers and continued within that tradition. Their confession and commitment to confessional identity differed, but both are Pietists who could trace the source of their theology at least to Zinzendorf, Francke, Spener, and Arndt.

The nineteenth century was one of great political change and the partisan tensions of the age were played out between Schleiermacher and Palmer and their respective countries. They naturally viewed the ideal political form of a nation to be radically different as well. Schleiermacher supported a liberal politics while living in a monarchist system. Palmer viewed nearly all political involvement with disdain. Yet her outlook was distinctly American, paying little regard to royalty, as seen in her correspondence to Queen Victoria. Stylistically they differed as well. Schleiermacher and Palmer both wrote, but the pulpit was their primary vehicle for conveying their message. For Schleiermacher, who was ordained, this was his vocation, associated with shepherding his various flocks. He also had to make sure that whatever he wrote or preached would make it past his overseers, both civil and ecclesial. Palmer, as a woman, both advocated for female ordination and discounted the very notion of ordination as a necessary instrument to bring people to God. She also never directly shepherded anyone. Her encounters were always indirect, through revivals, publications, and group discussion at her Tuesday Meeting. Palmer also lacked any real oversight to her ministry. If there ever became a problem with her message she could disregard it and move along, though no such case is recorded.

Theologically they would have disagreed with one another as well. Schleiermacher often spoke poorly about the "twice born." He was not opposed to conversion experiences; rather he was opposed to the idea that a subsequent birth was a completed act of sanctification. This of course was the central point of Palmer's Altar Theology. Palmer was equally dismissive with notions of universal salvation, which Schleiermacher's theology implied. Schleiermacher lent his support for universal salvation when he interpreted humanity rather than individual men and women as the elect in Christ. Palmer would have also opposed Schleiermacher's theology based upon feeling. She was always opposed to trusting feelings as the cause or justification for a religious experience. Schleiermacher's feeling of absolute dependence was anathema to Palmer, who continually argued that feelings are a product of faith rather than faith themselves.

The value of philosophy would also remain a point of contention. Palmer gives no credence to understanding classical Greek philosophy. Her life and her works focused on personal devotions rather than philosophical speculation. Schleiermacher's theology was deeply connected to his understanding of philosophy. Not only was it Kant who first challenged his theology, but he also worked tirelessly on translating the works of Plato into German. It should come as no surprise that Schleiermacher viewed Christianity in relation to secular philosophy rather than the testimonies of converts as Palmer did. The same division exists when addressing biblical criticism. Schleiermacher's contribution to the field is scandalous in Palmer's eyes, who viewed scripture with unwavering devotion.

Their differences, while extensive, are rivaled only by the many points of continuity. The greatest area of agreement they had was on the position of the church. Though they each had a different denomination and a different church they called home, each believed that the church should be independent of the state. Schleiermacher opposed involvement of the crown, believing that it hampered the gospel. Palmer believed that political apparatus of America, and indeed all countries, was a pale shadow of God's vision for the church. Within the church both valued the laity as well. Palmer's entire vocation was a laity led revival movement. Schleiermacher believed the doctrine of the priesthood of all believers and held that all Christians offer the word to one another.

The actual form of the church was also something held in common. Both opposed opulence. While Schleiermacher never advocated for the four bare walls and a sermon motif that many Reform preachers did, he insisted that a physical church serve its people and this often included forgoing beautiful ornamentation. Palmer often criticized the extravagance of many churches, especially when she visited Europe, believing that it aided no one in their path towards salvation.

In many ways their signature theological contributions were also essentially the same, though expressed from a different vantage point. Phoebe's Altar Theology and Schleiermacher's feeling of utter dependence both appeared to be easy expressions of faith, but were in fact difficult tasks that they expected the Christian to undertake. Palmer's Altar Theology, while in part an instantaneous decision to live a perfect sanctified life, was something that could be lost, as Wesley argued. As much as a declaration of accomplishment coincided with this new birth, the newly sanctified Christian had the duty to remain upon the altar. Remaining on the altar of Christ requires constant vigilance. The same can be said of Schleiermacher's feeling of utter dependence. This sentiment is not a whimsical fleeting emotion, rather a feeling that consumes the person entirely. It consumes the Christian so much, they are dependent upon the source of the feeling, namely God. Remaining in a state of complete dependency requires great attention and a promethean effort that would even make Francke proud.

The final point of agreement between our nineteenth-century Pietists was their contribution to ethics. Schleiermacher wrote extensively about what a Christian ethic is to be. He did this not only in his sermons but also with his philosophical works. Palmer did the same thing, though without the philosophical construct surrounding her ethics. For Palmer the call to Holiness was a call to holy living, so much so that it became nearly synonymous with the temperance movement. Schleiermacher's consumption of alcohol would be scandalous to Palmer, but the belief that the Christian life was necessarily a pious ethical life is something they all shared.

INTERDENOMINATIONAL MOVEMENT AND THE LASTING LEGACY OF SCHLEIERMACHER AND PALMER

"Pietism represents the working out of a series of unresolved issues that the Reformation bequeathed to later generations of Protestants."[2]

—*Jonathan Strom*

Finally both were central to the ecumenical movement as well. Palmer's Holiness was entirely ecumenical, consisting of Methodists, Baptists, and Presbyterians. Schleiermacher advocated for a church union between Reform and Lutherans and developed the concept of the visible and invisible church. The members of the invisible church were not only Reform, but all Christians, and to an extent all people who have been redeemed. The ecumenical spirit of Schleiermacher potentially includes Catholics, a position from which Palmer balked.

The process of confessionalization seems to have come to an end with the nineteenth century. What was so important to many Protestant leaders at the dawn of the Reformation seemed to account for little to most people

2. Strom, "Common Priesthood," 42.

a few centuries later. The lines which separated Lutheran from Reform and Anglican were muted by a new trend in theology which worked within denominations and outside of them. The disregard for denominational fidelity that both Palmer and Schleiermacher possessed help launch interdenominational dialogue. For this dialogue the most important thing was how one chose to approach God; experience overtook rationalism or scholastic theology. This is why the theological debates between these three dominant magisterial branches, and the subsequent denominations which splintered off of these three, counted for little. Following Schleiermacher and Palmer, an experience of God took priority, and this experience crossed denominational lines. As stated in chapters one and two, Schleiermacher sought union between the Reform and Lutheran Churches in Germany, believing that many of the initial theological arguments which fueled the division were lost on the public, and even many of the church leaders. As addressed in chapters three and four, Palmer disregarded the divisions when she opened her Tuesday Meetings to all who wished to attend, regardless of confessional identity.

While the processes of confessionalization may have come to a close in the nineteenth century and the interdenominational spirit grew, this should not be interpreted as a point of peace and harmony amongst Protestants. Inter-denominationalism also could not agree with itself. The lines which separate may have been minimized by Schleiermacher, Palmer, and others including Finney and Moody, but new lines were erected and new divisions occurred. Confessional identity was truncated and the idea of becoming non-denominational only weakened the bond between member churches. With weaker ecclesial bodies divisions became easier. This included not only divisions within denominations but also amongst individual churches. Today the number of denominations and sub-denominations is striking. The evolution of interdenominationalism in America is most clearly evidenced with the treatment of Holiness. In America the division between Methodist, Presbyterian, and Baptist was eroded only to see those who advocated for Holiness kicked out of the denomination and the newly formed Holiness churches splitting again between a more conservative and liberal understanding of the doctrine.

While anyone who argues that interdenominationalism was a success has their work cut out for them, the same could be said when one tries to comprehend the impact of Schleiermacher and Palmer upon the broader Protestant world. The many differences between these two spiritual giants largely outweigh their similarities and the same could be said of their legacies. Indeed it would be very easy to simply respond that these legacies do not agree with one another, but in actuality these very different ideologies largely do in principle agree with one another. Holiness, liberalism, neo-liberals, neo-orthodox, Pentecostals, and fundamentalists all share a basic world view. All of them anticipate their ultimate cause lies in a God who still encounters them on a fairly regular basis. The history, as well as the other contributors to Holiness and liberalism, delivered these divergent systems.

Palmer's contribution to the Holiness movement, combined with Finney, produced the groundwork for Parham, Seymour, and Pentecostalism at the dawn of the twentieth century. When Palmer's Holiness is combined with Moody and Torrey, fundamentalism emerges. Both strands of the Holiness movement are direct inheritors of Palmer's Altar Theology and her interpretation of Wesley's Christian perfection. In many ways these conservative trends are the mirror image of their more liberal counterparts as addressed in the previous two chapters. Schleiermacher's liberalism produced Barth's neo-orthodoxy in response, as well as Tillich's neo-liberalism, in addition to the myriads of nineteenth-century liberal scholars, such as Ritschl and Herrmann, who advanced Schleiermacher's program further than he would have anticipated and likely in directions that needed a corrective, one that both Barth and Tillich offered. The different systems emerge partly due to who joins the chorus with Schleiermacher or Palmer, but their notes are distinctive and necessary for the chord to be played.

What Jonathan Strom says of Pietism remained true into the nineteenth century. The unresolved issues of the Reformation needed to be decided, especially given the shifting conflicts within the modern world. While earlier experiential Protestants redirected their denominations away from scholastic dogma and rationalism, it was Palmer and Schleiermacher who created new systems which broke outside of denominational lines. Their contributions to nineteenth century theology forever changed all Protestant responses. By the beginning of the twentieth century there were no mute voices on the legacy of Schleiermacher and Palmer, even if their names were forgotten or relegated to a footnote within these larger systems. Liberalism, Holiness, and interdenominationalism were just a few of the attempts to come to grips with the shifting religious landscape of the nineteenth century. By the dawn of the twentieth century, the influence of Schleiermacher and Palmer included neo-liberals, neo-orthodox, Pentecostals, and fundamentalists. Each of these were different voices who tried to address the unresolved issues not only of the Reformation but of Protestant Christianity in the modern world, voices that resembled in part their founders. Palmer and Schleiermacher inherited a Pietist faith from their fathers and reworked experiential Christianity, giving credence to what came before it and preparing Christianity to address the challenges of modernity. As a result, Schleiermacher and Palmer became the father and mother of the modern Protestant mindset.

Bibliography

Ahlstrom, Sydney E. *A Religious History of the American People.* 2nd ed. New Haven: Yale University Press, 2004.

Angela of Foligno. *Complete Works.* Edited by Paul Lachance. Classics of Western Spirituality. Mahwah, NJ: Paulist, 1993.

Antoun, Richard T. *Understanding Fundamentalism.* 2nd ed. Lanham, MD: Rowman & Littlefield, 2008.

Balmer, Randall. *Mine Eyes Have Seen the Glory: A Journey into the Evangelical Subculture in America.* Oxford: Oxford University Press, 2006.

Barth, Karl. *The Epistle to the Romans.* London: Oxford University Press, 1968.

————. *On Religion: The Revelation of God as the Sublimation of Religion.* London: T&T Clark, 2006.

————. *Protestant Theology in the Nineteenth Century.* Grand Rapids: Eerdmans, 1972.

————. *The Theology of Schleiermacher.* Grand Rapids: Eerdmans, 1982.

————. *The Word of God and the Word of Man.* Gloucester, MA: Peter Smith, 1978.

Becker, George. "Pietism's Confrontation with Enlightenment Rationalism: An Examination of the Relation between Ascetic Protestantism and Science." *Journal for the Scientific Study of Religion* 30.2 (1991) 139–58.

Behrens, Georg. "The Order of Nature in Pious Self-Consciousness: Schleiermacher's Apologetic Argument." *Religious Studies* 32.1 (1996) 93–108.

Belmonte, Kevin. *D. L. Moody—A Life: Innovator, Evangelist, World-Changer.* Chicago: Moody, 2014.

Berger, Peter L. *The Sacred Canopy: Elements of a Sociological Theory of Religion.* New York: Anchor, 1990.

Birdsall, Richard D. "The Second Great Awakening and the New England Social Order." *Church History* 39.3 (1970) 345–64.

Bizzell, Patricia. "Frances Willard, Phoebe Palmer, and the Ethos of the Methodist Woman Preacher." *Rhetoric Society Quarterly* 36.4 (2006) 377–98.

Blackaby, Henry T., and Richard Blackaby. *Experiencing God: Knowing and Doing the Will of God.* Nashville: Lifeway Christian Resources, 1990.

Blackbourn, David. *The Long Nineteenth Century.* Oxford: Oxford University Press, 1998.

Blackbourn, David, and Geoff Eley. *The Peculiarities of German History.* Oxford: Oxford University Press, 2003.

Bowie, Andrew. "The Philosophical significance of Schleiermacher's Hermeneutics." In *Cambridge Companion to Friedrich Schleiermacher*, edited by Jacqueline Marina, 73–90. Cambridge: Cambridge University Press, 2005.

Brandt, James. *All Things New Reform of Church and Society in Schleiermacher's Christian Ethics.* Louisville: Westminster John Knox, 2001.

Bratt, James D. "Religious Anti-Revivalism in Antebellum America." *Journal of the Early Republic* 24.1 (2004) 65–106.

———. "The Reorientation of American Protestantism, 1835–1845." *Church History* 67.1 (1998) 52–82.

Bright, Bill. *The Four Spiritual Laws.* Orlando: New Life, 1956.

Campbell, Debra. "Hannah Whitall Smith (1832–1911) Theology of the Mother-Hearted God." *Signs* 15.1 (1989) 79–101.

Campbell, Ted A. *Methodist Doctrine: The Essentials.* Nashville: Abingdon, 2011.

———. "The Way of Salvation and the Methodist Ethos Beyond John Wesley: A Study in Formal Consensus and Popular Reception." *The Arbury Journal* 63.1 (2008) 5–31.

Carwardine, Richard. "Methodists, Politics, and the Coming of the American Civil War." *Church History* 669.3 (2000) 578–609.

Case, Jay R. "And Ever the Twain Shall Meet: The Holiness Missionary Movement and the Birth of World Pentecostalism, 1870–1920." *Religion and American Culture: A Journal of Interpretation* 16.2 (2006) 125–60.

Chapman, Mark. "Charles Hodge's Reception of Schleiermacher." In *Schleiermacher's Influences on American Thought and Religious Life, 1835–1920*, edited by Jeffrey A. Wilcox, et al., 244–93. Vol. 1. Eugene, OR: Pickwick, 2013.

Christian, C. W. *Friedrich Schleiermacher.* Makers of the Modern Theological Mind. Waco, TX: Word, 1979.

Clark, Christopher. "Confessional Policy and the Limits of State Action: Frederick William III and the Prussian Church Union 1817–40." *The Historical Journal* 39.4 (1996) 985–1004.

———. "The Wars of Liberation in Prussian Memory: Reflections on the Memorialization of War in Early Nineteenth-Century Germany." *The Journal of Modern History* 68.3 (1996) 550–76.

Collins Winn, Christian T., et al. *The Pietist Impulse in Christianity.* Eugene, OR: Wipf and Stock, 2011.

Cott, Nancy F. "Young Women in the Second Great Awakening in New England." *Feminist Studies* 3.1/2 (1975) 15–29.

Cramer, Kevin. *The Thirty Years War & German Memory in the Nineteenth Century.* Lincoln: University of Nebraska Press, 2007.

Crapazano, Vincent. *Serving the Word: Literalism in America from the Puilpit to the Bench.* New York: New Press, 2000.

Crouter, Richard. *Friedrich Schleiermacher Between Enlightenment and Romanticism.* Cambridge, England: Cambridge Press, 2005.

———. "Hegel and Schleiermacher at Berlin: A Many-Sided Debate." *Journal of the American Academy of Religion* 48.1 (1980) 19–43.

———. "Schleiermacher and the Theology of Bourgeois Society: A Critique of the Critics." *The Journal of Religion* 66.3 (1986) 302–23.

———. "Shaping an Academic Discipline: the Brief Outline on the Study of Theology." In *Cambridge Companion to Friedrich Schleiermacher*, edited by Jacqueline Marina, 109–29. Cambridge: Cambridge University Press, 2005.

Damick, Andrew Stephen. *Orthodoxy and Heterodoxy: Exploring Belief Systems through the Lens of the Ancient Christian Faith.* Chesterton, IL: Conciliar, 2011.

Daum, Andreas W. "Wissenschaft and Knowledge." In *Germany, 1800–1870,* edited by Jonathan Sperber, 137–62. Short Oxford History of Germany. Oxford: Oxford University Press, 2004.

Davis, George T. B. "Dr. R. A. Torrey." In *Torrey and Alexander: The Story of a World-Wide Revival,* by George T. B. Davis. New York: Fleming H. Revell, 1905. https://www.wholesomewords.org/biography/btorrey6.pdf.

Dawley, Alan. *Struggles For Justice: Social Responsibility and the Liberal State.* Cambridge: Belknap Press of Harvard University Press, 1991.

Dayton, Donald W. *American Holiness Movement.* Wilmore, KY: First Fruits, 2012.

———. "Pentecostal/Charismatic Renewal and Social Change: A Western Perspective." *Transformation* 5.4 (1988) 7–13.

———. *Theological Roots of Pentecostalism.* Grand Rapids, MI: Baker Academic, 1987.

de Tocqueville, Alexis. *Democracy in America: The Complete and Unabridged Volumes I and II.* New York: Bantam Classics, 2000.

de Vries, Dawn. "Schleiermacher's 'Christmas Eve Dialogue': Bourgeois Ideology or Feminist Theology?" *The Journal of Religion* 69.2 (1989) 169–83.

de Vries, Dawn, and B. A. Gerrish. "Providence and Grace: Schleiermacher on Justification and Election." In *Cambridge Companion to Friedrich Schleiermacher,* edited by Jacqueline Marina, 189–208. Cambridge: Cambridge University Press, 2005.

Deichmann, Wendy J. "American Methodism in the Twentieth Century: Reform, Redefinition, and Renewal." In *Cambridge Companion to American Methodism,* edited by Jason E. Vickers, 97–118. Cambridge: Cambridge University Press, 2013.

Delumeau, Jean. *Catholicism between Luther & Voltaire: A New View of the Counter-Reformation.* London: Burns & Oates, 1977.

Dieter, Melvin. *The Nineteenth-Century Holiness Movement.* Vol. 4 of *Great Holiness Classics.* Edited by Melvin Dieter. Kansas City, MO: Beacon Hill, 2011.

Dole, Andrew C. *Schleiermacher on Religion and the Natural Order.* New York: Oxford University Press, 2010.

Dorsett, Lyle W. "D. L. Moody: More than an Evangelist." In *Mr. Moody and the Evangelical Tradition,* edited by Timothy George, 31–39. London: T&T Clark International, 2004.

Drummond, Andrew Landale. *German Protestantism Since Luther.* London: Epworth, 1951.

Drummond, Lewis A. "D. L. Moody and Revivalism." In *Mr. Moody and the Evangelical Tradition,* edited by Timothy George, 93–107. London: T&T Clark International, 2004.

Dumont, Louis. *German Ideology: From France to Germany and Back.* Chicago: University of Chicago Press, 1994.

Durkheim, Emile. *The Elementary Forms of Religious Life.* New York: Free Press, 1915.

Erb, Peter, ed. *The Pietists: Selected Writings.* Mahwah, NJ: Paulist, 1983.

Erdman, Charles R. "The Church and Socialism." In *The Fundamentals: A Testimony To The Truth,* edited by R.A. Torrey, 97–109. Vol. 4. Grand Rapids, MI: Baker, 2003.

Fichte, Johann Gottlieb. *Addresses to the German Nation*. Chicago: Open Court, 1922.

Finke, Roger, and Rodney Stark. "How the Upstart Sects Won America: 1776–1850." *Journal for the Scientific Study of Religion* 28.1 (1989) 27–44.

Finney, Charles G. *The Autobiography of Charles G. Finney*. Grand Rapids: Bethany, 1977.

Foner, Eric. *The New American History*. Philadelphia: Temple University Press, 1997.

Forster, Michael. "Friedrich Daniel Ernst Schleiermacher." *Stanford Encyclopedia of Philosophy*, April 17, 2002. Edited by Edward N. Zalta. http://plato.stanford.edu/archives/sum2015/entries/schleiermacher.

Francis, Russell E. "The Religious Revival of 1858 in Philadelphia." *The Pennsylvania Magazine of History and Biography* 70.1 (1946) 52–77.

Frielander, David, Friedrich Schleiermacher, and Wilhelm Abraham Teller. *A Debate of Jewish Emancipation and Christian Theology in Old Berlin*. Edited and translated by Richard Crouter and Julie Klassen. Indianapolis: Hackett, 2004.

Gaustad, Edwin, and Leigh Schmidt. *The Religious History of America: The Heart of the American Story from Colonial Times to Today*. New York: Harper One, 2004.

Gawthrop, Richard L. *Pietism and The Making of Eighteenth-Century Prussia*. Cambridge: Cambridge University Press, 1993.

George, Timothy, ed. *Mr. Moody and the Evangelical Tradition*. London: T&T Clark, 2004.

Gerrish, B. A. "The Atoning Life of Christ: Schleiermacher and John Williamson Nevin on Incarnation and Atonement." In *Schleiermacher's Influences on American Thought and Religious Life, 1835–1920*, edited by Jeffrey A. Wilcox, et al., 217–43. Vol. 1. Eugene, OR: Pickwick, 2013.

———. *A Prince of the Church: Schleiermacher and the Beginnings of Modern Theology*. Eugene, OR: Wipf and Stock, 1984.

Gibson, George M. "The Challenge of Present-Day Fundamentalism." *Journal of Bible and Religion* 12.2 (1945) 67–71.

Goethe, Johann Wolfgang von. *Goethe's Faust*. Translated by Walter Kaufman. New York: Anchor, 1961.

Goodwyn, Lawrence. *The Populist Moment: A Short History of the Agrarian Revolt in America*. Oxford: Oxford University Press, 1978.

Gundry, Stanley N. "Demythologizing Moody." In *Mr. Moody and the Evangelical Tradition*, edited by Timothy George, 13–31. London: T&T Clark International, 2004.

Gunther Brown, Candy. "Publicizing Domestic Piety: The Cultural Work of Religious Texts in the Woman's Building Library." *Libraries & Culture* 41.1 (2006) 35–54.

Habermas, Jurgen. *The Structural Transformation of the Public Sphere: An Inquiry into a Category of Bourgeois Society*. Cambridge, MA: MIT Press, 1991.

Hagan, Anette I. *Eternal Blessedness for All? A Historical-Systematic Examination of Schleiermacher's Understanding of Predestination*. Eugene, OR: Pickwick, 2013.

Hahn, Steven. *A Nation Under Our Feet: Black Political Struggles in the Rural South from Slavery to the Great Migration*. Cambridge, MA: Belknap Press of Harvard University Press, 2003.

Hambrick-Stowe, Charles E. *Charles G. Finney and the Spirit of American Evangelicalism*. Grand Rapids: Eerdmans, 1996.

Hankins, Barry, ed. *Evangelicalism and Fundamentalism: A Documentary Reader*. New York: New York University Press, 2008.

Harrington, Joel F., and Helmut Walser Smith. "Confessionalization, Community, and State Building in Germany, 1555–1870." *The Journal of Modern History* 69.1 (1997) 77–101.

Hart, D. G. "When Is a Fundamentalist a Modernist? J. Gresham Machen, Cultural Modernism, and Conservative Protestantism." *Journal of the American Academy of Religion* 65.3 (1997) 605–33.

Hatch, Nathan O. "The Puzzle of American Methodism." *Church History* 63.2 (1994) 175–89.

Heath, Elaine A. *Naked Faith: The Mystical Theology of Phoebe Palmer.* Eugene, OR: Pickwick, 2009.

Hegel, Georg Wilhelm Friedrich. *The Consummate Religion.* Vol. 3 of *Lectures on the Philosophy of Religion.* Edited by Peter C. Hodgson. Berkeley, CA: University of California Press, 1985.

Heidegger, Martin. *Being and Time.* San Francisco: Harper San Francisco, 1962.

Helmer, Christine. "Mysticism and Metaphysics: Schleiermacher and a Historical-Theological Trajectory." *The Journal of Religion* 83.4 (2003) 517–38.

Hick, John. "Soul-Making Theodicy." In *Philosophy of Religion,* edited by Michael Peterson, et al., 357–65. Oxford: Oxford Univerisity Press, 2014.

Hinson-Hasty, Elizabeth. "In Each the Work of All, and in All the Work of Each: Sin and Salvation in Schleiermacher and Rauschenbusch." In *Schleiermacher's Influences on American Thought and Religious Life, 1835–1920,* edited by Jeffrey A. Wilcox, et al., 370–92. Vol. 1. Eugene, OR: Pickwick, 2013.

Hinze, Bradford. *Narrating History, Developing Doctrine: Friedrich Schleiermacher and Johann Sebastian Drey.* Atlanta, GA: Scholars, 1993.

Hofstadter, Richard. *The Age of Reform: From Bryan to F. D. R.* New York: Vintage, 1955.

Holscher, Lucian. "The Religious Divide: Piety in Nineteenth-Century Germany." In *Protestants, Catholics, and Jews in Germany 1800–1914,* edited by Helmut Walser Smith, 33–49. Oxford: Berg, 2001.

Hope, Nicholas. *German and Scandinavian Protestantism, 1700–1918.* Oxford: Clarendon, 1999.

Hovet, Theodore. "Phoebe Palmer's 'Altar Phraseology' and the Spiritual Dimension of Woman's Sphere." *The Journal of Religion* 63.3 (1983) 264–80.

Hughes, George. *Fragrant Memories of the Tuesday Meeting and Guide to Holiness.* New York: Palmer & Hughes, 1886.

Jackson Lears, T. J. *No Place of Grace: Antimodernism and the Transformation of American Culture 1880–1920.* Chicago: University of Chicago Press, 1981.

James, William. "Pragmatism." In *William James: Writings 1902–1910,* edited by Bruce Kuklick, 479–625. New York: Library of America, 1987.

———. "The Varieties of Religious Experience." In *William James: Writings 1902–1910,* edited by Bruce Kuklick, 1–478. New York: Library of America, 1987.

Johnson, Claudia D. "Hawthorne and Nineteenth-Century Perfectionism." *American Literature* 44.4 (1973) 585–95.

Johnson, Paul E., and Sean Wilentz. *The Kingdom of Matthias.* Oxford: Oxford University Press, 1994.

Jones, Charles Edwin. *Perfectionist Persuasion: The Holiness Movement and American Methodism, 1867–1936.* Metuchen, NJ: Scarecrow, 1974.

Jungkeit, Steven R. *Spaces of Modern Theology: Geography and Power in Schleiermacher's World.* New York: Palgrave Macmillan, 2012.

Kant, Immanuel. *Critique of Pure Reason*. London: Penguin Classics, 2008.

Karant-Nunn, Susan C. *The Reformation of Feeling: Shaping the Religious Emotions in Early Modern Germany*. Oxford: Oxford University Press, 2010.

Kelsey, Catherine L. "Methodism in America (1766–1840): Parallels and Anticipations Regarding Schleiermacher's Influence." In *Schleiermacher's Influences on American Thought and Religious Life, 1835–1920*, edited by Jeffrey A. Wilcox, et al., 17–50. Vol. 1. Eugene, OR: Pickwick, 2013.

———. *Schleiermacher's Preaching, Dogmatics, and Biblical Criticism: The Interpretation of Jesus Christ in the Gospel of John*. Eugene, OR: Pickwick, 2007.

Kierner, Cynthia A. "Woman's Piety within Patriarchy: The Religious Life of Martha Hancock Wheat of Bedford County." *The Virginia Magazine of History and Biography* 100.1 (1992) 79–89.

Knight, Henry H., III. *Anticipating Heaven Below: Optimism of Grace from Wesley to the Pentecostals*. Eugene, OR: Cascade, 2014.

Krieger, Leonard. *The German Idea of Freedom: History of a Political Tradition*. Chicago: University of Chicago Press, 1957.

Leibniz, Gottfried W. "Selections from *The Theodicy*." In *The Philosophical Works of Leibniz*, by Gottfried W. Leibniz. Translated by George M. Duncan, 194–97, 202–4. New Haven: Tuttle, Morehouse & Taylor, 1890.

Lewis, I. M. *Ecstatic Religion: An Anthropological Study of Spirit Possession and Shamanism*. Middlesex: Penguin, 1971.

Livingston, James. *The Enlightenment and the Nineteenth-Century*. Vol. 1 of *Modern Christian Thought*. Upper Saddle River, NJ: Prentice Hall, 2006.

Long, Kathryn. "The Power of Interpretation: The Revival of 1857–58 and the Historiography of Revivalism in America." *Religion and American Culture: A Journal of Interpretation* 4.1 (1994) 77–105.

Luther, Martin. "Temporal Authority: To What Extent It Should Be Obeyed." In *Martin Luther's Basic Theological Writings*, edited by Timothy F. Lull, 655–704. Minneapolis: Fortress, 1989.

Machen, J. Gresham. *Christianity & Liberalism*. Grand Rapids: Eerdmans, 1985.

Mahan, Asa. *Baptism of the Holy Spirit, God's Provision of Power*. Philadephia: Williams, 2002.

———. *The Scripture Doctrine of Christian Perfection*. Boston: D. S. King, 1839.

Marina, Jacqueline, ed. *Cambridge Companion to Friedrich Schleiermacher*. Cambridge: Cambridge University Press, 2005.

———. "Christology and Anthropology in Friedrich Schleiermacher." In *Cambridge Companion to Friedrich Schleiermacher*, edited by Jacqueline Marina, 151–71. Cambridge: Cambridge University Press, 2005.

———. "Schleiermacher on the Outpourings of the Inner Fire: Experiential Expressivism and Religious Pluralism." *Religious Studies* 40.2 (2004) 125–43.

Massey, Marilyn Chapin. *Feminine Soul: The Fate of an Ideal*. Boston: Beacon, 1985.

McGrath, Alister. *The Christian Theology Reader*. 3rd ed. Oxford: Blackwell, 2006.

Medhurst, T.W. "Is Romanism Christianity?" In *The Fundamentals: A Testimony To The Truth*, edited by R. A. Torrey, 288–301. Vol. 3. Grand Rapids, MI: Baker, 2003.

Melton, James Van Horn. *The Rise of the Public in Enlightenment Europe*. Cambridge: Cambridge University Press, 2001.

Menand, Louis. *The Metaphysical Club: A Story of Ideas in America*. New York: FSG, 2001.

Merritt, Timothy. *The Christian's Manual: A Treatise on Christian Perfection, with Directions for Obtaining That State*. Ann Arbor, MI: University of Michigan Library, 1824.

Moody, Dwight L. *Moody's Stories, Incidents, and Illustrations*. Chicago: Moody, 1884.

———. *Secret Power or the Secret of Success in Christian Life and Work*. New York: Fleming H. Revell, 1881.

———. *Sovereign Grace: Its Source, Its Nature, and its Effects*. New York: Fleming H Revell, 1891.

———. *The Way to God*. Chicago: Moody, 1884.

Morton, Marsha. "German Romanticism: The Search for 'A Quiet Place.'" *Art Institute of Chicago Museum Studies* 28.1 (2002) 8–23, 106–7.

Musser, Donald W., and Joseph L Price. *Tillich*. Abingdon Pillars of Theology. Nashville: Abingdon, 2010.

Nash, Arnold S. *Protestant Thought in the Twentieth Century: Whence & Whither?* New York: Macmillan, 1951.

Naumann, F. *Zur Einführung, Schleiermacher der Philosoph des Glaubens*. Edited by A. Titius, et al. Translated by Karl Barth. Berlin: Schoneberg, 1910.

Niebuhr, Richard R. "Schleiermacher: Theology as Human Reflection." *The Harvard Theological Review* 55.1 (1962) 21–49.

———. *Schleiermacher on Christ and Religion*. Eugene, OR: Wipf and Stock, 1964.

Noll, Mark A. *The Rise of Evangelicalism: The Age of Edwards, Whitfield, and the Wesleys*. Downers Grove, IL: InterVarsity, 2003.

Origen. *The Sacred Writings of Origen*. Altenmünster, Germany: Jazzybee Verlag, 2016.

Otto, Rudolf. *The Idea of the Holy*. London: Oxford University Press, 1972.

Palmer, Phoebe. *Faith and Its Effects: Or, Fragments from My Portfolio*. London: Alexander Heylin, 1856.

———. *Four Years in the Old World*. New York: Foster & Palmer Jr., 1867.

———. *Full Salvation: Its Doctrine and Duties*. Salem, OH: Schmul, 1979.

———. *Holiness to the Lord*. New York: MacDonald & Palmer, n.d.

———. *How They Entered Canaan*. Holiness Data Ministry, 1994.

———. *Incidental Illustrations of the Economy of Salvation, its Doctrines and Duties*. Toronto: G. R. Sanderson Wesleyan, 1855.

———. *Israel's Speedy Restoration and Conversion Contemplated: Or, Signs of the Times*. New York: John A. Gray, 1854.

———. *Mary: Or, The Young Christian*. New York: Carlgon & Porter, 1840.

———. *A Mother's Gift: Or, A Wreath for my Darlings*. New York: W. C. Palmer Jr., 1875.

———. *The Parting Gift to Fellow Laborers and Young Converts*. New York: W. C. Palmer, 1869.

———, ed. *Pioneer Experiences: Or, The Gift of Power Received by Faith. Illustrated and Confirmed by the Testimonies of Eighty Living Ministers of Various Denominations*. New York: W. C. Palmer Jr., 1868.

———. *Present to My Christian Friend on Entire Devotion to God*. London: William Nichols, 1857.

———. *The Promise of the Father*. Salem, OH: Schmul, 1981.

———. *Recollections and Gathered Fragments of Mrs. Lydia N. Cox of Williamsburg, L. I*. New York: Piercy & Reed, 1845.

————. *Selected Writings.* Edited by Thomas C. Oden. Sources of American Spirituality. Mahwah, NJ: Paulist, 1988.

————. *Some Account of the Recent Revival in the North of England and Glasgow.* Manchester: W. Bremner, 1860.

————. *Sweet Mary.* London: Simpkin, Marshal, & Co., 1862.

————. *The Tongue of Fire on the Daughers of the Lord: Or, Questions in Relation to the Duty of the Christian Chruch in Regard to the Privileges of her Female Membership.* New York: W. C. Palmer Jr., 1869.

————. *The Useful Disciple: Or, A Narrative of Mrs. Mary Gardner.* London: Alexander Heylin, 1857.

————. *The Way of Holiness.* New York: Piercy and Reed, 1843.

Palmer, Phoebe, and Jeremy Boynton. *Sanctification Practical: A Book for the Times.* New York: Foster and Palmer, Jr., 1867.

Palmer, Phoebe, and Walter C. Palmer. *Life and Letters of Leonidas L. Hamline, DD, Late One of the Bishops of the Methodist Episcopal Church.* New York: Carlton & Porter, 1866.

Parham, Charles F. *The Everlasting Gospel.* Cedar Rapids, IA: Pentecostal, 2013.

————. *A Voice Crying in the Wilderness.* Cedar Rapids, IA: Pentecostal, 2013.

Pierson, A. T. *The Keswick Movement: In Precept & Practice.* Memphis: NPL, 1903.

Prat, Ferdinand. "Origen and Origenism." In *The Catholic Encyclopedia.* Vol. 11. New York: Robert Appleton, 1911. http://www.newadvent.org/cathen/11306b.htm.

Raack, R. C. "Schleiermacher's Political Thought and Activity, 1806–1813." *Church History* 28.4 (1959) 374–90.

Randall, Ian. "Lay People in Revival: A Case Study of the '1859' Revival." *Transformation* 26.4 (2009) 217–31.

Raser, Harold E. *Phoebe Palmer Her Life and Thought.* Lewiston/Queenston: Edwin Mellen, 1987.

Redeker, Martin. *Schleiermacher: Life and Thought.* Translated by John Wallhausser. Philadelphia: Fortress, 1973.

Riesebrodt, Martin. *Pious Passion: The Emergence of Modern Fundamentalism in the United States and Iran.* Berkeley, CA: University of California Press, 1990.

Rilliams, Robert R. *Schleiermacher the Theologian: The Construction of the Doctrine of God.* Philadelphia: Fortress, 1978.

Rogers, Richard Lee. "The Urban Threshold and the Second Great Awakening: Revivalism in New York State, 1825–1835." *Journal for the Scientific Study of Religion* 49.4 (2010) 694–709.

Ruthven, Malise. *Fundamentalism: The Search for Meaning.* Oxford: Oxford University Press, 2004.

Ryie, Charles Caldwell. *Neo-Orthodoxy: An Evangelical Evaluation of Barthianism.* Chicago: Moody, 1956.

Sauter, Michael. *Vision of the Enlightenment: The Edict on Religion of 1788 and the Politics of the Public Sphere in Eighteenth Century Prussia.* Leiden: Brill, 2009.

Schleiermacher, Friedrich. *Brief Outline on the Study of Theology.* Translated by Terrence N. Tice. Richmond, VA: John Knox, 1966.

————. *The Christian Faith.* Edinburgh: T&T Clark, 1999.

————. *Christmas Eve: A Dialogue on the Celebration of Christmas.* Translated by Terrence N. Tice. Eugene, OR: Cascade, 2010.

———. *Fifteen Sermons of Friedrich Schleiermacher delivered to Celebrate the Beginning of a New Year.* Edited by Edwina Lawler. Lewiston, NY: Edwin Mellen, 2003.

———. *Friedrich Schleiermacher: Pioneer of Modern Theology.* Edited by Keith Clements. Minneapolis: Fortress, 1991.

———. *Hermeneutics and Criticism and Other Writings.* Translated by Andrew Bowie. Cambridge: Cambridge University Press, 1998.

———. *Lectures on Philosophical Ethics.* Edited by Robert B. Louden. Translated by Louise Adey Huish. Cambridge: Cambridge University Press, 2002.

———. *The Life of Schleiermacher, As Unfolded In His Autobiography And Letters.* Translated by Fredessica Rowan. 2 vols. London: Smith, Elder, and Co., 1860.

———. *On the Doctrine of Election With Special Reference to the Aphorisms of Dr. Bretschneider.* Translated by Allen G. Jorgenson and Iain G. Nicol. Louisville: Westminster John Knox, 2012.

———. *On The Glaubenslehre.* Translated by James Duke and Francis Fiorenza. Atlanta, GA: Scholars, 1981.

———. *On Religion: Speeches to Its Cultured Despisers.* Louisville: Westminster John Knox, 1994.

———. *Schleiermacher's Soliloquies.* Translated by Horace Leland Friess. Eugene, OR: Wipf and Stock, 2002.

———. *Selected Sermons of Schleiermacher.* Edited by W. Robertson Nicoll. Translated by Mary F. Wilson. New York, NY: Funk & Wagnalls, 1890.

———. *Servant of the Word: Selected Sermons of Friedrich Schleiermacher.* Edited and translated by Dawn DeVries. Philadelphia: Fortress, 1987.

Scott, Leland H. "Methodist Theology in America in the Nineteenth Century." *Church History* 25.3 (1956) 267–68.

Selbie, W. B. *Schleiermacher: A Critical and Historical Study.* New York: E.P. Dutton & Co., 1913.

Seymour, William. *Azusa Street Papers.* 1906–1908. Reprint, n.p.: Pentacostalbooks. com, 2013

Sherman, Robert. "Isaak August Dorner on Divine Immutability: A Missing Link between Schleiermacher and Barth." *The Journal of Religion* 77.3 (1997) 380–401.

———. *The Shift to Modernity: Christ and the Doctrine of Creation in the Theologies of Schleiermacher and Barth.* New York: T&T Clark, 2005.

Smith, Helmut Walser. *Continuities of German History.* Cambridge: Cambridge University Press, 2008.

Smith, Timothy L. *Revivalism and Social Reform In Mid-Nineteenth-Century America.* New York: Abingdon, 1957.

———. "Righteousness and Hope: Christian Holiness and the Millennial Vision in America, 1800–1900." *American Quarterly* 31.1 (1979) 21–45.

Spencer, Carole D. "Evangelism, Feminism, and Social Reform: The Quaker Woman Minister and the Holiness Revival." *Friends Historical Association* 80.1 (1991) 24–48.

Stark, Rodney, and Roger Finke. *The Churching of America 1776–2005: Winners and Losers in Our Religious Economy.* New Brunswick, NJ: Rutgers University Press, 2008.

Stockard, Jean, et al. "Moving from Sect to Church: Variations in Views regarding Sanctification among Wesleyan/Holiness Clergy." *Review of Religious Research* 43.1 (2001) 70–92.

Stoeffler, Ernest F. *The Rise of Evangelical Pietism*. Leiden: Brill, 1971.

Strom, Jonathan. "The Common Priesthood and the Pietist Challange for Minisry and Laity." In *The Pietist Impulse in Christianity*, edited by Christian T. Collins Winn, et al., 42–59. Eugene, OR: Pickwick, 2011.

Strong, Douglas M. "American Methodism in the Nineteenth Century: Expansion and Fragmentation." In *Cambridge Companion to American Methodism*, edited by Jason E. Vickers, 63–96. Cambridge: Cambridge University Press, 2013.

Styers, Randall. *Making Magic: Religion, Magic & Science in the Modern World*. Oxford: Oxford University Press, 2004.

Sweeting, Don. "The Great Turning Point in the Life of D. L. Moody." In *Mr. Moody and the Evangelical Tradition*, edited by Timothy George, 39–51. London: T&T Clark International, 2004.

Synan, Vinson. *The Holiness-Pentecostal Tradition: Charismatic Movements in the Twentieth Century*. Grand Rapids: Eerdmans, 1997.

Tauler, John. *The Following of Christ*. Edited by Paul A. Boer Sr. Translated by J. R. Morell. n.p.: Veritatis Splendor, 2012.

Thandeka. *The Embodied Self: Schleiermacher's Solution to Kant's Issue of the Empirical Self*. Albany, NY: State University of New York Press, 1995.

Thornton, Wallace, Jr. *The Conservative Holiness Movement: A Historical Appraisal*. Beach Grove, IN: Wallace Thornton Jr., 2014.

Tice, Terrence N. *Schleiermacher*. Nashville, TN: Abingdon, 2006.

———. "Schleiermacher on History and Comparative Method." In *Schleiermacher's Influences on American Thought and Religious Life, 1835–1920*, edited by Jeffrey A. Wilcox, et al., 37–70. Vol. 3. Eugene, OR: Pickwick, 2014.

———. "The 'Schleiermacher Renaissance' Begins to Take Hold, Selectively, in American Thought and Life: Part One: Prefatory Remarks on Secular, Apologetic, and Constructive Theology (Dewy, Knudson, and Brown)." In *Schleiermacher's Influences on American Thought and Religious Life, 1835–1920*, edited by Jeffrey A. Wilcox, et al., 113–49. Vol. 2. Eugene, OR: Pickwick, 2014.

———. "Schleiermacher's Interpretation of Christmas: 'Christmas Eve,' 'The Christian Faith,' and the Christmas Sermons." *The Journal of Religion* 47.2 (1967) 100–26.

Tillich, Paul. *A Complete History of Christian Thought*. New York: Harper & Row, 1968.

———. *The Courage to Be*. New Haven: Yale Univeristy Press, 1952.

———. *Dynamics of Faith*. New York: Harper Colophon, 1957.

———. *The Eternal Now*. New York: Scribner's Sons, 1963.

———. *The New Being*. New York: Scribner's Sons, 1955.

———. *Perspectives on Nineteenth and Twentieth-Century Protestant Theology*. New York: Harper & Row, 1967.

———. *The Protestant Era*. Chicago: University of Chicago Press, 1948.

———. *Systematic Theology*. 3 vols. Chicago: University of Chicago Press, 1951–1963.

Torrey, Ruben A., ed. *The Fundamentals: A Testimony To The Truth*. 4 vols. Grand Rapids, MI: Baker, 2003.

———. *How to Pray*. Crossreach, 2016.

Trachtenberg, Alan. *The Incorporation of America: Culture and Society in the Gilded Age*. New York: Hill and Wang, 2007.

Turner, Michael K. "Revivalism and Preaching." In *Cambridge Companion to American Methodism*, edited by Jason E. Vickers, 119–38. Cambridge: Cambridge University Press, 2013.

Vial, Theodore M. "Friedrich Schleiermacher on the Central Place of Worship in Theology." *The Harvard Theological Review* 91.1 (1998) 59–73.

———. "Schleiermacher and the State." In *Cambridge Companion to Friedrich Schleiermacher*, edited by Jacqueline Marina, 269–87. Cambridge: Cambridge University Press, 2005.

Vickers, Jason E., ed. *Cambridge Companion to American Methodism.* Cambridge: Cambridge University Press, 2013.

Wallhausser, John. "Schleiermacher's Critique of Ethical Reason: Toward a Systematic Ethics." *The Journal of Religious Ethics* 17.2 (1989) 25–39.

Warner, Laceye C. "American Methodist Women: Roles and Contributions." In *Cambridge Companion to American Methodism*, edited by Jason E. Vickers, 316–35. Cambridge: Cambridge University Press, 2013.

Weber, Max. *The Protestant Ethic and the "Spirit" of Capitalism.* London: Penguin, 2002.

Webster, John, ed. *The Cambridge Companion to Karl Barth.* Cambridge: Cambridge University Press, 2000.

Wehler, Hans-Ulrich. *The German Empire 1871–1918.* Oxford: Berg, 1997.

Welch, Claude. "The Problem of a History of Nineteenth-Century Theology." *The Journal of Religion* 52.1 (1972) 1–21.

———. *Protestant Thought in the Nineteenth Century.* 2 Vols. Eugene, OR: Wipf & Stock, 1972–1985.

Wellman, Gordon Boit. "Schleiermacher Today." *The Journal of Religion* 18.2 (1938) 161–73.

Wesley, John. "The Almost Christian." In *The Essential Works of John Wesley: Selected Books, Sermons, and Other Writings*, edited by Alice Russie, 171–78. Uhrichsville, OH: Barbour, 2011.

———. *Character of a Methodist.* Bristol: Gale Ecco, 1742.

———. "Christian Perfection." In *The Essential Works of John Wesley: Selected Books, Sermons, and Other Writings*, edited by Alice Russie, 397–414. Uhrichsville, OH: Barbour, 2011.

———. "On Perfection." In *The Essential Works of John Wesley: Selected Books, Sermons, and Other Writings*, edited by Alice Russie, 415–28. Uhrichsville, OH: Barbour, 2011.

———. *A Plain Account of Christian Perfection.* Edited by Frank Banfield. Vancouver: Eremitical, 2009.

Wheatley, Richard. *The Life and Letters of Mrs. Phoebe Palmer.* New York: W. C. Palmer Jr., 1876.

White, Charles Edward. *The Beauty of Holiness: Phoebe Palmer as Theologian, Revivalist, Feminist, and Humanitarian.* Grand Rapids: Francis Asbury, 1986.

Wilcox, Jeffrey A., et al. *Schleiermacher's Influences on American Thought and Religious Life.* 3 vols. Eugene, OR: Pickwick, 2013–2014.

Williams, Robert R. *Schleiermacher the Theologian: The Construction of the Doctrine of God.* Philadelphia: Fortress, 1978.

Wilson, George W. *Methodist Theology vs. Methodist Theologians.* Sydney: Wentworth, 2016.

Wyman, Walter E., Jr. "Sin and Redemption." In *Cambridge Companion to Friedrich Schleiermacher*, edited by Jacqueline Marina, 129–50. Cambridge: Cambridge University Press, 2005.

Zinzendorf, Nikolaus Ludwig von. *Christian Life and Witness: Count Zinzendorf's 1738 Berlin Speeches*. Edited by Gary S. Kinkel. Eugene, OR: Pickwick, 2010.